John Christie of Rillington Place

TAMESIDE M.B.C. LIBRARIES	
01766281	
Bertrams	18/12/2013
364.15232C	£12.99
HAT	

John Christie of Rillington Place

Biography of a Serial Killer

JONATHAN OATES

First published in Great Britain in 2012 by
WHARNCLIFFE TRUE CRIME
An imprint of
Pen & Sword Books Ltd
47 Church Street
Barnsley
South Yorkshire
S70 2AS

Copyright © Jonathan Oates, 2012

ISBN 978-1-84563-141-3 (H/B)
ISBN 978-1-78159-288-5 (P/B)

The right of Jonathan Oates to be identified as the author of this work has been asserted by him in accordance with the Copyright, Designs and Patents Act 1988.

A CIP catalogue record for this book is available from the British Library.

All rights reserved. No part of this book may be reproduced or transmitted in any form or by any means, electronic or mechanical including photocopying, recording or by any information storage and retrieval system, without permission from the Publisher in writing.

Typeset by Concept, Huddersfield, West Yorkshire.
Printed and bound in England by CPI Group (UK) Ltd, Croydon, CR0 4YY.

Pen & Sword Books Ltd incorporates the imprints of Pen & Sword Aviation, Pen & Sword Family History, Pen & Sword Maritime, Pen & Sword Military, Pen & Sword Discovery, Wharncliffe Local History, Wharncliffe True Crime, Wharncliffe Transport, Pen & Sword Select, Pen & Sword Military Classics, Leo Cooper, The Praetorian Press, Remember When, Seaforth Publishing and Frontline Publishing.

For a complete list of Pen & Sword titles please contact
PEN & SWORD BOOKS LIMITED
47 Church Street, Barnsley, South Yorkshire, S70 2AS, England
E-mail: enquiries@pen-and-sword.co.uk
Website: www.pen-and-sword.co.uk

Contents

List of Plates

Ernest John Christie.

Mary Hannah Christie, née Halliday, 1917.

Ethel, Percy and Mary Christie.

Black Boy House, 2010.

All Souls' Church, Halifax, *c*.1900.

Halifax Post Office, *c*.1920.

John Christie, 1921.

RAF Uxbridge.

Empire Cinema, Uxbridge.

Hillingdon School, 1930s.

Southall Park, 1920s.

Uxbridge Magistrates' Court.

Wandsworth Prison, 1980s.

No. 23 Oxford Gardens, Notting Hill.

Map of Notting Hill, 1914.

Christie's police record, 1939–1943.

Beryl Evans's birth certificate.

GPO Savings Bank, Blythe Road.

John Christie, c.1950.

Kathleen Maloney.

Maureen Briggs.

Hectorina MacLennan.

Alexander Pomeroy Baker.

Acknowledgements

I would like to thank Ian Baker, Alexander Barron, John Curnow, Jack Delves, Dr John Hargreaves, Professor David Kynaston, Paul Lang, Virginia Mason, Alice MacLennan, Robin Odell, Ken Pearce and Patricia Pichler for their help and the interest they have taken in this book. I also want to acknowledge the assistance of the staff at Calderdale Archives, Gunnersbury Cemetery, Wakefield Archives, Kensington Library, Hammersmith and Fulham Archives, Glamorgan Record Office, Southampton Library, Sheffield Library, Hull Library, the British Newspaper Library, the National Archives and at all the other archives and libraries where I have made enquiries. Finally, this book would not have been possible without the help and encouragement of Rupert Harding, the commissioning editor.

The book is dedicated to the memory of all those who lost their lives at 10 Rillington Place between 1943 and 1953.

Introduction

'From Hell, Hull and Halifax
Good Lord deliver us'.[1]

Halifax's John Christie is probably Britain's most notorious single serial killer of the twentieth century. This is not just because he murdered at least six women and concealed their corpses in his house and garden – the Wests of 25 Cromwell Street, Gloucester, did likewise more recently and had more numerous victims – nor because he was the most prolific, as Dr Shipman holds that dubious honour, but because he is alleged to have allowed an innocent man, Timothy Evans, to hang.

Much has been written about Christie's crimes, so readers may ask why there is a need for this book. Yet very few authors have used any of the voluminous police and judicial archives of the case which are at the National Archives, to say nothing of newspaper accounts and other sources for Christie's life. Previous writers have repeated old arguments and 'facts', and myths have been perpetuated which conflict with the evidence. Also, authors have tended to concentrate on the murders of Geraldine and Beryl Evans in 1949 and so other aspects of Christie's life and criminal career have been sidelined.

This book aims to correct these oversights, by using evidence from many more sources than have been previously used. These include police, prison and judicial files created at the time of the murders, contemporary newspapers, transcripts of trials and sources well known to the genealogist for tracking down an individual's history. It gives more weight to Christie's life and crimes outside the years 1949–1950, and in doing so gives a fuller and more accurate picture of the man and his criminal activities over three decades. It is a more intimate picture, though not necessarily one that makes him any more likeable. We shall see how he was perceived by those who met him, how he justified and explained his actions, and what motivated him. The book also sheds more light on Christie's family and his victims. This is a biography, not an examination of the police investigation nor of the judicial enquiries, though both will be outlined.

The chapters are arranged chronologically, beginning with Christie's Yorkshire boyhood and war service. The next chapter examines his career of petty crime. Chapter 3 considers his time as a police officer and his first murders. The following chapters survey what happened when the Evanses began to live in the same house as the Christies, the discovery of the murder of Geraldine and Beryl and the trial of Evans. The later chapters concern Christie's final murderous spree, his arrest, trial and execution. Finally, the controversies which arose from these murders are explored. The portrayal of Christie in fiction and popular culture is also examined.

I have known about Christie and his crimes since my schooldays in the early 1980s – and have been horrified by them. In later life, I watched the film *Ten Rillington Place* one night, alone. When I began the first of ten books about true crime, I swore never to touch the Christie case – it was so awful. However, a reading of Colin Wilson's *Written in Blood* indicated that there was much more to this case than a miscarriage of justice, if indeed that were the case.

It is important to recall the words of the Attorney General at the outset of Christie's trial in 1953:

> you must try your utmost to shut out of your mind everything you have read or heard, or even thought, about the case or about Christie himself. You must approach the whole matter, so far as you possibly can, with an open mind. As our old English legal phrase puts it, you must hearken to the evidence as it is laid before you. It is no use pretending about these things ... every one of us ... almost without exception, must have read something ... about Rillington Place.[2]

So, with as open a mind as possible, let us begin at the beginning.

Chapter 1

A Yorkshire Youth
1899–1920

'An ordinary, quiet boy. There was nothing
extraordinary about him at all'.[1]

Christie's roots were in Scotland. His paternal grandfather, also called John, was born in Kilmarnock in 1835. When he was ten, his father, Robert, sent his son to Kidderminster as an apprentice in the carpet trade. John later became a manager. He married Eliza, three years his senior. They had two boys and one girl. One of the sons was Ernest John Christie, born on 12 November 1862. The family moved to Halifax in the West Riding of Yorkshire in 1877 and in 1880 resided at 10 Chester Road. On 12 December 1881, at Salem Methodist chapel, Ernest, now a carpet designer (like his father) and employed by John Crossley and Sons Carpets, Dean Clough (again, just like his father, who retired from the firm in 1898), married Mary Hannah Halliday, aged eighteen. She had been born in Queensbury and was the daughter of David Halliday (1836–1911), a Liberal Halifax councillor (1880–1882) and businessman employing fifty-seven men in a boot factory (Halliday's and Midgeley's), who lived at number 24 Chester Road. Both Halliday and John Christie were fervent Liberals. Ernest was not, but the couple may have met because of their fathers' shared political interests. The newly married couple lived with her parents until about 1884. From then on they and their growing family led a peripatetic existence; although they remained in Halifax, they lived from about 1885–1893 in 54 Salisbury Place (very close to Chester Road), in the Northowram district. In the next two decades they had seven children. These were Percy (1882–1970), a bank clerk by 1901 and later a bank manager in Leeds, Florence, known as Cissie (1884–1949), Effie (1886–1918), Elsie (1890–probably before 1953), Winifred (1896–1968), John (1899–1953) and finally Phyllis, known as Dolly

(1900–1973). All had their mother's maiden name as their second Christian name; in John's case alone it was his third name.[2]

John Reginald Halliday Christie was born on Saturday 8 April 1899 (not 1898 as often stated) at Black Boy House, Turner Lane, in the Ackroyden district of Halifax, to the north-east of the town centre, where the family resided from about 1893–1901. The birth was registered on 19 May and the house still stands. They then moved to a house named Warmleigh Hall, located on Roper Lane, Queensbury, and in 1907 reached the summit of their social pretensions when they resided at Iona House, Boothtown. Yet in 1910 they returned to their more modest roots of three decades earlier, moving back to Chester Road. They lived first at number 30, which had nine rooms, but by 1915 they had moved again, to number 67. Elsie had by now (1911) left home and was boarding with a widow in Morley and was employed as brassworker, while Percy had risen to become a bank cashier at the Halifax Commercial Bank and had also left home. The other five children remained with their parents. Florence was a schoolteacher at a county council school. Effie's employment is not stated. Winifred, Phyllis and John were still at school. It is often stated that the Christies were a middle-class family, though as they did not employ a live-in servant, this seems unlikely. Ernest Christie was a skilled artisan, earning (between 1916 and 1918), £3 per week, rising to £3 15s in 1921, which was hardly the salary of a member of the professional classes. On the other hand, though, Christie was later reported as saying, 'The material side of the home ... was good'.[3]

Christie's father was heavily involved in local affairs, as his obituary notes. He was the first superintendent of the Halifax branch of the St John's Ambulance brigade and was an ambulance steward for many years, being awarded a silver cup and gold medal for his services. When young he was involved in the local anti-vaccination movement. He was awarded a thank you gold medal by Sir Robert Baden-Powell for his work for the Boy Scout movement and had been judge for the boys in the ambulance parade. He was trustee for Akroyden Square, judged at local allotment shows and was a keen Esperantist. He was chairman of the old folks' treat committee at Akroyden and Shibden. Finally he was a founding member of the local Conservative Association and had been honorary treasurer of the local branch of the Primrose League. All of this would have been a lot for a young lad to aspire to and may have led to Christie junior developing an inferiority complex. The family's standing could only have been improved further by the eldest son marrying a councillor's daughter in 1911 and having a sumptuous wedding and reception, and by another daughter marrying the son of a late councillor. In 1953 it was stated the family was memorable due to 'its size and also because of the musical and artistic abilities shown by some of the children'.[4]

There is no reference here to any involvement in any religious organisation. There is no record in the parish registers for All Souls', the parish they resided in, of the baptisms of any of the seven children (though Winifred was baptised in Aldershot in 1919), and only Winifred and Florence were married there, though Percy married at the parish church in 1911, as did Phyllis in 1923, and Effie married at St Thomas'.[5]

Most of what is known of Christie's childhood is that which he related himself. Harry Procter, a journalist for *The Sunday Pictorial* took notes of conversations with Christie and published that information in 1953. Christie also mentioned his childhood to those who interviewed him after his arrest. It is also worth stating, in the words of F. Tennyson-Jesse, writing in 1957, 'it is impossible to take any statement of Christie's as true unless it is corroborated by someone else'. This view is shared by this author, and is stressed here, because previous authors have retold his childhood without such qualification, as if it were all verified fact. It is not unknown for criminals to give misleading accounts of their youth but, on the other hand, it has been said that Christie was always happy to talk about any topic unless it might incriminate him. Regrettably none of his immediate family left written accounts of family life.[6]

There seem to have been a number of important formative aspects of Christie's early life: his relationship with his parents; seeing his first corpse and his first attempts at sex.

Christie described his parents as 'Victorians of the old school, highly regarded by the neighbours'. He had fond memories of his mother, 'a wonderful woman who lived for the happiness of others'. He recalled that when neighbours were in trouble they would come to her. Jack Delves recalls her as being kind and gentle. Christie was his mother's favourite. His recollection of his father was mixed. On one hand he seems to have admired him, writing that he was 'a brilliant man at work and at First Aid', being known at the factory as 'Dr Christie', and drank little. On the other hand, he was stern, strict and proud, 'I always lived in dread of him'. Christie's fear of his father was shared by his siblings. Ernest had no favourites. Christie recalled his father leading the family to church, marshalling his children as if they were so many bandsmen. He had a terrible temper and his children were afraid to speak to him, unless there was a favourable opportunity to do so, and his wife often had to protect the children. She could be told off by her husband for doing so, however. On Sunday afternoon their father would read the newspaper in the front room and would expect to do so in peace (admittedly not uncommon). On one occasion, the young Christie was accused by his father of stealing tomatoes, with the result that he was 'given a good hiding'. Later his mother convinced Ernest of his innocence and the wronged boy was given a shilling by his father. At the age of seven the young Christie was given another beating because he had been in the park with his favourite sister, Phyllis. It should be noted, however, that fathers of the time were expected to administer physical punishment to their children if they committed misdemeanours and Ernest Christie was probably no harsher than most fathers of his generation. Christie later said, 'Father very strict but only beat me twice'. He certainly seems to have been nervous, later recalling, 'As a child I was very nervous at night and often when in bed I appeared to see a spot of light in front of me and used to hide my head under the sheets'. This habit continued in later life. It is also worth noting that he worked in the garden with his father both before and after school, suggesting there was perhaps some affinity between them. Christie claimed that he got on well with his brother and sisters, and allegedly Florence always consulted him with her worries and troubles, though quite why a woman fifteen years his senior should do so is unclear. His health was generally good, though aged ten he suffered rheumatic fever and was absent from school for five months, yet he made a full recovery. In 1915 he was ill with pneumonia.[7]

One pivotal moment in Christie's early life was being taken to see the newly deceased corpse of his maternal grandfather, David Halliday, who died, aged seventy-five, on 24 March 1911, at the Christie house, after a lengthy illness. This was the first corpse the boy had ever seen in his life and he later said that it made a profound impression on his young mind. He did not see his grandfather die, but was taken to the parlour to see his body laid out on a trestle table, not an uncommon custom at the time. Christie later recalled that 'all my life I never experienced fear or horror at the sight of a corpse. On the contrary I have seen many and they hold an interest and fascination over me. The first one when I was about eight [actually nearly twelve] years old and quite clearly I remember. I was not in any way worried or perturbed. It was a grandfather of mine and I was permitted to see him after he was laid out'. Denis Nilsen, killer of fifteen men in 1978–83, recalled a similar experience in his childhood, too. In another example of his fascination with death, Christie went with others of his age to the local cemetery and they peered through gaps in the children's vault, looking at the tiny coffins. A friend later said, 'They seemed to have a peculiar fascination for him.' Unlike a live human being, a corpse poses no threat and a living man has power over the deceased.[8]

Christie's early attempts at sexual experience came in either 1915 or 1916. He recalled, 'I was never a sexy type'. In Halifax there was a lover's lane, or the 'Duck walk', where youths would meet with those of the opposite sex, and it was common for a group of lads to frequent this 'monkey run'. However, the young Christie did not find a mate and was thus taunted by his fellows. 'Such remarks made me feel I was not like other boys'. When at last he did 'pick up' a girl, in Savile Park, they kissed and cuddled. Yet, whereas Christie lacked confidence and experience, she was 'a mill girl ... whose morals were rather free'. There was no sex. Unfortunately for his ego, she told his friends (one account says she told his – regrettably unnamed – best friend) that he was slow. He recalled that they laughed and called him 'rude nick names' that even after forty years he could not bear to repeat in public, and unfavourable comparisons were made between himself and the other boys. According to Procter, he was called 'No Dick Reggie'. He later explained, 'all my life since I have had this fear of appearing ridiculous as a lover'. He was 'doubtful of my own sexual capabilities and these fears became very real doubts'. Procter later claimed 'It caused his hatred and fear of women. I believe it caused him to commit murder', but this is probably to overstate the matter. However, his sexual problems were not physical but psychological; there was nothing wrong with him anatomically. It was not until 1916 or 1917 that he lost his virginity when he and some friends visited prostitutes in Halifax.[9]

A psychiatrist suggested that Christie suffered from the Oedipus complex; that he hated his father yet loved his mother and that this early experience conditioned his future behaviour. Christie later told Dr Odess, his GP, that he had received no form of sex education (not unusual at the time) and felt inferior to his fellows both then and later.[10]

Not all of Christie's childhood and youth was unremittingly grim. He claimed that life was better when the family moved to the Boothtown district of Halifax in 1907. The young Christie (if not his family) was much associated with All Souls' Church. In Sunday School, he later recalled, 'I learned the ten Commandments – the sixth Commandment – Thou shalt not kill – always fascinated me'. He was a member of the church dramatic society, the choir (John George Haigh (1909–1949), another multiple murderer of the 1940s, had also been a young chorister). His brother sang in the choir of Halifax's parish church. He was also in the 30th Halifax Scout group, which was associated with the church and where he was eventually, and briefly, an assistant leader and was made a King's Scout (the highest award then in Scouting). He gained the Woodman's badge and the First Aid badge. He also joined the local branch of the St John's Ambulance Brigade aged fourteen. It is possible that Christie took part in all these activities to escape his father, but alternatively he may have been trying to emulate him and have been encouraged by him, for the elder Christie was also a First Aid enthusiast and was involved in Scouting too. Christie attended Boothtown junior school, Crown Road, as did his siblings, before winning a scholarship to Halifax Secondary School (now Clare Hall). According to his own account, he was a good scholar, being top of the form in Mathematics and Algebra, and was good at History and Woodwork. He was certainly intelligent, possessing an IQ of 128. But he was not merely bookish; he also played in the school teams for football and enjoyed sports, but was never team captain. However, although he got on well with his fellows, he did not make many friends. With the benefit of hindsight, a former schoolmate later said, 'A queer lad; he never knocked about like the rest of us' and another said of him, 'He kept himself to himself. He was never popular'. Christie later said, 'I was therefore happy on my own but not all the time', and he disliked crowds, having one or two close friends. He was never in trouble, though.

Christie left school on 22 April 1913, aged just over fourteen (at a time when the minimum leaving age was twelve), with a 'reasonably good' record. He worked as an operator at Green's Picture Halls in Sowerby Bridge from 1914 to 1916. It was probably just the sort of job to appeal to his technical mind. Another source states his first job was as a warehouse boy at Messrs John Foster and Sons, boot manufacturers, for eighteen months before taking up work at the cinema. It has also been said that Christie worked at the same factory as his father, but was sacked for theft; however the copious staff archives of the company do not list him as an employee, so this story can be dismissed. Christie has also been accused of theft whilst working as a clerk for the police, aged seventeen, but again, there is no evidence for such an assertion, so it should be disregarded.[11]

The young man's interests were chiefly solitary. Christie's favourite films were low brow; westerns and comedies. His film idols in the 1950s were a fairly conventional selection: Virginia Mayo, Gregory Peck and Adolphe Menjou. In later life he mentioned his admiration for another film star, Eric Portman (1903–1969), who also grew up in Chester Road, Halifax, and liked his role in *Wanted for Murder*, a film about a serial strangler of women, of 1947. Christie stated he was, 'very fond of reading and photography, also mechanical articles such as radio and clocks to be repaired and wouldn't give up something until I had repaired it and put it right and fond of making things for the home'. He allegedly avoided fiction, preferring books on technical topics, such as medicine, electricity and gardening (a hobby that he and his father enjoyed). Yet a friend declared, 'I don't remember his being a great reader, and I never heard him talk about his books'. It was also his claim that he was a friend to animals, liking dogs and cats and helping sick animals belonging to neighbours. Possibly this was an attempt to curry favour with the reading public in order to make his posthumous reputation look less black, but in later life he did have a cat and a dog, so his claim to be an animal lover may not be wholly false (Nilsen and Myra Hindley were also animal lovers and had pet dogs). Unfortunately there are no surviving archives relevant to his school, church or Scouting activities, nor do we have any other accounts of his family life.[12]

Perhaps the statement that best sums up his youth is one made by a neighbour. Mr Brooks remarked, 'An ordinary, quiet boy. There was nothing extraordinary about him at all.' He was remembered, decades later, as only 'a slim, rather shy young man'. Yet this was only his external appearance; the inner self was unknown.[13]

The First World War began in 1914. Christie enlisted as a private in the Nottinghamshire and Derbyshire Regiment, number 106733, on 19 September 1916, aged nearly seventeen and a half. On the following day he was entered on the reserve, but was not mobilised until 12 April 1917, just after his eighteenth birthday. Why did Christie put his name down so soon – and not wait until he received his call-up papers? It could have been through a sense of patriotism, but is more likely that he saw it as an escape from his dull surroundings and from a distressing youth. Perhaps, too, he saw service in the army as a way of proving his manhood. He may also have been keen to enlist because of a wish to come into contact with death on a grand scale.[14]

He then served in the United Kingdom and became a friend to one Dennis Hague. The two young men met on the same day that each arrived at Rugeley, Staffordshire, for their training. Hague recalled, 'We joined what was then called the Boys' Battalion, because all the men in it were all aged seventeen or eighteen'. They were picked out as signallers and passed their exams, so were sent to a practice camp at Redmires, near Sheffield. They slept in the same hut there, and often went on signal training together. Hague recalled, 'I remember one day Christie came running up and read a signal that the officer was flagging from some distance away. Christie said, "The lieutenant's signalling 'Put those cigarettes out'"'. They were transferred to Brockton, then to Minster, Kent, then Ashford. In the latter, they lived in billets in the same road, Beever Road, though not in the same house. Hague described Christie thus, 'Slim with reddish hair and a fresh complexion. I used to call him cherry face he had such a high colour'. He liked him: 'I thought he was a jovial fellow. The whole time I knew him he was never angry with anybody, and he always had a smile on his face'. Regarding women, Hague said, 'I cannot remember anything abnormal or unhealthy about Christie's attitude to the opposite sex'. He recalled Christie often spending his evenings off going alone to cinemas and surmising 'I think it was at this time he met his wife'. This seems unlikely; as will later be noted, Christie probably only met the woman he would later wed after the war. It is probable that he sought out the company of prostitutes at this time – they often hung around near army encampments – although he later said he had but 'infrequent intercourse with prostitutes' as a soldier. However, Christie did well in the army. He later wrote, 'Did you know that Sergeant Watson begged me to give him my books when we went away? He said to my parents that they were so good that he would always treasure them. I wonder what became of them'. Christie later reminisced with Hague, 'I remember that park, it was where I used to wheel the baby from my civilian billet in his pram on Sunday afternoon. Do you remember the other men used to pull my leg?' Hague also recalled Christie's excellent memory; a point worth the reader recalling later in this book. Dr John Matheson later reported, 'He says he was offered promotion three times but refused because he did not want to leave his pals'. This is not impossible – as the war progressed, the army offered the chance of commissions to educated and intelligent men and Christie certainly fitted the bill. Allegedly he won shooting competitions, but we have no evidence for any of this but his own word. However, in March 1918 the German army launched its last major offensive on the Western Front. Extra troops were needed to stem these onslaughts and prevent a German victory. Christie was among those sent to France and Flanders, arriving on 2 April 1918. Hague and Christie were separated and never met again until 1953 when the latter was in the condemned cell.[15]

Christie was posted to D Company in the 2/6 Battalion of the Sherwood Foresters on 13 April and joined his unit in the field exactly one week later. The battalion was withdrawn to Calais on 7 May and was then broken up, men being assigned to other units as required. Christie found himself in a battalion of the Duke of Wellington's Regiment. He was employed as a signaller at battalion headquarters (as with the cinema projectionist's job, this required a degree of technical intelligence).[16]

The work was dangerous indeed and his active service was of short duration. Christie was injured by the blast of a mustard gas shell; it is stated this occurred in May and in the following month, perhaps near Mont Kemmal. He later claimed that he was unable to speak in the following three and a half years and suffered from blindness and hysteria. However, the reality was that he was not blinded: 'There is no evidence that Christie suffered or was treated for any eye complaint' and only suffered from a temporary loss of speech; for some time afterwards, he spoke with a whisper. It was said that he also 'complains of coughs in damp weather and sore throat and loss of voice'. It was stated he was suffering from the 'Effects of gas poisoning'. On 18 June he was sent to a medical station, and on 28 June he was at the 35th General Hospital, Calais. He was given menthol treatment. By the end of the next month he was back in England, at Stoke Military Hospital, before going to the King's Lancashire Military Convalescent Hospital on 8 August; clearly he was almost cured and was discharged from hospital on 27 August. He may have suffered a short relapse, because on 28 March 1919, when employed in the paymaster's department, he was admitted to Lichfield Military Hospital. Even so, he was discharged after a few days. Back in barracks, Christie was not the perfect soldier; on 31 August 1919 he was absent from parade and on 16 September broke out of barracks while under open arrest for the earlier offence, and was gone for two days. For this dereliction of duty he forfeited eighteen days' pay. Such ill-discipline was common among the bored soldiery who yearned to be discharged. However, he was fully demobilised on 22 October 1919. He was awarded a weekly disability pension of 8s for twenty-six weeks, the same from 28 April 1920, then likewise from 27 October 1920 until 1 February 1921. His brother Percy visited him in hospital; perhaps the last time the two ever met.[17]

Christie's army character was assessed as 'very good', though it was not especially distinguished. As with all men who served abroad, he was awarded the Victory and British medals. Hague later recalled, 'before we left England, one of the instructors asked Christie to leave his exercise book to be shown to other recruits as an example of care and neatness'. Christie later recalled that at this time he became convinced that the death penalty as a punishment for murder was wrong and that doctors should be able to treat killers, considering murder to be a disease, though this may be only a later thought, when he was in the shadow of the gallows.[18]

Once back in Halifax in the autumn of 1919, Christie returned to his job as a cinema projectionist, this time at the Theatre de Luxe, Northgate, in the centre of Halifax, but by the following year he was a clerk for Messrs Sutcliffe's woollen mill. He later explained that he had no desire to be inactive. Christie was then listed as residing with his parents and Winifred (née Christie) and Harold Delves and presumably Phyllis (his other siblings, having married, had left home by now). There may have been problems in the family, as Percy later recalled that he never saw his brother again after 1919 – he did not even attend his brother's wedding. Winifred left with her husband for India in the same year and never saw her younger brother again. Jack Delves recalled his father telling him that on one occasion Ernest Christie had assaulted him with a bayonet, which gives an insight into the latter's character. In the meantime, Ernest had inherited £3,077 from his father, who had returned to Kidderminster on his retirement in 1898, to take up farming there, and died in December 1917, aged eighty-two. He probably never saw his grandson and namesake.[19]

At this time, a very important person came into Christie's life. This was Ethel Simpson, who was born at 30 St Luke Street, Halifax, on 28 March 1898. Her parents were William, a machinist in an iron foundry (in 1920, he was described as being a foreman at an engineering works; also as being a clerk) and his wife, Amy Martha, née Baker, both of whom were born in 1857. She had an elder brother, Henry (born in 1891) and a sister, Lily (1896–1980), both of whom had been born in Bradford, as had their father. In 1901 the family lived at 3 Ashfield Crescent, Charlestown, Halifax. Tragedy struck the family in 1904 when William died. Seven years later, they lived at 2 Havelock Street in three rooms. All three children were then in work; Henry as an assistant sanitary employee (in later life he sang on the BBC), Lily as a textile designer and the thirteen-year-old Ethel as a school milliner's errand girl. In 1920, she was a general clerk, residing at 10 Woodside Crescent.[20]

Ethel and Christie may have met because they lived in streets only a stone's throw from each other in that part of Halifax which was north of the town centre. It has also been suggested that they met at an evening class, learning typing, in 1914, or that they met whilst working in the same mill in 1920. Christie said that the courtship lasted only a few months and that they had been lovers before marriage, but on another occasion he said they had known one another for several years and there was no sex before marriage. He later recalled, 'I courted my wife ... with a note book and pencil', such were his speech difficulties, 'and she became good at lip reading'. We should recall that after the First World War the number of marriageable young men was greatly reduced, so a girl wanting husband, as most did, could not afford to set her sights too high. As for Christie's reasons for marriage, one must surely have been Ethel's good looks. Although we are accustomed to seeing pictures of the middle-aged Ethel, she was not always so. There is a picture of her which shows her as she was in the early 1920s. She is distinctly pretty and fashionably attired. Christie himself recalled that she was 'a charming and pretty girl and had many offers of marriage'. This latter comment may, of course, be mere vanity on his part. She was also a competent typist, with two shorthand diplomas to her name; she was also to gain four testimonials to her office skills, and had been to technical college. Her intellectual tastes were middle brow; later in life she possessed a copy of *The Penny Poets*, a cheap illustrated book.[21]

Christie married Ethel on 10 May 1920. Allegedly the registrar, 'watched my lips at the wedding ceremony.' The witnesses at the ceremony, Clifford Shearing and Fred Lumb, were from neither of their families, suggesting disapproval; nor was it noted in the local press as all his siblings' weddings were. Curiously enough, they married at Halifax Registry Office, not at All Souls' church, where Christie had recently taught at the Sunday School. Possibly he had grown apart from the church and certainly Christie never refers to church-going in adult life. It is hard to be sure about much in this marriage, lacking as we do much of anyone's testimony except Christie's. He had glowing memories of it, recalling that Ethel 'made me an excellent wife and was devoted to me'. According to him, they had a few differences 'but they never amounted to much', and no quarrels. He said he helped with household duties, such as washing, cleaning and polishing, even shopping for food. He would even assist with meals. If all this is true, then he was certainly a model husband (he claimed Ethel saw him in this light) and, for the time, a very unusual one. Yet he was recorded as shopping in 1949 by Joan Vincent, so his claim may well be true. He was a keen amateur photographer and certainly took many photographs of Ethel for his album; of her on the beach at Brighton, at London Airport, in the garden and in the park. All these pictures were taken in middle age and show her to be respectable, modest, plump and matronly, no longer the pretty girl she was in her youth.[22]

The newlyweds moved to 9 Brunswick Road (now demolished), near to the town centre. Perhaps now, after all his difficult experiences with his father, the mockery from his fellows and his war wounds, Christie had found a secure berth; being both married and employed as a clerk. However, Christie later recalled he had 'great difficulty' with sex and only had relations once a week. Early in the marriage, we do not know exactly when, Ethel suffered a miscarriage. They were never to have any children, despite Christie later stating that he did want them and to this end they did not use contraceptives.[23]

Christie had something of a Jekyll and Hyde existence. On one hand there was the respectable Jekyll, a member of the Boy Scouts and active in the church; but on the other there was Hyde who visited prostitutes. But his upbringing, as far as we know, offers no indication of his future crimes. Many serial killers have had very troubled childhoods, with either a lack of a father figure, or abuse. Many committed acts of violence against animals or other children when very young. None of this seems to have occurred in Christie's case (nor that of later fellow serial killer, Dr Shipman). It was a stern upbringing, but not a cruel or unusual one. He seemed a very ordinary lad, though a quiet one. Dr Hobson stated, 'There is nothing of psychiatric significance in Christie's family history'.[24]

Chapter 2

Christie's First Crimes
1921–39

'It half stunned me. It was all the world like an explosion.
Everything seemed to go black for a second.'[1]

The years following Christie's marriage saw him descend from humdrum respectability into the murky world of crime, in both Halifax and London, though to begin with his misdemeanours were of a relatively minor nature. Previous writers have paid little attention to these years, but they are important in chronicling Christie's criminal career. In contrast to the events of the first chapter, we are on firmer ground here, for Christie's activities are documented by authorities rather more reliable than himself.

Christie was of a restless disposition. On 10 January 1921, he was enrolled as a temporary postman at Halifax, and was paid £2 18s 2d per week. He later recalled that the amount of walking involved was 'too much for me as my left knee was not quite alright after the war injury', but his medical records make no reference to any leg wound. On 1 February he went before the medical board again, and was deemed to be suffering only 6–14 per cent effects of gas. He was recorded as 'states he is much better ... voice is husky in wet weather'. He was given a final weekly pension of 7s 6d for the next seventy weeks. However, Christie's life took a turn for the worse on Tuesday 5 April 1921, when he appeared at Halifax Magistrates' Court (Dr Shipman also had his first court appearance here in 1976) before Mr Greenwood Gibson on two counts of stealing postal orders. Detective Inspector Sykes provided evidence to the effect that on 20 February, two postal orders to the value of 3s 4d and 1s 11d, and on 26 March, those to the value of 1s 3d and 7s, had been stolen by the aforesaid Christie. He added that there might be other charges and that he would need another week to complete his case. Bail was granted for £20 and two people (perhaps Christie's parents) came forward to stand as sureties for £10 each. It is interesting to note that the accused was not mentioned by name in *The Halifax Courier*, which reported the court case over two issues, and he was referred to as the 'son of very respectable people and there was no fear of him not attending to meet the charges'.[2]

A week later, the case resumed, this time before Mr J. Brearley. Frederick John Fallowfield Curtis, on behalf of the Postmaster General, made the case for the prosecution. Joseph Henry Mackrell, a solicitor, pleaded guilty for the prisoner. He was accused on three separate counts; the theft of a postal order to the value of 1s 6d, and stamps worth 5s; the second being postal orders worth 11s and stamps worth 4s, and finally for a postal order of 13s 2d. Questions had arisen because letters were going missing from Halifax Post Office and a Mr Drennan had been called upon to make enquiries. On 4 April he had found a letter in a public lavatory at Crossley Street in central Halifax. This was a letter which Christie should have delivered. Drennan then followed Christie home and had a detective search him, which Christie consented to readily. Four postal orders were found on his person. Several other postal orders, together with cheques and dividends, were found at the house. They totalled several hundred pounds, including a £100 Bank of England warrant, cheques to the value of £600 and money orders worth £14 10s. Very few had been cashed and only £1-worth had been lost.[3]

The defence rested on the prisoner's previously exemplary character. The court was told that he had been a Sunday School teacher prior to his marriage, and had served in the war with a creditable record, where he had been severely gassed. Since then it was stated that he had been in poor health and had suffered from memory loss and dizziness. No reason for the thefts was given, and it was argued that this was a point in his favour, as he had not spent his ill-gotten gains on gambling and drinking. The verdict was that Christie was guilty and he was sentenced to three terms of imprisonment, each of three months, to run concurrently, and without hard labour. The relatively mild sentence was undoubtedly due to his previous good character and his creditable military service. He spent the next three months (12 April – 27 June 1921) in Manchester Prison. Later serial killers such as Ian Brady and Dr Shipman were also imprisoned there. Christie himself never offered any form of excuse for his actions. Possibly he wanted to abuse the little power he had been given. Or he may have craved excitement: he was a clever man, but his job and family life were probably mundane and petty theft may have appealed to his nature. The Christies certainly did not lack money as a household; apart from his wages, he was in receipt of a weekly government gratuity of 7s 6d because of his war injuries and Ethel earned 35s per week. Many ex-servicemen with good war records fell into petty crime because they lacked self-discipline, and perhaps Christie was among them.[4]

Christie's prison record sheet notes that on departure he returned to his parents' house at Chester Road. However, he did not reside for long with them. We do not know where he lived (he was not resident in the Halifax workhouse nor with his parents), nor how he was occupied, from 1921 to 1923. Christie related in 1953 that he and his wife lived together. He may have been living from hand to mouth, his criminal record inhibiting his employment opportunities.[5]

His next brush with the law occurred less than two years later. It has often been stated that this second crime was one of obtaining money under false pretences and using violence. However, although the former is true, the latter has no substance in fact. What happened was that Christie stayed in a guest house in Halifax from 7 to 13 January. The guest house was run by Doris Moore, possibly at 26 St John's Place. Apparently he had booked a room for himself and his wife for a week, and stayed for two or three nights by himself. On one evening he had a supper of eggs, bread and butter and tea, having the same the next day, but with bacon for breakfast. The food cost 2s. Christie had claimed he was on business in Halifax as an electrical engineer, but when pressed for payment had to admit he had none. He then promised to go to the bank to draw on equally non-existent funds.[6]

On 15 January he appeared before the magistrates' court again. As before, Brearley presided. Christie claimed there was no charge against him because he had booked the room for a week and that time had not expired. He had not intended to defraud. In any case, his mother had paid the landlady his bill, so no one had suffered. Christie was again leniently dealt with 'on a promise to pull himself together and make a man of himself', and was urged to show willpower and determination in going straight. He escaped gaol. He was put on probation for twelve months and thanked the magistrates. Once again, his name was not mentioned in the press, nor was the landlady's.[7]

Christie left Halifax forever in 1923. It is not certain why or exactly when he did so. He later said that it was because Ethel had had an affair, but he did not blame her because she had been drinking at the time. Apparently: 'There was some trouble which I did not want to mention. My wife was having an affair with her employer [one Mr Garside] and I left her. I know it was correct because I tackled the man and he admitted it'. Ethel was then working, presumably as a typist, at Garside Engineering Company, Ironbridge Road, Bradford. As with all Christie's statements which are unsupported by other evidence, this is suspect. However, it is not impossible; Ethel was an attractive young woman, who may well have been annoyed by her husband's criminality and so fell for another man, though her relatives later disputed it. The affair caused Christie, or so he said, to lose his voice for six months, because 'of the emotional disturbance consequent upon marital disharmony' and separation from his wife. Even if the story of his wife's affair is true, it may have been only a cover for his real reason for leaving the town.[8]

In a newspaper report of 1924 it was claimed that 'His parents were very respectable and had done all they could to put him straight ... After his parents had done everything they could for him, he broke into their house and stole jewellery'. Charges were not pressed. Christie briefly worked as a painter in Manchester, but soon moved to London, perhaps attracted by the anonymity of the capital and the better prospects it offered him. It was initially an aimless existence, as he later said, 'First I started travelling around, just walking from one place to another. I lived on savings [proceeds of theft?] and I didn't know where to settle'. He lived in rented rooms.[9]

Christie led a peripatetic life in London from 1923–33. He did not put down roots anywhere and made no lasting friends. At one point he was injured by a taxi in a traffic accident in central London. One account suggests he was cycling through the busy streets and was knocked down; the other that he was knocked over when crossing the road and became unconscious. In both cases he was treated at Charing Cross Hospital. He later had operations, for an injury to his left knee (Westminster Hospital) and also his right shoulder/collar bone (St Thomas' Hospital), leaving a permanent scar on his right shoulder. However, we only have Christie's word that these events happened, and since hospital patient records are either non-existent or closed for 100 years it is not yet possible to verify them. Yet the scar and partially missing clavicle were real enough.[10]

On 13 December 1923 Christie joined the RAF, service number 356,827, as an aircraftman second class. Oddly enough he gave his birthday as 8 April 1896. He was assigned to T Squadron, based at Uxbridge, where the RAF Central Depot was located. Signal units were based there in this period and given that Christie had been a signaller in the army in the previous decade it is no surprise that he was employed in the Electrical and Wireless School from 27 February 1924. He later claimed he enlisted because he wanted to be posted abroad so he could escape his criminal habits. Although his character was described as being very good, he claimed he was discharged due to bad health caused by his being gassed in 1918, though this may well be merely an excuse. Certainly he spent some of his brief service career in military hospitals, at Netley and then at RAF Hatton on 27 May 1924. Possibly his restless nature led him to being bored by the routine of military life in peacetime and he was discharged on 15 August 1924. Strangely, for some of the same time (20 December 1923 to 20 February 1924), he was also employed at the Empire Cinema on Vine Street, Uxbridge, as an operator.[11]

Christie was soon up to his old tricks. He was then living in Southall, on the fringes of west London. On Sunday 24 August, he had gone to the cinema where he was once employed and worked on the dynamo; Mr Needham, the assistant there, needing help to repair it, though this had not been authorised by John Polley, the manager. When Elizabeth Miller locked up for the night, Christie must have concealed himself inside, for the next morning she found the front door unbolted. Polley arrived at his office the following afternoon and discovered a chair obstructing his office door and a pipe and RAF glove on his desk. The cash, mainly coppers, which should have been in the till waiting to be banked, was missing, as were cigarettes, chocolate, glass cutters and money (worth £5 18s 2d in total). Some business cards left by salesmen were also missing.[12]

Furthermore, on 11 September, James Collins's twelve-year-old son left his bicycle (worth £3 10s) outside Hillingdon and Cowley Boys' School, Hillingdon Road, Uxbridge, in view of the road (and just opposite the RAF base), at 1.30pm. By 3.00pm it had vanished. Christie was the thief. Presumably he was motivated by simple financial gain, due to being unemployed.[13]

PC Thrusell found Christie lying on the grass at Southall Park, a few miles to the east of Uxbridge, on Monday 15 September, and asked him for his name and address. Christie replied, 'Wilson'. Thrusell went on to explain that a man of his description had been seen loitering in the vicinity of the school on the afternoon of the theft.

Christie denied he was there then, but admitted that he had sold a bicycle for a friend of his in Uxbridge, but he did not know where this alleged friend lived. He was arrested and on his person were found glass cutters and business cards (identified by Polley as his). When he was charged with the theft, on 16 September, before Howard Button at Uxbridge Magistrates' Court, he persisted in his denial. He was remanded in custody until the following week.[14]

The chief witness was Ernest Henry Elliott, of Southall, who ran a furniture business in nearby Hayes. He had been approached by Christie, who told him he was trying to sell a bicycle for a friend. Elliott agreed to sell it in his shop, and displayed it in the window, to sell for 35s. Next day Christie returned to ask if a sale had been made. It had not, but he said he needed money for a tram fare to Uxbridge, where he claimed he worked. Elliot gave him the money, but Christie returned later that day to say that he had lost his job due to being late and Elliott gave him 3s 6d and told him not to worry. The bicycle was sold on Saturday 13 September. Christie turned up to collect the money, saying that his friend could not attend. Elliott became suspicious and told the police, with the result that an arrest was made as related. At the trial the bicycle was identified by the boy's father.[15]

Christie pleaded not guilty and persisted in his story about helping out a friend in need, blaming the 'friend' for not having appeared at Elliott's, so 'I have to stand here and bear the brunt of the charge'. The friend was called Jack Smith, address unknown. Christie gave a description of the man but he could not be traced. He had apparently known this man since 15 August on leaving the RAF. Christie also said that he had left the cinema with Needham. His story was disbelieved and he was then (22 September) found guilty of both charges and asked to be dealt with leniently, claiming he would mend his ways.[16]

Christie was given two sentences of six and three months, with hard labour, the sentences to run consecutively. This was harsh; later sentences handed down to him in 1929 and 1933 were less so. Christie was sent to Wandsworth prison, where he was noted as being five feet eight, with blue eyes and brown hair, and his occupation was that of a 'motor driver'. It was noted that he had a good education, was from Halifax and was an Anglican, though the latter was purely nominal.[17]

Leaving gaol on remission on 11 May 1925 (the sentence expired on 21 June), Christie found a job as an electrician, employed by Messrs Hellyar and Sons Ltd, of 169 Church Road, Barnes. Doubtless his interest in matters electrical and his previous technical work in cinemas and in the RAF stood him in good stead. He worked for them for eight weeks. His next registered employment was as a lorry driver for a transport firm in Fulham, and he worked there from about January 1927 to May 1929. The reason for his eventual dismissal was his first violent crime.[18]

Meanwhile, life was fast changing for the Christie family in Halifax; though whether Christie was aware of it – or cared – is another question. There is certainly no evidence that he ever returned to Halifax. On 12 February 1928, Ernest Christie died, 'after a long and painful illness' at his home at 67 Chester Road. Christie may not have been unaware of this, for he later recalled his father dying after being paralysed in the legs. It is interesting to note that his will, which left £663 13s 6d (net), was entirely made out to his wife (who was also his executrix); the six remaining children were not mentioned at all. His widow died in Stockport in 1944 (Christie recalled, 'I loved her very much') with the Delves family. One family member remembered her looking at a picture of Christie in his policeman's uniform on her dressing table and saying, 'Oh, that's my little Reggie' (Christie was usually referred to as Reg or Reggie by family and friends). She deputised Percy to try and find Christie, but he was unsuccessful.[19]

Elsewhere in Yorkshire, life was moving on for Christie's wife, too. In 1924 she was employed by the English Electric Company, Phoenix Works, off Thornton Road in central Bradford. She never spoke about her husband whilst she was there. Emily Willis, a fellow employee, recalled 'She spoke of her sister and her sister's child. She was always talking about the child to whom she appeared deeply attached'. She was made redundant in about 1928. Then she moved to Sheffield to live with her brother, Henry Simpson Waddington (he had adopted the latter name in 1938 – some writers have mistaken it for Ethel's maiden name), a clerk employed by the council, resident at 63 Hinde House Lane. Her mother (who died in 1931), sister and her husband (Lily and Arthur Bartle) were at number 61. They thought Ethel was 'quiet and reserved' and 'seemed quite happy'. She stayed with them until about 1933, but also lived at a house in Earl Marshall Road. She is said to have reported her husband missing and applied, presumably unsuccessfully, for maintenance.[20]

However, Ethel, though employed as a shorthand typist at one of the steel works in Saville Street, Sheffield, and earning a good wage of £3 10s per week, had her own fish to fry. Vaughan Brindley, who was about four years her junior, met her in 1928. He later stated, 'I started keeping company with a girl called Ethel Christie whom I met at a dance at the Abbeydale Ballroom, Sheffield'. Brindley was single and 'began to court her'. The two went to the cinema, to the theatre, to dances and had trips to the countryside together. It was not until three months had passed that he noticed a wedding ring, and when he commented (he had believed her to be single), 'she broke down and cried'. She said that she had been married, but that her husband had been injured by poison gas in the War and had later died of his wounds.' She added that she had fallen in love with Brindley.[21]

Their romance blossomed nonetheless. They made love regularly. Although they never lived together, they did holiday together; in places such as Blackpool and Bournemouth. They had weekends away in Derbyshire, Brindley recalling, 'We lived as man and wife, registering as Mr and Mrs Christie'. By 1932, Brindley's job prospects had improved and he now felt in a position to marry. However, he did want to have children, and although he had never used contraceptives on the numerous occasions that they had had sex, Ethel had never become pregnant. He feared that she might not be capable of bearing a child. Ethel told him that she had once had a miscarriage when she was married. Ethel wanted marriage and she approached Brindley's father, asking him to use his influence on his son. This enraged Brindley and they quarrelled. The two split by the end of 1932.[22]

Despite this, in 1953 Brindley, now married and a father of two, had fond memories of Ethel, though he did not want these made public. He said Ethel was 'a refined, well bred and educated young woman. She was extremely attractive'. She was also respectable and did not frequent pubs, nor did she smoke. He added that she had a 'timid, sensitive nature' but was an 'extremely competent shorthand typist'. This adds a new dimension to our knowledge of Ethel; confirming what Christie said of her as regards her looks, but also indicating her efficiency as a worker and her need for male attention. He added that she kept a diary at this time, but unfortunately it is not known to have survived.[23]

It was probably in 1928 that Christie was in his second, and only other co-habiting relationship with a woman. In the following year he committed his first known violent crime. Mrs Maud Cole, who did not live with her husband, was travelling to Margate in a charabanc, presumably in the summer of 1928. She met Christie on this trip and they began to live together, at a flat at 6 Almeric Road, Battersea, together with her unnamed schoolboy son. Apparently Christie and

Mrs Cole were very fond of each other. It is often stated that Mrs Cole was a prostitute, but there is no evidence for this, and, as we shall note, she referred to going out in the daytime to work. It is hard to imagine that Christie, as a possessive man, would have tolerated such a profession. It might also be added that a clause of the Vagrancy Act of 1898 had made living off immoral earnings a crime and Christie was not charged with this, despite the court's evident animosity towards him.[24]

The couple had their problems, chiefly stemming from Christie's parsimony. Apparently he only ever contributed about a shilling towards housekeeping costs. At first this did not matter too much. Mrs Cole went out to work, and Christie was out of the flat for most of the time that he lived there, so he did not cost her much, she later said. He had been in work for the first fortnight he had lived with her, but apparently not thereafter (this is Mrs Cole's version; as noted above he was in work). Mrs Cole was, however, not possessed of infinite patience, and told him he should look for work. She said that he refused to do so. In late April, it was decided that he should leave. Christie did not take this well, and assured her that if he could not have her, then no one would.[25]

Matters came to a head on 1 May. In the morning of that day, Christie took master Cole's cricket bat out of the corner and said, 'This is a strong bat'. He said no more about it. At lunchtime, Mrs Cole brought Christie some fried chips – apparently he did not like fish – which he sat down and ate. He then left the table, whilst Mrs Cole remained seated. She then felt a blow to her head and she fell over. She later said, 'It half stunned me. It was all the world like an explosion. Everything seemed to go black for a second'. Rising, she felt Christie's fingers in her mouth, injuring her lip. She screamed and the noise of the scuffle was heard by Richard Boswell, who lived in the flat above Mrs Cole's.[26]

Boswell saw Mrs Cole at her door. Blood was streaming from her head. Two hands were pushing her out of the room. The door was then locked from the inside. Mrs Cole told Boswell, 'Don't let him get at me. He's trying to murder me'. Boswell took her to his flat and then called the police. PC Davidson, 563L, arrived at ten to one and found that the door to the flat was locked. He forced the door open, but found there was no one there. Marks on the window sill showed that someone had recently vacated the flat by that means. Christie was later arrested by DS Swain at Victoria Street. Meanwhile, Mrs Cole was taken to

Bolingbroke Hospital, where she was seen to by Dr John Ives, who saw that she had a scalp wound, five inches long. It needed five stitches and he sent her to St James' Infirmary. However, she was told that there would be no permanent injury. It was when she was in the recovery ward there that she was visited by Christie. He told her that it was an accident, but she disagreed and he then walked out. He later wrote her a letter, declaring that he would receive three years in prison and a flogging for what he had done.[27]

Christie was brought before Mr Campion at the South Western Magistrates' Court on Monday 13 May, charged with causing grievous bodily harm. Dr Ives and Mrs Cole gave their evidence, the essence of which has already been recounted. The clerk of the court read a written statement from Christie. He claimed that he was only swinging the cricket bat to test it and thought he had merely hit the back of the chair, not Mrs Cole. He went on to say that he did not realise that she was injured until she fell over and he picked her up. He then said he lost control of himself and panicked, fleeing through the window. The blow 'was an absolute accident'.[28]

Campion did not believe Christie's story, believing him to be a liar and a coward. He pointed out that Mrs Cole had been good to him and that 'he was fond of her as much as he could be fond of anyone'. He said that the assault was 'a murderous attack' and that with a little more force, it could have broken through her skull and killed her. Reading the letter quoted two paragraphs above, Campion regretted he could not sentence Christie to corporal punishment (not abolished until 1948, so it is unclear why it could not have been administered), 'though it was a thing that would impress itself strongly on a man of his cowardly temperament'. Instead, he imposed the maximum sentence he could, which was to give him six months in prison, with hard labour. Needless to say, it brought his driving job to an end. He was again sent to Wandsworth Prison, and the same facts were noted about him in the prison ledger, except that under 'Education', was written 'RWM', meaning he could read and write and was able to do mathematics.[29]

Christie returned to driving once he was released on remission on 14 October (the sentence expired on 12 November). From 8 July to 27 September 1930, Christie was working as a coach driver for the United Services Transport Company, based at Clapham Road. He was dismissed due to his slackness. A few weeks later, he found another job as a driver, this time with Messrs Waring and Gillow Ltd, Oxford

Street. Although he was with them until 23 May 1932, he was not fired but had to leave because of a rearrangement of staff.[30]

It has been suggested that Christie may have commenced his murderous career in London in the 1930s. The only murder which he may possibly have committed is the strangulation of Dora Lloyd, a middle-aged prostitute, on 21 February 1932, in her flat in Maida Vale. The man last seen with her was about thirty-five, five feet nine, medium build, clean shaven, wore horn-rimmed spectacles and 'spoke in a very nice and gentlemanly manner'. He may have lived in Wimbledon or Kensington, and wore an overcoat and a trilby. The motive was unclear as the victim had been neither robbed nor raped. Whilst some of these characteristics fit Christie (type of victim, method of murder, appearance and voice), they would probably fit many other men in London too. It is also the case that Christie did not wear glasses in 1932; he is first noted attending an optician in 1937, and it was not until 1948 that he became bespectacled. He was certainly not mentioned as a suspect in the police file covering the case. So, Christie was almost certainly innocent of this murder.[31]

Christie returned to west London in 1932. From 20 July to 17 September that year he was employed as a lorry driver once more, this time being employed by Clifford's (Fulham) Ltd, a haulage company on the Great West Road in Brentford. Then he switched to the employ of Sir Robert MacAlpine and Sons (London) Ltd, contractors, based in Cranford (or so he said: one record states he was not in registered employment for the following year).[32]

On Sunday 22 October 1933, Albert Henry Thomas, a cashier in MacAlpine's employ, noticed that a Morris Oxford car, worth £70, was missing from a garage there. The car, and Christie, were seen on the following day by Charles Albert Morton, of Calvert Brickworks, in Calvert, Buckinghamshire (near Twyford). It was 6.45pm and Christie asked him for permission to pull inside the works, so he could sleep in the car, because he claimed he had been driving since six that morning. He told Morton, 'You know me, I used to cart bricks from here with Clifford's lorries. I have left now and am working for MacAlpines'.[33]

Morton remembered him and Christie reminded him, 'My name is Christie'. He said that he had become very tired because of all the driving he had done and was feeling faint and giddy. He was given permission to park inside the works gates. Christie added, 'Thank you. If I had stayed along the road or in a field the police or someone will disturb me'. Christie drove through the now open gates and parked the car. Within half an hour, he was asleep.[34]

However, Christie's story did not ring true. Morton contacted the police. At 8.15pm, PC Taverner of the Buckinghamshire Police arrived and went to the brickfield, where he roused the sleeping Christie and asked what he was doing. 'Just having a sleep. Mr Morton said that I could come in here'. The constable asked him for his licence and insurance papers, but Christie could not provide them, saying that his driving licence had expired and that he lacked any motor insurance. He was then told that the car had been stolen. Christie feigned innocence, as ever, replying, 'I was picked up by another man, who has gone to look for lodgings, and he left me here to drive the car into the yard'.[35]

The car was taken to Harlington Police station where it was identified by Thomas on the following day. Christie was formally charged and found himself, on 1 November, once again at Uxbridge Magistrates' Court, where he was described as being 'a motor driver of no fixed abode'. Rowland Richard Robbins, CBE, was chairman of the court, where the charges were stealing and receiving the car, driving without a licence and lacking third-party insurance. There was also the charge of breaking and entering into the garage in the pursuance of theft, but this was dropped. For once, Christie pleaded guilty to all charges and apologized for his misdemeanours. DS Templeman told the court that the accused had four previous convictions. Christie was found guilty and sent to prison for three months, with hard labour, for the theft of the car. For the other offences, he was given the choice of either a 10s fine or seven days in prison. Choosing the latter, he was told that this sentence would run concurrently. This also meant that he would be disqualified from driving for a year. For the third and final time, he was sent to Wandsworth prison.[36]

It will be noted that there is no reference to Christie stealing the car from a priest, as has been stated by previous authors. This is because the contemporary report does not refer to it. Furthermore, such was the poverty of Catholic clergymen that very few, if any, would have owned a car at this period. One version of the story, reported in the press in 1953, is that a priest employed Christie as chauffeur and his wife as housekeeper after the former came out of prison, and that Christie repaid his kindness by theft. As stated above, Christie was employed elsewhere and his wife was still in Sheffield.[37]

This was the last petty offence committed by Christie and indeed he is not known to have carried out any other criminal act for another decade. One reason for this was his reconciliation with his estranged wife, who visited him in prison. According to Christie:

> At her visit to Wandsworth it was agreed, that the past on both sides should be put behind us ... At the visit she said it was a question of divorce or coming together again. I asked her which she preferred and she said coming together again ... After a couple of weeks we felt as if we had never been parted.

This occurred on Ethel's initiative, possibly because her romance with Brindley had collapsed. Her sister recalled, 'John Reginald Christie was eventually traced to London and my sister joined him there and they resumed normal married life'. He did not mention his assault on Mrs Cole. He was released from prison on remission on 17 January 1934 (sentence expired on 31 January). Christie clearly always behaved well when under the thumb and so was always released early. He and Ethel had moved to Notting Hill by the end of 1934 and the two were certainly living together in 1936, for they are then recorded at 23 Oxford Gardens, after having resided briefly at 173 Clarendon Road, and probably at other addresses, prior to this. In these instances they lived in just the one room. Christie also (in December 1934) signed up with Dr Matthew Odess of 30 Colville Square, who was to remain his physician for the rest of his life. He recalled treating Christie for insomnia in 1936, and Christie claimed he helped him with his shoulder. His first appointment was on 15 December 1934 for eczema of the foot; in 1936 there were four visits: headache, colds, temperatures and insomnia. There were three appointments in 1937; four in 1938 and a staggering ten in 1939. He also saw an optician in 1937.[38]

According to Christie he and Ethel lived happily enough:

> If when I saw her coming home at night and she was out I always was very careful to have the tea ready for her. Was very careful about that. She had sore feet and so as soon as she came in she could sit down and rest her feet and have her tea. I used to sit at the window watching for her so as to have the tea ready as soon as she came in. If we had been out to Regent's Park when she came in I would get water for her feet so that she could bathe them. One Xmas she had a bilious attack and I got the Xmas dinner ready.[39]

It was in 1937 (not December 1938 as previously thought) that the Christies moved from living in Oxford Gardens to that address forever associated with Christie – 10 Rillington Place.

Before going any further with the Christie story, we should briefly consider the history of the house which will unwittingly form the setting for the tragedies which follow.

Rillington Place was a small road in Notting Hill – formed of ten houses on each side of the road, just off St Mark's Road, with the southern side, from St Mark's Road, numbered from one to ten and the northern side from eleven to twenty. The houses were built in early 1869 by a number of builders, and initially had an annual rental value of £28. The houses in the street were of a dull conformity. The front doors all opened onto the pavement. They had a frontage of seventeen feet and were twenty-six feet long, with a back yard/garden of a further twenty-eight feet. They have been described as 'doll's houses' due to their small size. Each had a washroom and a toilet at the rear. Number 10 and some of the other houses were still uninhabited a year after their erection, and it was not until 1871 that the houses were all populated. The Charles Booth 'poverty map' of the 1890s has the street coloured purple, indicating that there were working people inhabiting the street, neither rich nor poor. At the end of the road, near number 10, was Bartle's iron foundry, with its large chimney.[40]

Contemporary middle-class descriptions of the district are unflattering. One said it was 'an area of West London that in many ways parallels Whitechapel to the east, except that it was once an eminently respectable neighbourhood which has since declined'. Another reported that the house was 'a squalid house in a seedy neighbourhood'. Of the house it was said:

10 Rillington Place was a tiny shabby house, where the paint needed renewing, where there was no bathroom and only one WC on the garden level for all the inhabitants ... Being a cul-de-sac, Rillington Place, was the natural playground ... of the children of the neighbourhood ... On summer days when the evenings are mild the housewives sit out on broken chairs or on the kerb edge and call to acquaintances passing in slippers and curlers. The yellow brick of the mean terraced houses, which face each other across the littered street, is stained and the doors and windows are ill fitting, for the foundations are gradually sinking. At the end of the cul-de-sac is a wall and behind it shows an ugly factory

chimney. Beyond the wall the ground falls away to a level well below that of Rillington Place.

No. 10 is the last house on the left hand side … There are no cellars, the staircase is narrow, and it is impossible for anybody to do much about the house without the other inhabitants hearing. On the ground floor there is an ugly Victorian bay window to the front room of the house, surrounded by crumbling sandstone. This was the room the Christies used as their sitting-room; their bedroom was behind it with a window looking out on the back-yard and the garden; and a tiny kitchen, a mere box of a room, was beyond it on the other side of the narrow passageway which led out to the garden and the communal water closet … It is of importance that in front of the bay window on the ground floor there was a manhole cover of heavy iron set into the paving over the drains. Set into the front wall beneath the window, below the level of the sitting-room, was a ventilator grating.[41]

Of course, in much of this it was no worse than much of the housing stock in the neighbourhood. When, in 1953, there were proposals for slum clearance in north Kensington, the street was not on the list. A positive spin was given in an auctioneer's sale catalogue of 1932 which advertised numbers 12 and 13 for sale. It referred to them thus, 'Just off St Mark's Road and close to Ladbroke Grove (Metropolitan) station and frequent bus routes' and 'The Attractive Non-Basement Bay windowed property'. It was suggested that for one tenant, weekly rent could be 24s 8d.[42]

The house was certainly in a poverty-stricken district; one of the worst in London. On average, 1.3 people shared each room in 1931 and 14.8 per cent lived below the poverty line, which was the highest proportion anywhere in west London and far above the average for the city. The death rate was high, at 13.8 per 1,000, and infant mortality was 77 per 1,000; both among the highest for London. There were few open spaces for recreation. As a report stated, 'North and west of Notting Hill High Street is a mixed middle and working class district, which in the Notting Dale region includes some of the most notorious slums in London. Since the War some new blocks and cottages have replaced slums in this region, but north of it is still bad'.[43]

There had already been a hideous crime committed in this district, which had received national attention. This was the murder by strangulation and the sexual assault of ten-year-old Vera Page of 22 Blenheim

Crescent in December 1931. No one was ever convicted of this terrible crime. The chief suspect, Percy Orlando Rush (1891–1961), lived in the district at 128 Talbot Road until 1947.[44]

No. 10 Rillington Place was divided into three floors and each housed one household. In 1937, the landlord was Arthur George Partridge, who owned several properties on the street, each with an annual rental value of £28. Charles Herbert Kitchener (1877–1964), once a van guard at Paddington for the GWR, resided on the first floor, as he had done since about 1920. From 1920–1924, he had lived with Sarah Kitchener. On the ground floor lived an elderly woman, one Alice Aldridge, and on the second floor were Edward and Winifred Smith. He moved to the ground floor on her death in late 1936. Sometime afterwards, but before autumn 1937, the Christies began to rent the two rooms on the second floor, and in December 1938 they took the rooms on the ground floor when vacated by Smith (who had lived in the house since 1929). The second-floor rooms were then taken by Kathleen and Stanley Clowes. Christie later recollected, 'We occupy the ground floor which consists of a bedroom, living room and a kitchen'. Ethel put a picture of her mother on the living room wall. They paid 12s per week rent.[45]

Christie and Ethel settled down, again, as in 1920. In September 1936 Christie had taken the job of foreman at the Commodore Cinema at King Street, Hammersmith (the fourth cinema he was employed at, and since demolished). He worked there for almost three years and this spell of employment was only interrupted by the outbreak of war, though during 1937 several hundred pounds were stolen from the safe in his office (two men were arrested for this crime). It was in 1939 that Christie and Ethel acquired a fawn-coloured Irish terrier (later to be joined by a cat), doubtless much to Christie's content and probably because he wanted the additional companionship they unconditionally offered.[46]

It had been a tumultuous two decades. Christie had committed at least two offences in Halifax, and probably the even more heinous one of stealing from his parents, then decamped to London. He had been injured in a road accident, and then lived a peripatetic existence, mainly making a living from various driving jobs, all of which were relatively short-lived. They were also punctuated by three prison sentences for theft and violent assault. The latter incident demonstrates Christie's foul temper – like that of his father. However, with the arrival of Ethel in about 1934, after a separation of a decade, and, from 1936, permanent employment and a secure address at 10 Rillington Place, his life seemed to have made a return to a humdrum, tolerable kind of existence. Outwardly he was as respectable as ever and neighbours later recalled him 'as quite an upstanding bloke'.

Chapter 3

Christie's First Murders
1939–46

*'Once again, I experienced that quiet peaceful thrill.
I had no regrets'.*[1]

On the first day of September 1939, the Blitzkrieg on Poland began as the German army advanced eastwards, thus beginning the Second World War. On the same day, Christie, having already registered his interest, responded to the call for more police manpower in the capital and enrolled as a Wartime Reserve Constable, number 07732. Initially he had applied to be a full-time ARP Warden in Paddington, but he was turned down.[2]

Christie never explained why he took this step. Possibly it was because it would give him a position of power, or opportunities for crime, or because he wished to avoid conscription into the armed forces. The latter is less likely because the ages for conscription were between eighteen and forty-one and he was at the upper end of this age range when war began. A man with his illnesses was unlikely to have been classed as being A1 fit. It was during the Second World War that Christie resumed his criminal career, but this time he turned to the far more serious offence of murder. However, he was now far more cunning and successfully concealed his misdeeds on both occasions.

Those with a criminal record are usually barred from entry into the police force in any capacity, and Christie had five previous convictions. Yet his record was not checked, and he served as a constable for over four years. This is easy to explain. The urgent demand for additional manpower and the difficulty of checking paper records for the 20,000 men who formed the war reserve constabulary meant that men with convictions could easily slip through the net.

Christie's police service, as with his army and RAF service, seems to have been creditable enough. He was attached to the Harrow Road

Police Station, which was in district X, Paddington. Christie was an enthusiastic officer, and said to a colleague, 'If I were a younger man I would like to be a regular CID man. There must be a thrill in tracking down a murderer'. It was stated, 'His conduct was assessed as very good, and he was commended on two occasions for his ability relating to criminal offences'. These were for arresting a man who was giving false air-raid warnings and for work on a case of bicycle theft. A magistrate commended Christie for the way in which he gave evidence in court and this was incorporated in a wireless programme about police work. He also obtained a First Aid Certificate. Frederick Byers, later a detective inspector, recalled:

> it would have been on several occasions that he was paired with me on various duties. A War Reserve Policeman was normally paired with a time serving one when detailed to go on fixed points and similar duties. He was as far as I remember a good War Reserve Policeman and did his work well. He was always well turned out as compared with War Reserve Policemen generally ...
> I believe Christie worked on plain clothes duties.

He added that he was 'efficient and tidy' and said that there was nothing eccentric or odd about him. However, Byers remarked: 'I didn't like him. I wouldn't like to put a finger on it, just one of those things, you either like or dislike'. Another former colleague, George Outram, recalled that Christie made many complaints about cars parking in Rillington Place. This reflects the puritanical side of Christie. However, Outram remembered another side of Christie's character. 'He used to go out picking up prostitutes'. This happened a lot, and the behaviour continued after Christie left the police. On one occasion, Outram and Christie were in Westbourne Grove and the former was about to arrest a woman he suspected of prostitution. Christie said, 'That's my wife,' and so Outram desisted. He later learnt that Christie had been lying. In 1953, one Daniel Heaney recalled that Christie reminisced about his experiences in this sphere: 'he was able to make friends of a number of prostitutes in the West End area, and ... he had a happy arrangement with them where he would turn a blind eye to their activities, and he could have a good time'.[3]

Christie recalled a terrifying incident during his war service:

> I was shaken on two occasions by bombs dropping while on duty. On the second occasion I was nearly overcome by gas from a

fractured main in the street, while getting people to a Rest Centre. On the first time I was in Kilburn Lane when a bomb exploded in Harrow Road approximately a hundred yards away. I was knocked down but carried on helping in rescue work.

One Francis Ross recalled travelling with Christie and other 'specials' in mobile canteens during air raids. He later said that Christie often complained about money matters and the two became friends. Christie could be officious and so was not universally popular. Tom Jarrett recalled, 'It gave him a certain status and a sense of power over ordinary people. He liked to flash his warrant card and boast about the number of people he had "knocked off"'. Mrs McFadden of 3 Rillington Place later recalled, 'often he tried to use his police authority to tell us to do what he wanted. He threatened to report practically everybody in the street for some lighting or other supposed irregularity'. He later claimed he continued as a friend to animals; on seeing a man hitting a dog in 1941, he struck the man in the face with his fist. Two years later, when he saw a dog being injured by a bus, he took the animal to the People's Dispensary for Sick Animals. What is clear is that Christie looked back at his time as a police officer with pride, and, as we shall note, he often mentioned it to those with whom he came into contact. He even sent a photograph of himself in his uniform to his mother; a rare instance of his making contact with his estranged family.[4]

The Christies visited Ethel's relatives in Sheffield together during 1940–41. Christie later recalled:

When you had a bad Blitz and the High Street was wrecked, I was on leave from our Metropolitan Police and was spending time in Firth Park. I went to the police station and offered my services after producing my warrant card. What a time it was. It was like London often and seemed like a busman's holiday.[5]

It was also at this time that the Christies began to spend their Christmasses in Sheffield. This was at Ethel's aunt's, Emily Legg's, in Duke Street. She recalled, 'They seemed quite happy'.[6]

John Girandot, who lived at 220 Lancaster Road and whose garden was near Christie's, also remembered him from this time. Girandot recalled, 'I have had quite a lot of disagreements with him over various matters', chiefly Christie's habit of throwing stones over the garden fence. He stated, 'Whilst he was serving in the Police War

Reserve, he offered to fight me, but when I went round to his address, he failed to open the door'. The two never came to actual blows.[7]

We have already noted that Christie often visited his doctor because of a variety of illnesses. His time in the police was no exception to this rule. Although he passed the police medical examination as being in good health, during his service of four years, four months he took 108 days off because of sickness, on ten occasions (peaking in 1942 with four lengthy absences from work); for influenza, chills and tonsillitis. In fact he was first sick on the day after enlisting, and was to be off work until 10 December. However, he was only off for twelve days in the following year and for five days in 1941. He also suffered two injuries; hurting his nose when walking into a letter box at night time on 13 October 1941 and being hit on the upper lip on 30 June 1943.[8]

Christie also found the time to have an affair with one of his female colleagues, one Gladys Jones, a married woman (born in 1911), but allegedly separated from her husband since 1937. She later recalled, 'We formed an acquaintanceship [in 1942 or 1943], I do not wish to go into any details respecting my acquaintanceship with Christie, but he was cited as co-respondent in the divorce action'. Christie often visited her in her rooms at 196 Ladbroke Grove, but never stayed the night there. It has been said that this affair ended in 1943 with her husband, a soldier, finding Christie and hitting him, but as we shall later note this occurred later and the affair lasted until the war's end. In any case, Christie's rival, David Iorweth Jones, served in the RAF.[9]

Another woman had an important part to play in Christie's life. This was Ruth Margarete Christina Fuerst, who had been born on 2 August 1922 in Bad-Voeslau, Lower Austria. Her father was Ludwig Fuerst (1879–1951), a painter, who had married Fredericke Altmann (born in 1891). Ruth was their second of at least three children. She attended the Higher Elementary School there from 1932–36; having to leave because she was half Jewish (a *mischling*), probably on her mother's side. In 1937 she was at a school in Hamburg when she was separated from her family. She was tall (five feet and nine inches) and slender, but suffered from deformed legs and bad blood, so was excused sports at school. When she was six or seven she injured herself at school accidentally with a pencil, which left a small scar above one of her eyes. There was also dental treatment, resulting in a crown, possibly carried out by Dr Heinrich Blaschke in 1930 for 80s, and this was later to play an important part in her identification. She was fond of jewellery and wore a charm bracelet and also wore a Christian cross around her neck, but was described as being without religion. However, racially she was part Jew and in March 1938 Nazi Germany annexed Austria in what was known as the Anschluss. Jewish property was confiscated. It was time for far-sighted Jews to leave the country and many did so. Ruth moved to Vienna on 1 October 1938 and stayed at 2 Nestroplatz there until leaving for England. It is likely that the family broke up, with her parents going to the USA and residing in New York by 1951. Ruth believed they died in a concentration camp. Fortunately, the Swedish Mission assisted in her emigration to England.[10]

Ruth arrived in Britain as a refugee on 8 June 1939, with Edith Willis of 92 Oakwood Road, Golders Green, as her guarantor, who referred to her thus, 'very difficult to manage and was very keen on the company of men'. She was designated as an alien, number EZ 356710. Initially she was employed at the Prince of Wales Hotel, De Vere Gardens, Kensington, where she was described as a 'very reserved type of girl who formed no close friendships and who studied nursing and medical books during her off duty periods'. Between 1 August and 2 October 1939 she worked as a student nurse at St Gabriel's Home, Westgate on Sea, Kent, where she was described as 'very intelligent and alert'. Then she went to live with the Revd and Mrs Le Bas at Elswick, Lancashire. They found her to be 'morose and sullen', unhappy and uninterested in domestic work. They put this down to a mental illness and sent her to a London specialist.[11]

On 8 December 1939 Ruth appeared before a tribunal (all Austrians and Germans in the country had to attend a tribunal, a process intended to weed out spies) and declared she was a refugee from Nazi persecution. No immediate action was taken against her. It was a different story in the following year when invasion loomed. As with all other Germans and Austrians in Britain, Ruth was put in an internment camp. In her case, this was on the Isle of Man, from 15 June to 23 December 1940. When she regained her freedom, she gravitated towards London and was given police number 764019. It was here, in December 1941, whilst working in the Mayfair Hotel, possibly as a waitress, that she met Anastasio Isiedoran, a Cypriot waiter employed in a Soho restaurant. She had a daughter by him, named Christina Sonya and born on 9 October 1942 at the West End Lane Home for Unmarried Mothers. The baby was taken to St Christopher's Residential School, Tunbridge Wells, and was later adopted.[12]

Ruth met an old friend, one Paula Eisenstadt, of 30 Orsett Terrace, W2 (where Ruth once lived), in February or March 1943. Paula thought Ruth, who was then employed as a waitress and living at 141 Elgin Crescent, was 'very hard up' and was 'a girl who could be easily influenced by a stronger character'. She gave Ruth some handkerchiefs.

Later in 1943 Ruth was living in a room at 41 Oxford Gardens, Notting Hill, not far from Rillington Place and therefore within Christie's regular orbit. She worked at John Bolding and Sons, Grosvenor Works, Britannia/Davies Street, WC1, from 30 March to the week ending 29 June 1943, as a capstan operator. Christie believed 'she was in some factory making sewing machines or something'. This was a munitions factory and she worked on the night shift. Although deemed 'a very attractive girl', she was a poor time-keeper. She told her colleagues that she had had a German husband, but that he had been killed in the war. It was on 25 May that she wrote her last letter to her mother in America. Apparently her final weekly wages were never collected. A colleague thought she left the job because she was about to marry; others that she was pregnant. It is not certain how she was employed after leaving the factory job; prostitution or petty theft are two possibilities. (Christie later said, 'she used to go out with American soldiers and one of them was responsible for the baby', though the latter is incorrect; perhaps the former is, too). However, neither of these may have been the case because there are no instances of any convictions, though this may have been the result of the police turning a blind eye, perhaps receiving payment in kind to do so. She was subject to authority and was reprimanded for not informing the police of her changes of address, as aliens were obliged to do. On the first occasion, 10 April 1942, there was a verbal warning; on the second, 13 May 1942, she was obliged to attend Marlborough Magistrates' Court, where she was bound over for future good behaviour.[13]

There are two accounts of how Christie met Ruth, both given by him. One account states that they had been acquainted since January 1943; the other implies it was later that year. One says that he was off duty and in plain clothes and met her at David Griffin's Refreshment Room, 110a Ladbroke Grove, 'I was off duty at the time and I used to go into the snack bar to see if I could find a man who was wanted for theft'. The other account claims that he met her whilst on his beat. She is often described as being a part-time prostitute, but Christie only said, 'I knew that some of her friends were prostitutes', but he would hardly be likely to mention that she was one if that had been the case.

However, she was in want of money and Christie said that she needed cash for the rent and he gave her 10s as a loan when it was requested, but added that she would have to come to his home to collect it – when Ethel was absent. Apparently she had visited there twice already. He claimed that they struck up a friendship and that she kept him company on his beat, and that they had lengthy conversations. According to him, she was fascinated by his uniform.[14]

Ruth was waiting for Christie on the doorstep on the appointed day; perhaps 21 August 1943 (Ethel was absent). They had tea in the kitchen and talked. Christie later said she was 'madly in love with me', despite knowing that he was married. He claimed that 'It was she who suggested that we should become lovers ... I was rather backward and shy'. Yet it may have been a simple cash transaction, and we know Christie enjoyed the company of prostitutes. They went to the bedroom. Christie later admitted, 'While I was having intercourse with her, I strangled her with a piece of rope. There was a struggle. But she died quickly'. Surveying his victim, he recalled, 'She looked more beautiful in death than life'. He added, 'I remember as I gazed down at the still form of my first victim experiencing a strange, peaceful thrill ... It was thrilling because I had embarked on the career I had chosen for myself – the career of murder'. Yet the killing was probably not part of a long-term plan, as he claimed ten years later. He was on duty and had not taken sick leave despite his record of doing so, suggesting this murder was not pre-meditated.[15]

After committing the crime, Christie was alarmed by the expulsion of her bodily fluids and wrapped her naked body in her coat and then hid the body under the floorboards of the front room. When Ethel's brother was in the house (he slept in the same room as the corpse), Christie remembered 'I became worried, wondering whether he would suspect anything'. Once Waddington left on the next day, and Ethel was at work, Christie took the body to the wash house behind the house. That evening he buried her three feet deep and planted things over the spot, and then he burnt her clothes. This was on the right-hand side of the garden, halfway towards the rockery. On the following night, he straightened the garden and raked it over. He later dug up the skull by accident, put it in the dustbin and covered it up. The dustbin was then buried and used as a place for burning rubbish. The neighbours saw him digging and they exchanged greetings. He was later asked, 'Is this the first person you killed in your life?' and Christie replied, 'I don't know', but it probably was.[16]

Ruth's disappearance was reported by her landlady, Julie Walker, probably when she failed to appear to pay the rent, and also on 1 September by the Friends Committee for Refugees and Aliens. Her particulars were circulated in *The Police Gazette* on 16 October, but only because she had failed to register as an alien. It was noted there that 'It is known that she is in bad health', but we don't know exactly what this was. No news of her was forthcoming. However, London, with its teeming millions, can be an anonymous place, and doubly so in the upheaval caused by war, when people come and go at short notice. So the disappearance of a single foreign young woman, with fourteen addresses in four years, without close friends or family, was not remarkable, especially because there was no suspicion of foul play.[17]

The question to ask is 'Why did Christie begin his murderous career in 1943?' Christie never gave an answer. The impetus for the murder may have been (according to one of his two versions of the event) that whilst the two were preparing for sex, there came a knock at the door. It was a telegram boy with a message about Ethel and her brother's imminent return. This may have panicked Christie, desperate not to be found *in flagrante delicto*, and may have led him to murder, especially if Ruth was suggesting a long-term arrangement. Certainly Christie claimed that she was rather more ardent than him, though whether this is because she wanted his money, saw him as a father figure/protector, especially as he was older and a policeman, or was due to genuine affection/infatuation, is unknown. Christie may thus have become a murderer by accident, but it was a role he was to relish.

Christie's underlying motive for the crime seems to have been partly sexual; a means of fulfilling his desires, which could be satisfied in no other way. He had always had a fascination for corpses. Dr Jack Hobson, a psychiatrist, later said, 'There is some evidence in the way he describes finding bodies when he was a Special Constable to suggest he had some abnormal feeling of fascination in seeing bodies'. He may also have been motivated by a desire for power. It is also worth noting that he had, for the first time in his life, the opportunity to kill in relative safety. He had a secure base which he could lure his victim to, where he could kill and dispose of the body safely, and his wife was absent. Finally, the social upheaval caused by war enabled him to meet his first two victims and kill them with impunity (also the case for Haigh in 1944). Once Ruth was dead there was no going back: revelation of his crime could mean his own death. The Rubicon had been truly crossed, and the enormity of Christie's act may have taken time to sink in. He had clearly enjoyed the murder and could not resist this part of his nature. He later wrote, 'some unknown force was urging me to do it. Was compelling me to go on', but this was probably his own nature as opposed to anything else.[18]

On 28 December, Christie voluntarily left the police force: 'He was released from the War Reserve for employment in industry'. It is not known why this happened; perhaps ill health was the reason as Christie was on sick leave from 27 November to 26 December with influenza. He began to work at the Ultra Electric Ltd factory on the Western Avenue, Park Royal, on the following day. It manufactured radios. He was employed as a despatch clerk and an inter-departmental driver. It was here, several months later, that he met his second victim.[19]

Muriel Amelia Eady was a different character to Ruth Fuerst. She was born in Plaistow on 14 October 1912, and was the youngest of four children of William Eady (born in 1875) and Fanny Hooper, who married in 1904. They were then living at 20 Baron Road, Plaistow. Muriel had an unfortunate start in life and her youth was not very happy. Her mother died in 1918. The children were split up, with Reginald (born 1907) and Ernest (born 1909) being sent to Shenfield Home, Sheffield, paid for by her father, while she was placed in Poplar Homes, Brentwood, although she later went to the Hutton School with her brothers. Her other brother, Leslie, died at a very young age. Her father was in the Merchant Navy and, because he was often at sea, he was unable to care for his children, though he occasionally visited his daughter, last seeing her in 1943. At the age of twelve she went to live with her father's sister-in-law, Mrs Ethel Souhami, at 48 Cresswick Road, Acton, on her father's approval. Ethel was strict and did not allow Muriel any male friends. She was only allowed out of the house to do shopping. Her cousin, Wilfred Dunn, who also lived in the house in Acton, remarked that she was 'rather a quiet sort of person and usually was rather reticent'. In about 1935, Muriel was working in Cambridge, perhaps in domestic service. When Mrs Souhami died, in March 1939, Muriel went to live at number 50, then afterwards went to another aunt, Martha Elizabeth Hooper, at 12 Roskell Road, Putney. Muriel was described as being five feet four inches tall, with brown hair, a fresh complexion, a straight nose, a round face and stout.[20]

Muriel's new life was an improvement on the old one. One Richard Grant recorded, 'after her aunt [Mrs Souhami]'s death, she changed

and started going out with men. She had a number of male acquaintances'. On one occasion in 1944, when she took her ten-year-old niece
to an amusement arcade near Putney Bridge, she was seen with a man
who was tall, slim and 'very reticent'. They were also seen at the Half
Moon pub on Lower Richmond Road, Putney. Dunn recalled her
talking about the prospect of marrying a 'middle-aged gentleman'
who was employed at her place of work. This man was never named,
but was described as being either a gatekeeper or watchman, who had
once served in the police force. This was possibly Ernest Lawson, who
was thirty-six in 1944 and was employed as the gatekeeper where
Muriel worked. He described himself as a friend. Muriel also talked of
going to Ireland with the brother of a friend called Pat who had died in
an air raid on Hammersmith.[21]

Muriel began to work at the Integral Auxiliary Equipment Company
at Chiswick in 1943, then started work at Ultra Electric, not very far
from her old home in Acton, on the assembly line, on 20 April 1944.
Why she chose to do so is unclear, because the journey from Putney
was a lengthy and time-consuming one. Christie later recalled, 'I got
friendly with a woman named Eady', the pair having met in the works
canteen over a cup of tea. He introduced her and a male friend of hers,
who was never named (probably Lawson), whom Christie referred to
as 'a nice fellow', to Ethel. The four often had tea at Rillington Place
and went to the cinema together once.[22]

Christie selected Muriel as his next victim and carefully planned his
second murder, later recalling that it was 'a really clever murder,
much cleverer than the first'. He took his time and was properly
cautious. He also took sick leave from 2–10 October, alleging bron-
chitis (he visited Dr Odess's locum thirteen times that year). Having
wormed his way into Muriel's confidence, he found that her weakness
was her health concerns – she suffered from catarrh. 'My knowledge
of medicine made it possible for me to talk convincingly about sickness
and disease and she readily believed I could cure her'. She was invited
to Rillington Place when Ethel was absent, Christie telling her that he
had the medical knowledge to cure her problem. He organised his
tools, preparing a glass jar with two rubber pipes attached; one leading
to perfumed water, another to the gas main. The perfumed water
disguised the taste of the lethal carbon monoxide.

On Saturday 7 October, Muriel had lunch with her aunt and left the
house at four that afternoon, saying, 'I shan't be late'. She was wearing
a black frock, black shoes, a camel-coloured coat and no hat, but

she left her belongings, her savings book (which account stood at £26 14s 9d) and money at home and clearly expected to return. Once the two were in the kitchen at Rillington Place, Christie gave her an inhalant which included Friars' Balsam, which she inhaled. As the coal gas took effect, she lost consciousness. However, Dr Camps, a pathologist, questioned this: 'it could have been done, but would have postulated a person of weak intellect who allowed it to be carried out without the curiosity of wondering what it was all about'. Be that as it may, Christie then took her into the bedroom, had sex with her and then strangled her. However, he later said that he couldn't remember whether he used gas on Ruth or Muriel, and whether it was inhaled in the bedroom or the kitchen. Again the body was buried in the garden, near Ruth; although it was temporarily lodged in the wash house first. Christie later noted, 'Once again, I experienced that quiet peaceful thrill. I had no regrets'. He was taking a risk, because Muriel might have told her aunt where she was going. Possibly Christie, perhaps consumed by lust, took the chance or had ascertained before the murder that she had not mentioned the location of her visit to anyone.[23] She certainly did not confide in her aunt.

There was no hue and cry. Muriel's employers initially assumed she was ill and on 25 October requested a medical certificate. Dunn reported his cousin as missing to the Putney police on 4 November and a report form was duly completed. Mrs Hooper thought that she might have been pregnant by her man friend. Her family believed she might have attended a dance hall in Putney which had been bombed by V2 rockets and not survived. Her father was told of her disappearance in 1945.[24]

Christie had chosen a method of murder he was to continue with. It suited his personality, with his interest in matters technical. Gas and a ligature were to be his trademarks for most of his murders. The amount of violence and force used was minimal; useful for a middle-aged man of limited physical strength. Strangulation also gives the strangler a feeling of power. We should also bear in mind that, although Christie was in no way the ladies' man he liked to style himself as, he was not outwardly socially repulsive. He was able to persuade two younger women to visit him on his own at home, and though cash may have been involved to an extent in the first instance, in the second it was not. He was clearly persuasive and convincing, with a veneer of knowledge and authority. He was also cautious, leaving fourteen months between the murders, and spent weeks cultivating Muriel's confidence. These murders were easy to commit and to conceal. There was never any investigation into them and, by the time of the inquests in 1953, only skeletons remained and they told no tales. However, it was to be several years before he killed again and this break from killing is unusual for serial killers. Possibly he had temporarily sated his lust, and certainly it was more difficult to satisfy these urges with his wife in the house most of the time, and with a return to the more stable years of peace.

It was in the winter of 1945 that Christie's extra-marital dalliance with Gladys Jones came to an abrupt end. The war being over, Jones's husband returned home from service in the Mediterranean, looking forward to a reunion with his wife. He heard about the affair and lay in wait for the couple returning to the flat. Jones later described what happened:

> It was a real scrap. Sometimes I was on the floor, sometimes it was Christie. There were no rules. Christie fought desperately – I will say that for him – but I was seeing red. While he was cosy in London and I was overseas he had broken up my home. It was a terrible homecoming for me and I paid Christie back in the only way I could – with my fist.

A neighbour reported, 'I believe Christie would have been in even worse shape but for the fact that someone dialled the police'. Jones later wondered whether his wife would have become Christie's next victim, but thought not, 'people knew of his association and he had been in trouble with his superiors at Harrow Road because of it'. The sequel to this incident was at the High Court, which Christie attended as the third party in the divorce proceedings, on 29 July 1947. He had to pay costs. Christie made a scene in court when he rose to his feet, stood with his head thrown back, clenched his hands and shouted 'Liar. He's telling lies' when he was mentioned by Jones. He had to be removed from court, yet persisted in his remonstrations outside the court. A decree nisi was granted on 1 August 1947.[25]

Christie remained in the employ of Ultra Electrics until 8 April 1946, though on 23 January 1945 he worked at the branch at Erskine Road, Chalk Farm ('driving a van too tedious'). On 21 May 1946 he rejoined the Post Office, which he had so ignominiously left in 1921. As with the police in 1939, no one checked his record, and he was employed as a Grade 2 clerk in the Post Office Savings Bank at Blythe Road, Shepherd's Bush. In August 1947 he was employed as a clerk at the

Post Office Savings Bank at Kew and was in the First Aid party there. Clifford Spurling, a colleague, later recalled, 'He told me that if I should get a girl in trouble he could perform an abortion operation. He said that he had done so before'. He was still apparently as ill as ever, with eight visits to the doctor in 1946 and nine in 1947, but only one in 1948. It was at this time that he began wearing glasses. Meanwhile, at 10 Rillington Place, the Clowes were no longer resident on the second floor and had been replaced by Henry Williams, who lived there from at least 1945 until the autumn of 1947. Patricia Pichler recalled Christie thus: 'he was the most respected person in the street . . . always in a suit and tie . . . what a nice man he was . . . very upstanding character'.[26]

Christie had now entered into another stage in his life. Although remaining, as in 1939, outwardly respectable, with a job, a wife and a fixed abode, and having had an apparently 'good' war, the reality, as always, was hidden beneath the surface. He associated with prostitutes, as he had earlier in life. More sinister was, of course, his descent into murder. But he had planned and executed his crimes well; choosing victims whose loss would not cause huge outcry, in the unsettled period of total war, and who could not be linked to him, though presumably he would have been seen with them. Although the first murder had been hasty in its execution, the second had set a pattern for most of his later murders in the use of gas to render his victims easier to deal with. Most importantly for him, there was no suspicion of murder. His crimes of the 1920s and 1930s had been detected and he had paid the penalty. On these two occasions he had escaped scot free. Yet there was a guilty secret in the back garden, which, if revealed, would have dire consequences for him.

Chapter 4

Enter the Evanses
1948–49

'We've got everything nice up here now,
and the Christies are alright'.[1]

The arrival of Timothy and Beryl Evans at 10 Rillington Place heralds a new phase in this narrative. They played a part in Christie's life and, more importantly, influenced how he has been seen since. The following narrative, which some will feel is controversial, is based on what seems to be the most likely explanation of the known facts. In order to set the scene for what happened, we must now turn from Christie and explore Timothy and Beryl's characters and behaviour.

Timothy John Evans was born on 20 November 1924 in Merthyr Vale, Glamorganshire. He was brought up as a Catholic. His mother had been born Thomasina Agnes Lynch in Merthyr in 1901. She married Daniel Evans twenty years later in the same place. Their first child was a daughter, Eleanor, born in 1921. Whilst Mrs Evans was pregnant with Timothy, on 25 April 1924, her husband deserted her. The family lived at 50 Mount Pleasant. She later met Penry Probert, who was about a year her senior, and had one son. They had a daughter, Mary, in 1929, and married in September 1933 (not in 1929 as customarily stated).[2]

Evans had been brought up in part by his stepfather, who had treated him well. He had no abnormal mental traits, but was a nail biter and known for temper tantrums. His schooling had been interrupted by bad health. When he was nine he cut his toe and this led him to spend time in numerous hospitals until he was seventeen: the Royal Infirmary, Mount Pleasant, Princess Louise Hospital, London, St Charles' Hospital and Moorland Hospital, and the result was that he was a poor scholar and lacked application. Unlike Christie, though, it seems he 'got on well with his school mates and was liked by them'. At school he enjoyed football and boxing.[3]

The Probert family moved to London. In 1936 they were recorded at 221 Portland Road, Notting Hill, then at 39 St Mark's Road. Evans briefly attended school in Kensington, but returned to Merthyr in the summer of 1936 and was looked after by his grandmother, Mary Lynch, at 71 Mount Pleasant. On 23 November 1938 Evans, having reached the age of fourteen, left Mount Pleasant School and joined his family at 210 Cornwall Crescent, Notting Hill. He was briefly employed as a van boy in north Kensington. However, in December he was back in Glamorganshire, working in a mine and earning 10s 6d per week. This did not last long and he returned to London, working as a lorry driver for the Air Ministry by 1945. The family lived at flat V15, Peabody Buildings in 1939 and were still there, albeit at R13, by 1945. Health problems led to him avoiding national service, but he was in the Home Guard and was a Civil Defence messenger for N91 Post Kensington.[4]

It was in London that Evans had his first sexual experiences, with a girlfriend to whom he was engaged aged eighteen, but she broke off with him. From 1942 until his marriage he often visited prostitutes. His other interests were conventional: spending time in pubs and cinemas, occasionally going to football matches and dog races. His stepfather said he got into bad company after leaving school; Evans denied this.[5]

Physically, he was five feet five inches tall, with black hair and brown eyes. He had an oval face and a fresh complexion. He was clean shaven.[6]

That Evans was untruthful is acknowledged by all who knew him. Cornelius Lynch, his uncle, later said, 'I know my nephew as a liar. This is generally known throughout the family'. His mother added that her son had 'a very vivid imagination and he is a terrible liar'. George Williams, the salesman who travelled with Evans on his van deliveries, said that Evans was 'a liar'. Evans would lie for financial gain.[7]

There has been much said about Evans's lack of intelligence. Certainly his schooling had been interrupted and he was no scholar. Yet he may well have not been wholly illiterate. He said himself, 'I had my tea and sat down and read the papers and listened to the wireless' and 'I had a letter from J. Broderick's telling me I was behind in my payments'. He also read football reports in the newspapers and possessed a watch. On the other hand he also claimed he was illiterate and asked others to read on his behalf.[8]

There were various tests later carried out in prison to assess his intelligence. He was assessed as having an IQ of sixty-five or seventy-five, and a mental age varying from ten-and-a-half to eleven or fourteen. His vocabulary amounted to 9,000 words. Another assessment concluded: 'Memory and attention good. Weak in simple arithmetical problems. Reasoning poor'. However, he was capable in his employment and in social situations, and was clearly not mentally defective. A medical report noted: 'His education is faulty owing to absences from school, the result of physical illness. But he is of average intelligence in spite of this. He is well informed on matters of ordinary interest and common knowledge'. He was described by the police as being 'quite worldly' and prison officials thought he was slightly under average intelligence.[9]

Cornelius Lynch said of his nephew, 'I know Timothy to have a very violent temper'. His mother did not deny this outright, saying, 'I don't think he is the type of man who would use violence', while his half-sister agreed that as a lad he was 'a bit rough with his temper'. Williams described Evans thus: 'He was highly strung, unbalanced of character and very nervous'. He was also a petty criminal, having stolen a car and driven it without insurance or a driving licence. At the West London Magistrates' Court on 25 April 1946 he was fined 60s. He also received stolen goods from Charles and Joan Vincent of 164 Westbourne Road. Evans recalled that the latter 'asked me if I would look after the rug and brief case for them ... he got it from the flat next door ... until he found a customer for them. I said I would'. These items were stolen from James Nicol, a researcher of the same address, and valued at £19. Christie claimed that Evans sold stolen watches too. Yet his mother could ignore his faults when she said, 'He has never been in any trouble with the police. He has got a clean record'.[10]

Evans's work record was patchy. In 1946 he was described as being a car cleaner. He worked for Lancaster Road Food Products at 196 Lancaster Road from 23 July 1948 to 8 July 1949 as a van driver. His next employer was Angelo Esposito, a wine merchant of Edgware Road, from 11–25 July 1949. The weekly wage was £5, but Evans did not last long, as his employer said, 'He was not satisfactory whilst he worked for me'. Evans had persuaded his employer to lend him money on false pretences which he never repaid. On the other hand, Williams said that he was an 'excellent driver'. He then returned to Lancaster Road Food Products on 8 August. Emanuel Adler, his boss there, said that at first he was 'satisfactory and willing', but that later he was 'not particularly satisfied with Evans' work'. Evans was paid £5 5s per week, but often earned up to £7 with overtime, though his wife collected the basic wage each Friday.[11]

By 1947 the Probert family was living at 11 St Mark's Road, Notting Hill (the house no longer survives). It was in multiple occupancy, like 10 Rillington Place and most terraced housing in the district. With the two Proberts were his son John, and also Mary, Eleanor and Timothy Evans.[12]

Beryl Susan Thorley is an enigmatic character. She was born in Lewisham Hospital, south-east London, on 19 September 1929. Her father was William Thorley (1887–1957), then working for the London General Omnibus Company as a petrol filler attendant, and her mother was Elizabeth Simmonds (1895–1947), described as a house-keeper. They lived temporarily at 15 Halesworth Road, Lewisham, but only very briefly. The family lived a peripatetic existence in the 1930s with several addresses in south London. A son, Basil William, was born in about 1931 and there was a daughter born in about 1933. The family moved to north Kensington during the Second World War and Beryl attended St Mark's School (just opposite Rillington Place). By 1945 they lived at 112d Cambridge Gardens, Notting Hill, not far from the Christies and the Evanses. She was a very slightly built young woman, being five feet two inches high and weighing seven and a half stones. She worked at Thomas Wallis's of Oxford Street as a relief telephonist. She was also of an argumentative nature, as her husband said: 'she would never stop, once she had started a row'. However, she may well have been popular with the neighbours, for Procter later wrote that they were sorry to see her leave.[13]

Beryl's mother died in 1947 and the Thorleys split up. William Thorley moved to 10 Chapel Street, Brighton. He was now employed as a general hand at Victoria Railway Station. His son, who remained in west London, was a projectionist at the Royalty Cinema on Lancaster Road. He had been before the magistrates' court for larceny on 5 August 1949. He was also acquainted with Evans and the latter owed him £3 7s for a watch he gave him.[14]

Evans and Beryl met in January 1947 and, following a courtship centred around dance halls and cinemas, were married at Kensington Registry Office on 20 September 1947, when Beryl was just eighteen, possibly prompted by the break-up of her family. They initially lived with his family, but she soon fell pregnant. They needed accommodation because seven adults now shared two or three rooms, and they began their search in January 1948, buying furniture on hire purchase. On 9 March 1948 the two rooms on the top floor of 10 Rillington Place (about 300 yards from their current address) fell vacant. The Evanses found out about this and applied. Since their references were good, the agents accepted the offer on 24 March. The rent was 12s per week, payable in advance. It is possible that they were shown their rooms by Christie; certainly in 1950 he complained about having to show around prospective tenants, so maybe he did so in 1948.[15]

Apparently Kitchener had little liking for either of his fellow male tenants. He thought that one of them was Communist and the other was a Socialist (Kitchener was a Conservative). He also thought that both men were thieves, saying 'I was always missing little things', and, by what we know of them, Kitchener was probably right.[16]

Relations between the Christies and the Evanses were generally good as far as is known. Ethel recalled, 'since they have been here, I have been on very friendly terms with them, particularly Mrs Evans'. Christie remembered:

We were friendly acquaintances, nothing more. I went up that first afternoon to have a cup of tea as she had previously asked me once or twice. I believe it was a couple of days previously that she had asked me to go up and get some sugar she had saved up for me. When I was up there she said she had just made a cup of tea and asked me to have one. I had a cup of tea with her then and she told me to come up any time I wanted a cup of tea.

Apparently Beryl said, 'We've got everything nice up here now, and the Christies are alright'. The Evanses also allowed Christie to photograph them.[17]

Christie was not a great friend of Evans, recalling 'I had no ill feelings against Evans ... He wasn't my type ... I just didn't like to be seen with him. We weren't inclined to make them our friends' and the two couples never went out, but given the age difference this was perhaps unlikely in any case. He certainly expected the less intelligent and younger man to defer to him. Christie stated 'he showed great respect for me and always called me Mr'. However, 'I have always felt kindly towards the Evans family and have tried to show it in little ways ... They should have been grateful to me'. His act of kindness cited was to allow Beryl to park her pram in the Christie's front room rather than lug it up two floors.[18]

Baby Geraldine was born at Queen Charlotte's Hospital on 10 October 1948 and was baptized into the Catholic faith of her father's family. After her birth, her parents went to the cinema each Wednesday as Evans's mother babysat.[19]

Despite having a baby, Beryl was back at work in July 1949 and had a mild flirtation with another man. She teased her husband about this with the result that he slapped her face and made such a scene at her workplace that she was sacked. In late August, Beryl had been referred to the West London Magistrates' Court because of an assault by her husband. Thorley visited his daughter on 4 or 5 November and recalled, 'I do not believe they were very happily married'. He did not think it was 'a genuine friendship'. But another observer said, 'As far as I could tell they were reasonably happy together'. In contrast to her father's impression, at the same time, this witness said, 'She seemed in good spirits and said that she would be going away for a holiday with her daughter, Geraldine'. This would be to Bristol, with a friend of her husband's, possibly Evans's uncle and aunt who lived there. Basil Thorley, in 1965, said, 'I think Timothy and Beryl were fond of each other and Timothy was definitely very fond of Geraldine. They had their tiffs just like me and the wife and any other married couple, but I never thought there was anything serious in it'. Mary Westlake (Evans's half-sister) later said, 'I often used to visit them and they got on quite well together. There was only once when they had a quarrel and that was over money'. Evans himself said that the marriage at first was happy, but that owing to debt the marriage began to break up and he had frequent quarrels with his wife. This remark is perhaps nearest to the truth, spoken by the man best placed to know. It is also worth noting that men who have been described as loving husbands have murdered their wives; Christie being one example among many.[20]

Quarrels between Evans and Beryl were apparent to the other residents in the house; given its size, they could hardly fail to notice. Ethel stated:

> All the time the Evans' have lived at our address there have been frequent quarrels, some of which my husband and I have heard when their voices were raised, although we have not heard what was actually said. After some of these quarrels Mrs Evans would

tell me that she had rowed with her husband over his lying to her, his associating with other women and financial matters. The last time I heard them quarrel was on or about Sunday 13th [6th] November 1949, when they were shouting at each other and appeared to be having a violent quarrel. It lasted all day on and off.[21]

Her husband added his ha'porth:

Mr and Mrs Evans got on very badly together, they were always rowing and Mrs Evans has told my wife and I on more than one occasion that he has assaulted her and grabbed hold of her throat. She said he had a violent temper and one time would do her in.[22]

Evans also said likewise on 2 December. He began by referring to Beryl's 'moaning about me working long hours' and said that she had 'got herself into £20 debt'. He claimed she would not tell him to whom she owed the money. The couple were certainly in need of money. Evans elaborated:

I had a letter from J. Brodericks telling me I was behind in my payments for my furniture on the hire purchase. I asked her if she had been paying for the furniture and she said she had, then I showed her the letter I had received from Brodericks then she admitted she hadn't been paying it. I went down to see Brodericks myself to pay them my one pound a week and ten shillings off the arrears so then I left the furniture business to my wife. I then found she was in debt with the rent. I accused her of squandering the money so that started a terrific argument in my house. I told her if she didn't pull herself together I would leave her, so she said, 'You can leave any time you like', so I told her that she would be surprised some day if I walked out on her. One Sunday, early in November, I had a terrific row with her at home, so I washed and changed and went to the pub dinner-time. I stopped there till two o'clock. I came home, had my lunch, left again to go out, leaving my wife and baby at home, because I didn't want any more arguments … I went home sat down and switched the wireless on. I made myself a cup of tea. My wife was nagging till I went to bed at 10.00pm. I got up at 6.00am next day, made a cup of tea. My wife got up to make a feed for the baby at 6.15am. She gets up and starts an argument straight away. I took no notice of her and went into the bedroom to see the baby before going to work. My wife told me she was going to pack up and go down to her father in Brighton. I asked her what we was going to do with the baby, so she said she was going to take the baby down to Brighton with her so I said it would be a good job and a load of worry off my mind, so I went to work as usual so when I came home at night I just put the kettle on, I sat down my wife walked in so I said 'I thought you was going to Brighton?' She said, 'What for you to have a good time?' I took no notice of her. I went downstairs and fetched the pushchair up. I come upstairs she started an argument again. I told her if she didn't pack up I'd slap her face. With that she picked up a milk bottle to throw at me. I grabbed the bottle out of her hand, I pushed her, she fell in a chair in the kitchen, so I washed and changed and went out. I went to the pub and had a few drinks. I got home about 10.30pm. I walked in she started to row again, so I went straight to bed.[23]

Debts were certainly mounting up. Hire purchase payments were behind by £39 13s and rent arrears were £12 1s 6d, having last been paid on 18 July. The house agents took out a court summons to try and claim their money. Lucy Endecott, a sixteen-year-old blonde girl, said Evans always kept his wife short of money from his wages; he didn't give her the £5 per week he claimed to. Evans's mother said, 'She never seemed to have any money. I had to help her many times over money'. To add to these problems, Evans liked spending time in the pub, regularly drinking two or three pints on his way home, and in the autumn of 1949, it was claimed, 'he has been drinking rather heavily'.[24]

It has also been alleged by Evans's mother that Beryl was a poor housekeeper. Her daughter-in-law was apparently dirty in her habits and did not clean the rooms. Finally, 'She got no hot meal for him, except on one day a week. She did not do the washing up, but left heaps of dishes unwashed'. Evans's mother claimed her son 'was not used to that kind of life'. Mrs Probert and her daughters often had to help out.[25]

Clarke Vincent, a twenty-two-year-old grocer's assistant, recalled a conversation he had with Evans, who said '"I'm going off the track. If I ever get hold of Lucy, I'll smash her up or run her down with my lorry". On several occasions I have heard him say to Beryl, "I'll do you in". But Beryl said "he hadn't got the guts to do it".' Vincent added that there had been a time when Beryl had had to defend herself with a bread knife against her husband, and that she would have liked to have left him but couldn't because of the baby and a lack of money. He added that Evans 'was in a furious temper'.[26]

There is other evidence of Evans's bad temper. Rosina Swan, a neighbour, recalled seeing 'two figures fighting; sort of struggling together. She looked as if she was trying to get away from him and a neighbour opposite told me she saw it all and she thought he was trying to push her out of the window'. She said that Lucy Endecott 'often told me how Mr and Mrs Evans quarrelled. She could see them hitting one another'. Once Beryl threw a jar of baby cream at Evans, causing a cut on his forehead.[27]

Evans's involvement with Lucy, a cashier employed in Grosvenor Place and a friend of Beryl's, did not help matters between him and Beryl. His mother noted, 'My son and his wife were perfectly happy until August 1949'. Lucy briefly lodged with the Evanses in August 1949 and she had sex with him on the 28th of that month. They lived together for two days before she left him to return to her mother's. Her testimony gives an insight into Evans' character:

he said he was still going away and was going to get a room as Beryl and he were definitely going to part ... Beryl didn't want him to leave her although they were unhappy together. He used to stay out late at night and they were continually squabbling. They also used to row about money ... I know they used to have a lot of arguments about money and he used to lie to her a lot. [Evans said] 'I'll give you a good hiding for you going to the pictures and leaving the baby'. When they got home he set about her, and began hitting her with his hand across her face and body. He was in a furious temper. [Evans said] 'I'll put you through the bloody window'.[28]

On the evening of 28 August, Inspector Percy Parks visited the house because Evans, his wife, his mother and Lucy were arguing. Beryl said Lucy had slapped her and said, 'She has been carrying on with my husband and last night went to the pictures and afterwards slept in the kitchen with him'. Lucy replied, 'There is nothing wrong. I will have a medical examination'. Beryl was advised to attend the magistrates' court, which she did and received advice from the probation officer.[29]

Another major development was Beryl becoming pregnant again in the autumn of 1949. For this, we have the accounts of her husband and the Christies. On 30 November, Evans told the police at Merthyr Tydfil:

> About the beginning of October, my wife, Beryl Susan Evans, told me that she was expecting a baby. She told me that she was about three months gone. I said, 'If you are having a baby, well, you've had one, another one won't make any difference'. She then told me that she was going to try and get rid of it. I turned round and told her not to be silly that she'd make herself ill. Then she bought herself a syringe and started syringing herself. Then she said that didn't work and I said, 'I'm glad it won't work'. Then she said she was going to buy some tablets. I don't know what tablets she bought because she was always hiding them from me. She started to look very ill and I told her to go and see a doctor and she said she'd go when I was in work but when I'd come home and ask her if she'd been she'd always say that she hadn't.[30]

Another account was given by Ethel on 1 December. She recalled:

> About two months ago Mrs Evans told me that she was then two months pregnant and that she did not want another baby. She told me that she had already taken various pills that had been recommended to her by different people in an endeavour to secure the miscarriage, and that she had purchased a syringe with this object in view. Two of the people she mentioned were her mother in law, whose name I cannot remember, I know it's not Evans because Mr Evans was a son of her first marriage, and a Mrs Lawrence, who lived at 8, Rillington Place. She did not discuss what they told her to do. I advised Mrs Evans to stop trying to procure a miscarriage, but she seemed determined to go on with it, and even spoke of going somewhere for an illegal operation. She mentioned about the operation some time after she had told me of the various pills she was taking to secure her miscarriage. The exact words she used were, 'She would have an operation, but that it costs money'. I have an idea she mentioned going to Praed Street near St Mary's Hospital for the operation, but she never told me the address where she intended to go.[31]

Ethel told the story to her husband and he later recalled:

> About two months ago my wife told me that Mrs Evans was again pregnant and my wife informed me that she was acting very silly

in trying to bring about her own miscarriage by taking pills and was syringing herself with glycerine and carbolic soap.

Mrs Evans did tell the wife and I what she was doing about six weeks ago and I said to her, in my wife's presence, that she was looking a physical wreck and advised her to stop it. We warned her of the consequences and she promised both of us that she would stop taking the stuff. The next day, Mr Evans came down and said that any pills or similar things that he had found about the place he had destroyed.

All three witnesses agree that Beryl was pregnant, which it was later proved that she was, and that she did not want to have the baby and was taking not very successful steps to abort it. Finally, Evans's drinking, which increased towards the end of this year, cannot have helped relations much.[32]

It was not a happy household for the Evanses in the November of 1949. Debts, Evans's drinking and his affair had soured what had once been a happy married life. The fact that Beryl was pregnant added to their woes. Christie and his wife were all too aware of these circumstances, and their lives were to become more interwoven because of subsequent developments. However, on 4 November Thorley visited his sister and later reported, 'She seemed to be in good spirits and said that she would be going away for a holiday with her daughter'. It is possible that this planned escape precipitated the final crisis.[33]

Chapter 5

The Murders of Beryl and Geraldine Evans 1949

'I want to give myself up. I have disposed of my wife'.[1]

On 31 October, the firm of Messrs Larter and Sons, builders, began work on repairs to 10 Rillington Place. Initially they worked on the outside of the house, at the front of the premises. On 3 November, they started work on the wash house and water closet at the rear of the house. The old roofs were removed and new ones laid on the following days. Kitchener was in hospital at this time, as his eyesight was bad.[2]

Tuesday 8 November 1949 was to be a crucial day in the lives of all those dwelling within 10 Rillington Place. Christie was off work for the first two weeks of November and regularly saw his doctor, who was convinced he was genuinely ill with enteritis and fibrositis. He attended the surgery on 29 October, 1, 4, 8, 12 and 15 November. Christie recalled:

> On the Tuesday [8 November] I was in bed a lot of the time with the illness I had, which is enteritis and fibrositis in my back. I was in a great deal of pain and I rested as much as possible under doctor's instructions with a fire in my room day and night, and on Tuesday evening at about twenty past five I went up to the doctor, and my wife suggested going up later to the library.[3]

Christie claimed that when he had been at home, he was:

> In my pyjamas, and other times with the pain being so bad I was unable to lie down for any length of time, and I had to keep getting up, and I used to sit in front of the fire and try to get it to my back to get some relief, and then I would go back and lie down again in bed.

Whilst at home, Christie claimed to have seen no one apart from the workmen and his wife, although he caught a glimpse of Beryl leaving the house. He claimed his health was so bad that he had to go down on all fours to pick up a pin.[4]

It seems certain that Tuesday 8 November was the last day of Beryl's life. No one ever saw her alive after that day. She spent part of that day outside the house, as noted by three witnesses. A crucial statement came from Frederick James Jones, a builder's labourer, who recalled:

At about 10.00am on Wednesday 9th November [later amended to 8th November] 1949, whilst I was mixing up materials outside 10 Rillington Place, W11. With the front door open, I saw a young woman come downstairs with a baby in her arms and she was accompanied by another young woman. She put the baby in a pram, which was already outside the front door and I said to her, 'Mind how you go when you come back as I am going to lay a ladder up the stairs'. She replied, 'I'll get by that alright'. I did not pay any particular attention to this woman or her companion, and I could not recognise them again. Apart from saying the woman with the baby was small and thin, I cannot further describe her. This was the first and last time I saw these people.[5]

Ethel also made a statement about Beryl's movements that morning:

I saw Mrs Evans the following morning and she looked terribly ill, she did mention that a friend of hers called Joan who had made trouble between her and her husband, and that Joan was coming round that morning, and that she (Mrs Evans) did not want to see her. After Mrs Evans told me this she went back upstairs, and shortly after Joan came but Mrs Evans locked herself in her kitchen and refused to see her.[6]

Joan Vincent, an old school friend of Beryl's, was uncertain on which day she actually went to number 10, as she gave different dates (5, 7 and 8 November on different occasions), and had been to St Bernard's Hospital for her memory. She said:

I went to see Beryl Evans during a lunch hour. I reached the top of the stairs ... I called her name and tried to turn the handle of the door and I felt that somebody was pressing the door and holding it against me. I then remember thinking it must have been Beryl herself at the time, that perhaps she didn't want me in the flat at the moment, and I said, 'Well, if you don't want me to come in, I'll go'. But I had a nervous and uneasy feeling and felt very frightened at the time and hurried away from the house. I didn't meet anyone else in the house on that day.

Apparently she returned on the next day and saw Christie, who seemed 'aggressive and rude'. She noticed Beryl's pram in the Christies' living room. Christie told her, 'She isn't there. She has gone away. I expect she will write'.[7]

However, assuming the builder's statement is correct, Beryl may have returned at about noon, having avoided Joan, only to leave again later, though the second time she may have been alone. Mothers with small children usually want to spend time outside the home for the sake of variety. According to Christie, 'I last saw Mrs Evans about 8th November, 1949, when she was going out into the street. I took no special notice of this', but four days later he amended the statement to read, 'I last saw Mrs Beryl Evans round about 1pm on 8th November 1949, when she left our address with her daughter Geraldine. I was in our front room'. Ethel's recollection, made independently, is similar, but with one major difference: 'That afternoon Mrs Evans went out and asked me to keep an eye on her baby daughter who was in bed. She said she would not be out for long. However, she had not returned at 5.30pm'.[8]

Basil Thorley stated that his sister was expected at 4.30pm by their grandmother, Mrs Barnett, of 13 Bonchurch Road. She never kept that appointment. The question, of course, is why – and this we can never know. However, Evans said his wife was meant to visit her grandmother on the previous day, so it seems probable she did so on that day instead of the 8th and Thorley confused the two dates.[9]

We do not know when Beryl returned home; none of the workmen, nor the Christies saw her, so it was probably after the Christies had gone out that evening. Ethel Christie went to the public library on Ladbroke Grove and Christie himself went to the doctors at Colville Square (in order to extend his sick leave). Odess opened his surgery at 6.00pm. Christie was also a user of the library, as attested by his library card. Evans later gave the police at Notting Hill police station this account on 2 December:

> I come home at night about 6.30pm my wife started to argue again, so I hit across her face with my flat hand. She then hit me back with her hand. In a fit of temper I grabbed a piece of rope

from a chair which I had brought home off my van and strangled her with it. I then took her into the bedroom and laid her on the bed with the rope still tied round her neck. Before 10.00pm that night I carried my wife's body downstairs to the kitchen of Mr Kitchener's flat as I knew he was away in hospital.

He then fed Geraldine, put her to bed and had a smoke. He went out that night and returned late.

I then went downstairs when everything was quiet, to Mr Kitchener's kitchen. I wrapped my wife's body up in a blanket and a green tablecloth from off my kitchen table. I then tied it up with a piece of cord from out of my kitchen cupboard. I then slipped downstairs and opened the back door, then went up and carried my wife's body down to the wash-house and placed it under the sink. I then blocked the front of the sink up with pieces of wood so that the body wouldn't be seen. I locked the wash house door, I come in and shut the back door behind me. I then slipped back upstairs. The Christies who live on the ground floor were in bed.

Evans went to work next day, after feeding and changing Geraldine. Evans visited his mother at 5.30pm, as he usually did on Wednesdays (his mother usually babysat for them on this night as they went to the cinema). He told her, 'Mam, you won't see Beryl or the baby for a week or two. She has gone to Brighton to her dad's', and he said that Beryl would write to her from there. Three days later he called around again, between 10.00 and 10.30am. 'Are you ok?' asked his mother. 'Yes, I am going to Brighton tomorrow to see Beryl and the baby', Evans replied. Mrs Probert recalled that he 'seemed alright' but also 'quiet and moody'. Evans then 'looked straight at me' and said he might not be going to Brighton because he didn't have the money. Clearly he was lying, for Beryl was already dead.

Evans lied about his wife's whereabouts again on 10 November, when he quit his job, receiving his wages owing and telling his boss that his wife had gone to Bristol. On returning home:

I then went home picked up my baby from her cot in the bedroom, picked up my tie and strangled her with it. I then put the baby back in the cot and sat down in the kitchen and waited for the Christies downstairs to go to bed. At about twelve o'clock that night I took the baby downstairs to the wash-house and hid her body behind some wood. I then locked the wash-house door behind me. I then slipped back upstairs and laid on the bed all night, fully clothed.[10]

This was his fourth and final statement of what happened on that day. There has been much debate over this issue; with the majority view being that Christie killed the Evanses. Yet the above explanation meets the known facts (for instance, Evans could not have known where the corpses were and how they were concealed if he had not put them there himself) and the story Evans's defence rested upon does not. The quarrels and violence also tie in with what else we know about them (Lucy referred to Evans hitting his wife in the face). We shall examine Evans's other versions later in the chapter and see why they are implausible. Yet there are two odd points about the version above. Firstly, it seems unlikely that Beryl's corpse was in the wash house on the day of the murder; however, it could have been placed there later, as the workmen finished with the wash house before Evans left for Wales. Secondly, it must be questionable whether Geraldine was killed two days after her mother, because no one heard her cry out. It seems likely that she was killed on the same evening as her mother. Neither of these points of detail, though, detracts from Evans's guilt.

It is also significant that on 9 November Evans asked Mr Willis when the building work in the house would be completed and he told him it would be in two days' time. Evans saw Robert Hookway, a dealer in second-hand furniture of 319 Portobello Road, about selling the furniture in his rooms, which was not his because the hire purchase money had not all been paid. Hookway came to 10 Rillington Place, saw the furniture and offered £40, which Evans accepted. The furniture could not be collected until Monday 14 November. Hookway was impressed by Christie, with whom he occasionally had a drink, saying that he was 'a marvellous sort of bloke, sort of parsonical, full of scientific knowledge, that enormous dome and penetrating eyes, a very good mind, very refined and nice to talk to'. Evans met Basil Thorley and told him that Beryl was going to Bristol. He spent the weekend at various pubs, including the Kensington Park Hotel. He also went to the cinema. On 12 November, Christie went to the doctor, still suffering from fibrositis.[11]

On 14 November the furniture van came round and collected the goods at 3.00pm, and Evans received £40. Earlier that day, Albert

Rollings, a rag dealer from Ladbroke Grove, whom Evans had met on the previous day, collected various clothing belonging to Beryl that Evans had ripped up, but when he found a rattle, Evans said he would need to keep that for Geraldine. All that remained in the house was some crockery, Geraldine's pram, her small chair and a few baby clothes. Later that day Evans took his suitcase, went to the cinema and the pub, met Basil at the Royalty Cinema, Ladbroke Road and told him he had had a telegram from Beryl asking him to meet her in Bristol, then caught the 12.55 train from Paddington to Swansea, changing for Merthyr Vale. He arrived at about 6.40am and went to his uncle and aunt's house at 93 Mount Pleasant.[12]

Evans told the Lynches that he had been with his boss, but that the latter's car had broken down in Cardiff and so he might be with them for a few days. He told them that Beryl and Geraldine were in Brighton. Some of his evenings there were spent with his uncle in the pub, and he also saw William Costigan, an old friend. Evans gave Costigan's wife a necklace which belonged to his wife, and he was cagey about its source. He told them Geraldine was staying with friends in London. They all thought that Evans seemed relaxed and cheerful. On 28 November, Evans sold his wife's wedding ring at the branch of Messrs H. Samuel and Sons at 119 Merthyr Tydfil High Street. Mrs Violet Gwendoline Lynch later recalled, 'I asked him where his wife and baby were, and he said they were gone to Brighton for a holiday till Christmas'.[13]

Evans interrupted his sojourn on 21 November by returning briefly to London (about three or four days after Kitchener returned home). He called at 10 Rillington Place. This was probably on the next day. It was about 5.20 to 5.30pm and Christie was about to visit Dr Odess. The doorbell rang and he answered it. He later stated:

> ·Mr Evans was stood in the doorway. He said, 'I've just come straight down from Wales; I've come from Paddington Station. I've not seen anybody; I've come straight here'. I asked him in and I said, 'What on earth are you doing here?' He said, 'Beryl has walked out on me and I couldn't find a job, so I've been to Bristol, Cardiff, Birmingham and Coventry and back to Cardiff and couldn't find a job'. I said, 'Well, what you should have done was settled down somewhere, paid for rooms, accommodation, for a period of time and the money you had, the £60, would have kept you going until you got a job'. He said, 'Well, I've had to spend a

lot on travel'. I said, 'How much have you got left?' He said, 'About a couple of pounds'.

Christie gave the young man his opinion about how he had used his money (unstated). Evans seemed keen to travel back to Wales, and as Christie was travelling partially in the same direction, they both got on the 7a bus from Cambridge Gardens; Christie alighting at Portobello Road, Evans heading to Paddington Station. Apparently Christie paid both fares.[14]

Evans gave a different account of this episode. He said he returned to ask after Geraldine. 'He asked me what I was doing back in London, and I told him I had come up to find out about my daughter; and he told me my daughter was perfectly all right ... That was the only reason why I came to London'.[15]

Evans returned to his aunt and uncle's house on 23 November. His aunt recalled, 'I asked him did he see his wife and baby. He said, "Yes" and that his wife had walked out of the flat and left the baby in the cot in the bedroom. He did not say why. I asked him what he had done with the baby, and he said he gave it to some people from Newport to look after'.[16]

Christie was now a very ill man. The Registrar of St Thomas' Hospital wrote to Dr Odess on 19 November to state, 'I saw this patient ... He was complaining of pain in the right side of his back for the last three days. On examination I found he was in agony whenever he tried to bend down or bring the left lumbar muscles into use. There was extreme tenderness in the left lumbar region over the muscles. This is a case of muscular pain and I was able to give him considerable relief by an injection of local anaesthetic. I have referred him to the psychotherapy department'.[17]

Meanwhile, in Notting Hill, Mary Probert was worried about her half-brother and his family, whom she had not seen for some time. She went to number 10 on 29 November, but on knocking at the door received no answer. Yet she could see Ethel peering around the curtain. She came to the door and told Mary that she had last seen Beryl leaving the house on 8 November. She added, 'Beryl was not as nice as we thought she was', and went on to relate that she had once left Geraldine in the house alone and returned smelling of gin. Ethel had told her not to repeat such behaviour. She said that Beryl and Geraldine had gone to Brighton. Mary did not believe her. Christie then came on the scene and said, 'I [Mary] did not know what Timothy got up to' and she defended her brother by calling Christie a liar. Christie prevented his wife from saying something about Beryl, 'you shut your mouth' and claimed he knew Evans from his days in the police, which Mary denied. He also stopped her from entering the house.[18]

Evans's mother was confronted with the furniture company wanting its money from her as guarantor of her son's repayments, so she wrote to Mrs Lynch whilst not in the best of tempers, on 29 November. She reported that she had been told that Beryl and Geraldine were in Brighton with her father. She wrote that her son:

> is like his father no good to himself or anyone else so if you are mug enough to keep him for nothing that will be your fault I don't intend to keep him any more I have done my best for him & Beryl what thanks did I get his name stinks up here everywhere I go people asking for him for money he owes them I am ashamed to say he is my son.

Whether this was wholly written in the heat of the moment or whether this contained an insight into Evans's true character is a moot point. On 30 November, Mrs Lynch read the letter to Evans, who denied the allegations contained therein, but was visibly agitated and did not finish breakfast. He had another cup of tea and took the bus to Merthyr Tydfil with his aunt.[19]

That afternoon, Evans went to the police station there. He was seen by DC Gwynfyrn Howell Evans. Evans then dropped his bombshell:

> 'I want to give myself up. I have disposed of my wife'.
> 'What do you mean?'
> 'I put her down the drain'.

Evans was told to think before he continued, but he said 'I know what I am saying, I cannot sleep and want to get it off my chest'. Evans was then cautioned and asked if he wanted to make a written statement. He replied, 'I will tell you all about it and you can write it down. I am not very well educated and cannot read or write'.

Evans told his story to DC Evans and DS Gough, beginning at 3.20pm. He told them that his wife desired to abort her baby, then that he had met a man in a transport café, who gave him pills which would abort Beryl's unborn baby, but instead they killed her. He then claimed he put her corpse into the drain in the street, told lies about where his family was, and escaped to Wales. DC Evans thought that Evans took a long time over his statement, which was concluded at 5.10pm, and also believed that Evans was a 'terrible liar' who had been 'telling a cock and bull story'. It is worth noting that Evans's mother said he spoke quickly when he was being truthful and slowly when he lied. DC Evans was also concerned that Evans said little about Geraldine's whereabouts.[20]

Evans was arrested on suspicion of murder. He was then penni-less and did not have the teddy bear he later claimed he had bought for Geraldine. The police telephoned Scotland Yard, who in turn sent a message to the Notting Hill police station. Much was the same message as already noted, but with an addition, 'He [Evans] handed his fourteen month [actually thirteen months] old child to a man called Reginald Christie at the same address who stated he could have the child taken care of'. This was the first time that Christie was linked in public to the tragedy at Rillington Place. Meanwhile, in London, three officers tried to lift the manhole cover on the drain, but could not do so. The noise they made brought Christie to the door, and they asked him about the whereabouts of Beryl and Geraldine. Christie told them that they had left some time ago, and gave them the Proberts' address. They told this to their colleagues at Merthyr Tydfil, and Evans was duly informed. Eventually, using levers, the manhole cover was lifted, but nothing was there.[21]

At 9.00pm Evans stated that he had lied. 'I said that to protect a man called Christie. It's not true about the man in the cafe either. I will tell you the truth now'. Then there was another statement, made by Evans, and again before DC Evans and DS Gough, which began just before 10.00pm and took two hours:

> As I was coming home from work one night, that would be a week before my wife died, Reg Christie who lived on the ground floor below us approached me and said, 'I'd like to have a chat with you about your wife taking these tablets. I know what she's taking them for she's trying to get rid of the baby. If you or your wife had come to me in the first place I could have done it for you without any risk'. I turned around and said 'Well, I didn't think you knew anything about medical stuff'. So he told me that he was training to be a doctor before the war. Then he started showing me books and things on medical. I was just as wise because I couldn't understand one word of it because I couldn't read. Then he told

me that the stuff he used one out of every ten would die with it. I told him that I wasn't interested so I said goodnight to him and I went upstairs. When I got in my wife started talking to me about it. She said that she had been speaking to Mr Christie and asked me if he had spoken to me. I said 'Yes' and told her what he had spoke to me about. I turned round and told her that I told him I didn't want nothing to do with it and I told her she wasn't to have anything to do with it either. She turned around and told me to mind my own business and that she intended to get rid of it and that she trusted Mr Christie. She said he could do the job without any trouble at all.

On the Monday evening, that was the seventh of November when I came home from work my wife said that Mr Christie had made the arrangements for first thing Tuesday morning. I didn't argue with her, I just washed and changed and went to the K.P.H. until 10 o'clock. I came home and had supper and went to bed. She wanted to start an argument but I just took no notice. Just after six I got up the following morning to go to work. My wife got up with me. I had a cup of tea and a smoke and she told me, 'On your way down tell Mr Christie that everything is alright. If you don't tell him I'll go down and tell him myself'. So as I went down the stairs he came out to meet me and I said, 'Everything is alright'. Then I went to work. When I came home in the evening he was waiting for me at the bottom of the staircase. He said, 'Go on upstairs I'll come behind you'. When I lit the gas in the kitchen he said, 'It's bad news. It didn't work'. I asked him where was she. He said, 'Laying on the bed in the bedroom'. Then I asked him where was the baby. So he said, 'The baby's in the cot'. So I went in the bedroom I lit the gas then I saw the curtains had been drawn. I looked at my wife and saw that she was covered over with the eiderdown back to have a look at her. I could see that she was dead and that she had been bleeding from the mouth and nose and that she had been bleeding from the bottom part. She had a black skirt on and a check blouse and kind of a light blue jacket on. Christie was in the kitchen. I went over and picked my baby up. I wrapped the baby in a blanket and took her in the kitchen. In the meanwhile Mr Christie had lit the fire in the kitchen.

He said 'I'll speak to you after you feed the baby'. So I made the baby some tea and boiled an egg for her, then I changed the baby and put her to sit in front of the fire. Then I asked him how long my wife had been dead. He said, 'Since about three o'clock'. Then he told me that my wife's stomach was septic poisoned. He said, 'Another day and she'd have to have gone to hospital'. I asked him what he had done, but he wouldn't tell me. He then told me to stop in the kitchen and he closed the door and went out. He came back about a quarter of an hour later and told me he had forced the door of Mr Kitchener's flat and had put my wife's body in there. I asked him what he intended to do and he said 'I'll dispose of it down one of the drains'. He then said, 'You'd better go to bed and leave the rest to me'. He said, 'Get up and go to work in the morning as usual' and that he'd see about getting someone to look after my baby. I told him it was foolish to try and dispose of the body and he said, 'Well that's the only thing I can do or otherwise I'll get into trouble with the Police'.

Evans went to work whilst Christie looked after the baby. On Evans's return, Christie told him that he had contacted a young couple in East Acton who would be happy to look after Geraldine. On Thursday morning, Evans was feeding Geraldine, when: 'Christie came in. He said, "In the morning when you get up feed the baby and dress her then put her back in the cot, the people will be here just after nine in the morning to fetch her". He said, "I've told them to knock three knocks and I'll let them in."'

When Evans returned that evening, Christie told him that he had done as he planned, but the pram and Geraldine's clothes in a case would be handed over later that week. Evans saw his mother that evening and when asked about Geraldine, said that she and Beryl had gone on holiday. Later that night, Christie gave him additional information, 'Now the best thing you can do is to sell your furniture and get out of London somewhere'. Evans then related selling the furniture, leaving his job, and then going to Merthyr Vale.

He later said that he saw Christie, huffing and puffing, carrying Beryl's body down the stairs and into Kitchener's rooms.[22]

Those believing Evans to be innocent maintain this story to be true. Yet it does not appear to be a very intelligent method of shifting the blame from Evans to Christie, though Evans was not a very intelligent man. It would appear to be a tissue of lies for a number of reasons. Firstly, Christie was at the doctors when Evans claimed to have been having a meeting with him on 8 November. Secondly, Beryl was strangled and marks were clear around her neck. Evans gives lots of detail about his wife, but does not mention this. Thirdly, if Christie did kill Beryl, there would have been screams and other sounds heard by Ethel and the workmen. None were. Fourthly, how could Christie have moved the corpse? He dragged his other victims using a sheet – he was not a strong man. Fifthly, the above story suggests Evans was a weak man, easily malleable, but other evidence shows him to be manipulative, not vice versa. Sixthly, the dialogue and actions of Christie suggest him to have been simple-minded, yet we know he was not. Finally, can we believe that a loving father would have entrusted his daughter to a family of whom he had never heard and whose address he did not know? We should also note that the police thought Evans took a long time over this statement and his mother said that he usually took his time talking when he was lying.

This new information was passed to London, where a new investigation began, led by Detective Inspector James Neill Black, a police officer of twenty-two years' experience. In the night time they looked down the drains again and examined the garden for signs of recently disturbed earth. Nothing untoward was found. Police officers were stationed in and around the house and the occupants were questioned. Evans's rooms were also searched. Cuttings from four newspapers about the Donald Hume case were found in a cupboard – Hume was accused of murdering one Stanley Setty in October 1949, then scattering the latter's chopped up corpse into the Essex marshes. These cuttings showed pictures of the bundle in which the corpse had been wrapped; Black later recalled, 'he was very interested in the Setty case'. A briefcase which had been stolen in August from 164 Westbourne Park was also found. In the Christies' rooms were Geraldine's clothing, her pram and high chair. The Proberts were informed that morning that Evans had told them that they should ask Christie where Geraldine was.[23]

The police told the family that Evans was in custody in Wales and that he had made a statement about putting his wife down the drain. Both Christie and his wife were questioned separately by the police, with Christie accompanying them to Notting Hill Police Station from 11.00pm to 5.00am. A policeman was stationed at the house.[24]

Ethel explained about the troubles between Evans and his wife. She stated that Beryl had left the house at lunchtime on 8 November and that she saw Evans return late that same day (this is corroborated by Evans and Christie); Evans's whereabouts that evening are unknown.

When Evans returned to the house on 22 November, she said, 'I was in the house but I did not go to the door'. She said, 'I cannot think why Evans should suggest that she had [a miscarriage] and that my husband knew all about it. We were both on friendly terms with him … We have never had any friction with him'. The police were impressed by Ethel. 'In my opinion Mrs Christie was by no means under the dominance of her husband'.[25]

Meanwhile Christie was interviewed at the police station, where he told them he had been a policeman during the war, then about the Evanses' situation. He said his wife had spoken to Evans when he arrived on 22 November. He concluded, 'At no time have I assisted or attempted to abort Mrs Evans or any other woman … I cannot understand why Evans should make any accusation against me as I have really been very good to him in lots of ways'. Christie also said a little about the washroom:

> The wash room was a communal one, but actually it was only used for keeping rubbish and junk in. There was no key to it and the lock was rusted and broken and not usable. It could be open and shut by turning the handle but could not be locked. The wash house was only used for getting water to rinse out pails or put down the lavatory.[26]

It was later on that morning of 1 December that Chief Inspector George Jennings took charge of the case. A more thorough search of the house was made. In Christie's rooms they found a syringe, but tests proved it had not been used recently. Detective Chief Superintendent Thomas Barrett then ordered that Evans be recalled to London for questioning about the disappearance of his wife and child and Black and PS Corfield were accordingly despatched there.[27]

On 2 December the police made other discoveries. Christie later recalled, 'They found something in the outhouse and asked my wife go to the outhouse (wash house). She told me afterwards that they pointed to a bundle and asked her if she knew anything about it. She said that she did not and they asked her to touch it to see if she knew what it was. She said she touched it but didn't know what it was and she had never seen it before. An officer told us soon after that they had found a body'. Jennings stated:

> I searched an outbuilding on the ground floor at the rear of 10 Rillington Place … when I found a large package wrapped in a

green table cover and a blanket, and tied tightly with a sash cord, concealed by a quantity of timber under a sink. I removed the timber, pulled the package out into the back yard and discovered it contained the body of a woman doubled over with the head between the feet. Behind the door of this outbuilding concealed behind some timber, I found the body of a baby girl ...[28]

About this time, evidence of Christie's past misdeeds returned to haunt him. He recalled, 'Several years afterwards [after 1943] I was digging the garden and came across a bone which was broken in half. I knocked one piece into the ground next to a post in the garden'. He also later made the further revelation about this time:

my dog had been digging in the garden and I found the skull from the body of the woman Eady that I had buried in the nearest corner of the garden. I just covered it up with earth and later in the evening, when it was dark, I put my raincoat on. I went into the garden and got the skull and put it under my raincoat. I went out and put it in a bombed house, the last standing bombed house next to the tennis courts on St Mark's Road. There was a corrugated iron covering some bay windows and I dropped the skull through the window where the iron had been bent back. I heard it drop with a dull thud as though there were no floor-boards.[29]

It is likely that Christie was concerned that the police were on the premises and might find evidence of his two murders. Meanwhile, Evans was about to travel back to Notting Hill. Both men would be involved in the police investigations which ensued, as well as a trial for murder.

Chapter 6

The Murder Investigation 1949–50

'I know I made all those statements, mum, but only one of them is true. The one in which I said Christie had done it'.[1]

A murder investigation now began. Inspector Percy Law, a police photographer, took four photographs of the interior of the wash house and then the scene at the mortuary once the corpses had arrived there. PC Rogers drew a sketch plan of the house and grounds. The examination of the corpses was conducted by Dr Robert Donald Teare (1911–1979), one of the three leading post-1945 pathologists, 'a solid, likeable man with a good sense of humour, competent both in the field and the witness box' and he began work at 2pm at Rillington Place, continuing his work at Kensington Mortuary. The examination on Geraldine was straightforward. She had been strangled by a tie, tied with a bow knot, which remained around her neck when her corpse was located.[2]

The examination of Beryl was to prove more controversial, though the cause of death was obvious enough, as Teare stated: 'I came to the conclusion that the death of Mrs Beryl Evans was due to asphyxia due to strangulation by a ligature'. The body was clothed in a dress, jacket and blouse, the upper garments exposing parts of the body to view, and there were no knickers, though the latter did not surprise the doctors because many women entered prison without wearing such garments (nor was there a diaper, which Christie customarily affixed to his victims). It was uncertain what had been used to strangle her. The marks on the neck pointed to the attack coming from behind, with a rope about half an inch thick being used, though a twisted stocking could not be ruled out, though Teare thought this unlikely. There was a sixteen-week-old unborn male baby inside her, which had not been interfered with.[3]

There were other marks on the body too. There was an abrasion on the left front of the neck, where either the attacker had struck Beryl or where she had made a mark when trying to pull something away from her neck. There were bruises to the left thigh and also to the left leg below the knee. There was swelling above the right eye and upper lip, caused by a fist. Teare concluded that a struggle had occurred about twenty minutes before death, as otherwise there would have been no swelling to the face. He also noted that Beryl had not eaten for three to four hours before death. William Thorley officially identified the bodies, which were buried in the same coffin under a marked tombstone at Gunnersbury Cemetery at public expense on 8 December 1949.[4]

What the examination did not find was as significant as what it did. Firstly, because Teare was alert to the possibility that an abortion had occurred, he examined the vagina with a magnifying glass to try and find traces of semen. He found none. Professor Francis Edward Camps (1905–1972), another leading pathologist, agreed with his colleague's assessment. Secondly, and though it was not considered at the time, there were no other unusual marks on the body, and we will return to this point in Chapter 10.[5]

Jennings found other evidence and also said, 'I recall seeing football pools correspondence addressed to Evans which seem to indicate that Evans was a participant which would entail a certain amount of reading and writing'.[6]

Meanwhile, in Merthyr Tydfil, Black and Corfield arrived at the police station to collect Evans. Evans was handed over at 4.30pm, being told that this was in connection with the stolen briefcase. They travelled to London by train, and they talked about football, Evans being interested in Queen's Park Rangers (the police officers had been forbidden to discuss the murder case). They arrived at Paddington station at 9.30pm. Jennings met them there and they all drove over to Notting Hill Police Station, arriving at 9.45pm. Until then there had been no mention of the murders.[7]

At the station, two piles of clothing, Beryl's and Geraldine's, were laid out side by side, and the fatal tie was lying on top of the latter pile. Evans looked at the items 'and was slightly upset when he picked up these garments, but he was not unduly distressed', but said nothing. Jennings and Black did not say that the tie had been found around Geraldine's neck. Jennings introduced himself:

I am Chief Inspector Jennings, in charge of this case. At 11.50am today, I found the dead body of your wife, Beryl Evans concealed in a wash house at 10 Rillington Place, Notting Hill, also the body of your baby daughter Geraldine in the same outbuilding and this clothing was found on them. Later this day I was present at Kensington mortuary where it was established that the cause of death was strangulation in both cases. I have reason to believe that you were responsible for their deaths.

Evans only had a one word answer to this. It was: 'Yes'.

. Evans was then cautioned, before making the following statement, which is in direct contradiction to his previous ones:

She was incurring one debt after another and I could not stand it any longer, so I strangled her with a piece of rope and took her down to the flat below the same night whilst the old man was in hospital ... This was on Tuesday 8th November. On Thursday evening after I came home from work I strangled my baby in our bedroom with my tie.

He then signed and dated the document, adding, 'It is a great relief to get it off my chest. I feel better already. I can tell you the cause that led up to it'. Perhaps it is worth noting that no one told Evans how the two were strangled, yet he knew how – information known only to the police, the pathologist and the murderer – furthermore that he knew exactly where in the outhouse they were and by what they were hidden, though a quick-witted man might have deduced that. But was Evans quick-witted?[8]

At about ten that night, Evans made another statement. He spoke about debts and arguments, and the actual murders themselves, as has been already related in Chapter 5. As with the other confessions, he talked about selling his furniture and going down to Merthyr Vale. He signed each page of the confession and initialled alterations. It was read back to him. The time was recorded: 11.15pm.[9]

This confession, coming on top of the shorter one, may seem to be a conclusive statement of Evans's guilt, and the speed of it would also suggest this was truthful, according to his mother's general statement about her son's speed of conversation when being truthful. It is also interesting to note that Evans knew how his wife's body was behind wood under the sink and his daughter's behind the door, as no one had told him these facts. However, it has been argued that such a lengthy statement could not have been taken down in the time quoted by the police. However, Black noted that Evans was very quick in his speech and he had trouble in keeping up. Subsequent tests showed that it was possible to write so much down from dictation.[10]

Evans also made another statement attesting his guilt. PS Leonard Trevallian saw Evans in a cell at about 6.00am on 3 December, and said to him, 'Well one can understand possibly something happening to your wife, but to your baby, that sounds a bit much'. Evans replied: 'Well, it was the constant crying of the baby that got on my nerves. I just had to strangle it, I just had to put an end to it, I just couldn't put up with its crying'.

Trevallian recalled, 'When Evans confessed to me he was completely relaxed and this was not made under any tension'.[11]

The next morning, Evans's mother came to the police station to see her son, but was told she would have to wait until the next day when she could see him at Brixton prison. Evans was charged that morning with the murder of his wife and he replied, 'Yes, that's right'. En route to prison, Black recalled Evans saying to him, 'After I killed my wife, I took her wedding ring from her finger and sold it'. Black also recalled, 'he thought everybody had been very fair and every word that had been spoken had been the truth'.[12]

At the prison, Evans was seen by Dr John Campbell MacIntyre Matheson, who had been Principal Medical Officer there since 1929. He had to ascertain whether Evans was sane and so fit to plead his case in a court of law. He thought Evans seemed tired and upset and classed him as a 'high grade mental defective'. Later that day, Evans relaxed and it was noted 'Appears cheerful and converses with others. Watches games'.[13]

Matheson concluded thus: 'He appears to have led a careless improvident life since leaving school and his habits have deteriorated ... an inadequate psychopathic personality, which tends to make him act impulsively with little or no foresight or consideration for others'.

Matheson had two interviews with Evans, and he later wrote in conclusion, 'I feel, if I may use popular language, in my heart of hearts, Evans did murder his wife and child'.[14]

Evans's mother visited him in prison on 4 December, where he made a startling statement:

I did not touch her mum, Christie did it. I didn't even know the Laby was dead until the police brought me to Notting Hill.

Christie told me the baby was at East Acton. Don't trust Jennings, mum, he's a swine. Black's a gentleman.

He also said, 'I know I made all those statements, mum, but only one of them is true. The one in which I said Christie had done it'. His mother was concerned that her son had made so many differing statements, to which Evans replied, 'See Christie'. He made similar remarks to his sisters when they visited him, too.[15]

Numerous suggestions have been made about why, if Evans was innocent, he said otherwise to the police. They all rest partly on the assumption that Evans was a man of low mental capacity, though it is simplistic to label him as stupid, and that he was in a state of tension and guilt. Dr Jack Abbott Hobson, a psychiatrist, suggested that feelings of guilt might lead to a false confession, and that Evans might feel remorse for having concealed his wife's death for three weeks as well as neglecting Geraldine. He may have felt he needed to confess. Another possibility, advanced by Ludovic Kennedy, is that Evans was brainwashed by techniques familiar to those used by the Chinese Communists. Prisoners become suggestible to manipulation by their captors. But there is no evidence that Jennings and Black indulged in such tactics or were proficient in their use. Finally, it has been argued that the essentially weak Evans was preyed on by both the manipulative Christie and the bullying police, though Evans stated that Black acted well towards him. Jennings, however, did not think Evans seemed frightened or nervous, and believed he was 'quite worldly', but that on being shown the clothes, he seemed 'upset'. Black remarked, 'He was slightly upset when he picked up the garments and also the tie, but he was not unduly distressed'. He added, 'I can definitely say there was no influencing of Evans and no pressure of any kind was used in the interviews and I was frankly surprised at the readiness showed by Evans to tell us his story after he had been cautioned'. It is also odd that Evans showed no anger on hearing of the death of his daughter, suggestive again of guilt.[16]

The fear of police brutality has also been advanced. Evans declared, 'I thought unless I made that statement and said I had committed the murder of my little girl, I would be taken to the cells and knocked about'. Later it was argued that 'this man is an uneducated man and it may well be that his ideas of police methods are such as one perhaps associates with foreign countries rather than England'. However, Evans never mentioned that the police made any threat towards him, nor was he injured by them. Furthermore, Evans had been in police custody for the past two days and no one had threatened him at all. It has also been alleged that Evans said that he was kept up all night with the confession and only signed it because he no longer cared for his life when he knew Geraldine was dead.[17]

Evans seems not to have disliked his time in prison. He said, 'There are eighteen of us here, and we play dominoes and games of all kinds all day, but you have to watch Hume'. The record of his time in prison is unremarkable. He was deemed 'quiet and well behaved' and 'quite unassuming'. He had no complaints and settled into the daily routine. Daniel Heaney, a prison officer, remembered Evans as 'a likeable type of person'. 'He used to read the newspapers', but often asked Heaney to interpret for him. However, 'the way he put it to me, he was strongly involved in the killing of the child'.[18]

Hume, in prison for the murder of Samuel Setty, was a fellow inmate of Evans. He later alleged that he had spent time with Evans, whom he deemed, 'a bit of an idiot, this boy'. He advised Evans, 'Blame everyone but yourself'. Evans reputedly told him 'I've been thinking about what you said about sorting out a defence story. Will you help?' Evans denied murder, but Hume concluded, 'I am convinced that he and Christie together arranged to murder the child'. Hume also alleged that 'in the presence of several prisoners and witnesses, Evans admitted to killing his baby because it kept crying'.[19]

The police also questioned the workmen who had been on the premises in November, and their statements have often been used to indicate Evans's innocence. Frederick Willis, a plasterer, stated: 'I completed plastering the ceiling of the wash house about the middle of the morning on Wednesday 9th November ... I was constantly in and out of the wash house until we left the job on 11th November'. Frederick Jones, a builder's labourer, added:

> Whilst we were working on the wash house and water closet, once the wooden shires were up, it was impossible for anyone to put anything in there ... All the time we were there I saw nothing at all in the wash house other than the materials we were using and our tools ... After completing the work on Friday afternoon, the 11th November, I personally swept out the wash house and also cleaned out the copper which was in it. There was definitely nothing whatever in the wash house or the copper.[20]

This statement is important because it means that Evans cannot have put the corpses of his alleged victims there when he said he had, because Jones would have seen them, and he did not. This is not in itself proof of Evans's innocence: he could have put the corpses there after 11 November, as he did not leave the house until the 14th.

On the next day, the police questioned the workmen again. They were called to the police station again because Jennings, believing Evans's statement about putting the body of his wife in the wash house on 8 November, which contradicted the workmen's evidence, wanted to clarify matters. The men were kept waiting and were 'browned off'. Willis admitted he might have been in error: 'I feel now that it would have been quite possible for anything to have been under the sink in the corner with timber in front of the sink', and so concurred with Jennings, but Jones initially stuck to his original statement. Larter later said that his employees felt that they had been pressurized to alter their statements to fit the police view of the case.[21]

Christie and his wife made additional statements to the police. On 5 December, Ethel said that on the night of 8 November:

> I woke up and heard what seemed to be that someone overhead was moving furniture. I also heard a kind of thud somewhere, but could not place it as I was half asleep ... I did not pay much attention to the noise as I thought they were getting ready to move out silently as the landlord's agents had taken out a summonses against them for arrears of rent ... After 8th November 1949 I did not hear the baby cry at all. It would be possible for the baby to cry out without my hearing.[22]

Likewise, Christie made another statement. He said that he and his wife went out on the evening of 8 November. That night he too said that he heard noises:

> During the night I was awakened by a heavy thud from some-where else up above. It woke my wife and we discussed what the noise could have been. We also heard noises like heavy furniture being moved upstairs. I sat up in bed and looked out of the back window, but as I could not see anything, I lay down and dropped off to sleep again.[23]

It is possible that the two had forgotten about the sounds in the night time and sought to rectify their error, though it has been inferred that there was a conspiracy between them to deceive, with Christie influencing his wife to produce a statement corroborating his. Or the sounds were of Evans moving his wife's corpse, perhaps into Kitchener's rooms.

Three days later Christie made a final statement about the builders who worked in the house on 8–14 November. There were workmen's tools and equipment in his front room from 8–11 November. He declared that he never saw any of these things stored in the washroom or toilet.[24]

Superintendent Cherrill, a fingerprint expert, went to Rillington Place. There he met 'a fair haired, balding man wearing glasses [who] offered a chair. It was John Reginald Halliday Christie ... the soft voiced bespectacled man'. Meanwhile 'the pleasant, smiling Mrs Christie' brought him tea.[25]

At the West London Magistrates' Court on Thursday 15 December, Evans stood in the dock. He sat passively, his arms folded, and was charged with the murder of his wife and child. Maurice Crump was the prosecutor and he recounted the details of the case. One of the witnesses called was Christie, and he was given a seat because he protested that he was unwell. He told how he had heard a loud thud in the night of 8 November, how Evans told him about Beryl's departure and how Evans sold his furniture before departing on 14 November. Although Ethel was called upon to give evidence, she broke down when she first stepped into the witness box, explaining, 'I am rather upset about it'. Kennedy has assumed that this is evidence that she knew of her husband's guilt, but this seems unlikely. Rather it was probably natural distress at a double murder, including that of a baby, occurring under the same roof as herself. At the end of the hearing, Evans was remanded in custody until 22 December, when he was committed for trial.[26]

On the following Thursday, Evans was once again brought before the magistrates. Crump presented the case for the prosecution based on the statements taken by Jennings at Notting Hill on 2 December. One of the witnesses was Mrs Lynch, who told of Evans's visit on 15 November, his return to London on 21 November and his being back in Wales on 23 November. She was shown a ring and asked if she had ever seen it before. She said that she had seen it in her nephew's possession and she told them that he had said he had picked it up in Cheltenham. She then mentioned Mrs Probert's letter. There is also the allegation that Evans bought a teddy bear in Wales for Geraldine, but there is no evidence for this, as Jennings reported. 'With regard to such a toy ever existing, I personally have no recollection of it'. Jennings gave evidence of the discovery of the body and Evans's statement. Evans pleaded not guilty and reserved his defence concerning both charges. He was then formally committed for trial at the Old Bailey in the next month.[27]

Procter, then working for *The Daily Mail*, visited Christie at this time, and recalled, with the benefit of hindsight, that Christie 'smiled his thin, suspicious smile, and invited me into his kitchen'. He was 'anxious to talk … Then he became quite friendly. He smiled, a sickeningly, silly smile, and he gave me an unforgettably repulsive handshake, wet and limp'. Christie seemed very upset about the murders and said he prayed for the killer to be found. 'Who do you think murdered her?' he asked. Christie offered him tea and stated he could offer him nothing stronger. Christie was certainly upset about the police investigation. He recalled, 'they kept constant watch on me and accompanied my every move. I had no sleep at all'. Having two skeletons in the garden was certainly cause for concern. What we don't know is how much he knew – or suspected – about what Evans had done. If he knew something he could hardly have voiced his concerns to anyone: his knowledge of his garden's gruesome contents caused him hold his tongue.[28]

Meanwhile, on 6 December Muriel's skull had been found at 133 St Mark's Road, where Christie had deposited it. The coroner's report noted that it was the skull of a woman, and stated, 'extensive enquiries have been made by PS Garrod, Harrow Road Police Station, and no person was unaccounted for in air raid incidents at that address or in the vicinity'.[29]

In the meantime, Evans's lawyers learnt that the principal witness for the Crown would be Christie, and that he had been a War Reserve Constable. Jennings is alleged to have said, though he denied it, that Christie's evidence was 'purer than snow' or 'as good as gold'. Christie's previous criminal record was made known to the defence. The Brief to Counsel drew up the evidence and then discussed whether a plea of insanity should be attempted, whether Evans's story of the abortion attempt by Christie should be pursued, or whether a plea for the charge of manslaughter should be preferred. The former was discarded as Evans was not insane. Finally, Malcolm Morris, QC, was selected to lead the defence in court. It was decided that Evans's second confession at Merythr Tydfil should be taken as the truthful one, though as noted this was at odds with both known facts and reasonable probability.[30]

Christie has often been accused of being an abortionist. In a recent television programme (2011) former PS Trevellian strongly stated this as a fact and included Ethel as his accomplice. Yet the foundation for this is thin. Trevellian did state in 1965 'I gathered that Christie was associated with prostitutes, abortions and so on' but did not know this personally as fact. When Mrs Hide, a neighbour, tasked Ethel on the topic, she dismissed it: 'Fancy asking my Reg such a thing'. While Ethel's evidence may be questioned, that of Jennings ought not to be, for in 1953 he categorically stated that Christie was not an abortionist and he was best placed to know. In the want of positive evidence and this outright negative we can only conclude that whatever Christie's subsequent claims about being able to abort women, these were lies to lure potential victims to their deaths.[31]

Christie was about to be put into a position of responsibility and attract publicity, the like of which he had never before experienced. He was also about to be accused of murder.

Chapter 7

The Trial of Timothy Evans
1950

*'Well, Mr Christie, I have got to suggest to you, and
I do not want there to be any misapprehension about it,
that you are responsible for the death of Mrs Evans
and the little girl'.*[1]

Evans's trial began at the Old Bailey on Wednesday, 11 January 1950 and the judge was Mr Justice Lewis. It appeared to be a very ordinary case of domestic murder and received little media attention. As Procter recorded 'We in Fleet Street ... regarded the Evans case as ... dull, sordid, unglamorous, dreary'. Mr Christmas Humphreys, Senior Counsel to the Crown, led the case for the prosecution. He informed Morris that they would be proceeding with the indictment that Evans killed his daughter, so the defence of provocation/manslaughter could not be used. Lewis declared that evidence about the murder of Beryl could be used as it was felt to be relevant in this case too.[2]

Thus, on the first day of the trial, Evans pleaded not guilty. Humphreys then outlined the sequence of events as he saw them. He also stated how Evans had made four different statements; one in which 'he laid the whole blame with regard to the charge of the murder of the child on the shoulders of Mr Christie, who was living on the ground floor, saying that he killed his wife in the process of performing an illegal operation'. The jury were told that Beryl and Geraldine were never seen again after 8 November, that Evans left six days later and then went to the Merthyr Tydfil police station on 30 November. Here he made two different confessions, with the result that the police in London searched 10 Rillington Place, where the corpses of Beryl and Geraldine were found. Evans was brought back to Notting Hill and charged with the murders. He made two confessions there, admitting to committing both murders. Humphreys concluded his opening speech thus:

> You are concerned with the death of the baby. It is alleged he murdered the baby deliberately, as he himself set out not once but twice. You will have to consider whether you have any doubt that the story he there told was true. You will bear in mind that he begins with a story most of which he abandons, and that he goes on to tell a story, which is a terrible accusation, if it is true, of the murder by a man downstairs of his wife, and then he throws both these statements away and clearly confesses to the murder of his wife and child. You will listen to the evidence of the witnesses for the prosecution, and you will listen to any evidence which the accused may put forward through his counsel or by any other witnesses he may call, but when you have heard all of the evidence you may well think – and indeed, you must be certain in your minds that it is so – that he murdered this baby, and in that case you will find him guilty of wilful murder.[3]

Then the chief witness for the prosecution stepped into the witness box. This was Christie, described as being a 'ledger clerk'. The first part of his evidence concerned the layout of the premises, the fact that no one could have entered the garden without passing Christie's bed-room, and that he heard 'a very loud thud' in the night of 8 November: 'As though something was being moved, something heavy was being moved'. The jury was reminded that that was the last day Beryl and Geraldine were seen alive. Morris then asked Christie to 'keep your voice up'. Christie replied, 'I have a quiet voice; it is the reaction of gas poisoning in the last war'.[4]

There was some discussion about Christie relating how he had seen Evans on the night of 8 November and he claimed he was told that Beryl had gone to Bristol, and that Evans said that he had lost his job two days later. Christie gave evidence that Evans later sold his furniture and then left. Finally, Christie told how Evans had returned and how they had met at 10 Rillington Place.

Humphreys also spent some time building up sympathy towards Christie: 'You were under medical treatment at the time?'

'Yes, and still am'.

'Still are; you are not too well. What were you doing during the war, Mr Christie?'

'I was a police officer during the war'.

'For how long?'

'From 1st September, 1939, to December, 1943'.

'So for four years you were in the police?'

'Yes'.

'You are rather a sick man now?'

'Yes'.

The judge then asked about Christie's 'voice and gas', to which the witness replied: 'Yes; that was the first war; I was in the 1914 war'.

That was the end of the first day in court. That evening, Christie went to see his doctor and was in severe pain that night. Also, on that day, Evans said to Basil, 'I'm sorry, Baz'. Thorley was convinced that this was an admission of guilt.[5]

The trial continued into a second day on Thursday, 12 January, and Christie was cross-examined by Morris. He asked Christie if he knew anyone in Acton, particularly the young couple Evans claimed Christie had said he was going to give Geraldine to. This Christie emphatically denied. He was asked about the tie (which had a faint stripe) with which Geraldine had been killed, and again Christie denied all knowledge. He said that Evans had had a striped tie. Then Morris made the following suggestion:

Well, Mr Christie, I have got to suggest to you, and I do not want there to be any misapprehension about it, that you are responsible for the death of Mrs Evans and the little girl; or, if that is not so, at least that you know very much more about those deaths than you have said?

'That is a lie', retorted the indignant Christie.[6]

Christie's knowledge that Beryl desired an abortion was aired. He denied he had ever shown Evans any medical books or that he had claimed he had been training to be a doctor, 'No, that is nonsense'. Christie said that he had shown Evans a St John's Ambulance first aid book, but that was all. In that case, Morris asked, 'Can you suggest how in the world I am able to ask a question about it, how Evans could have known that you had a book with diagrams in it in your flat?' Christie began, 'Well, it might have been obvious ...' but Humphreys objected on the grounds that this was a hypothetical question about what someone might have known. Morris then had Christie state that he had been at home throughout 8 November, though Christie stated that he had been scarcely able to move about on that day. The judge then intervened: 'Mr Christie, would you be more comfortable sitting down giving your evidence?' He replied, 'I think I would, my lord'. Christie was asked about hearing the noises in the night of 8 November.[7]

Morris then launched into a more direct attack:

Perhaps I should have put this to you before about the events of the Tuesday evening; what I am suggesting to you happened then is that you carried the dead body of Mrs Evans with Evans' help down to Kitchener's flat on that evening?

'That is absolutely ridiculous, because ...' began Christie. The judge cut him short, merely wanting to know whether it was true or not, and Christie said it was untrue because he could barely move, 'the fibrositis in my back was so bad ... I could scarcely bend'.[8]

There was further examination about his conversations with Evans about selling the furniture and leaving. Christie mentioned a conversation he had had that morning with Basil Thorley, in which he had alleged he had recommended Hookway to Evans as a possible furniture dealer, and who had told him that Evans was a liar. Morris then made an attack on Christie's character:

Now, my lord, I have certain questions to ask this witness which I feel I must ask in view of the question which my learned friend asked him yesterday, which in my submission, was not a proper one, about his being in the Police Force during the last war. I regret to have to ask the questions, and it may be that your lordship will feel that our friends of the Press will not see fit to report this matter.[9]

'Mr Christie ... you are not, are you, a man of good character?'

'Well, I have had some trouble'.

'I apologise for having to ask you these questions, but I am afraid I must. On four occasions you have been convicted of offences of dishonesty, have you not?'

'Three'.

'Not four?'

'No'.

'Then perhaps I had better put them to you. Were you sentenced to three, three and three months' imprisonment concurrent in 1921 for stealing postal orders? Do you remember that?'

'Yes, I remember that'.

'Is that right?'

'Yes'.

'Bound over for false pretences in 1923 at Halifax?'

'Yes, I remember that'.

'Nine months' hard labour for stealing material and goods in 1924 at Uxbridge?'

'Yes'.

'And three months and various fines, with an alternative of imprisonment, also at Uxbridge, for stealing a motor car in 1933?'

'Yes, that is right'.

'Surely, Mr Christie, you could remember that. Four offences of dishonesty?'

'I had an idea it was three. I was not quite sure'.

'I see. But what is perhaps more important and relevant to this matter, is there another conviction recorded against you?'

'Yes'.

'And is that for malicious wounding, for which you were sentenced to six months' imprisonment in 1929?'

'Yes'.

'Now I must suggest this to you, because it is something which the accused will say in due course, when he comes to give his evidence, that you have told him – that you procured abortions for a number of young women?'

'That is wrong. This is a lie'.

Christie then went on to deny he had any medical knowledge apart from first aid skills and that he never claimed to have been training for a medical career.[10]

Finally, Humphreys attempted to salvage his witness's character:

'Now, only a word about your character. What were you doing in the First World War?'

'I was in the Army in the First World War'.

'Fighting for your country?'

'Yes, I was in the Duke of Wellington's Regiment and in the Notts and Derby, and I was gassed twice, and I was blinded for three months, and never spoke for three and a half years'.

As noted, Christie had been gassed, but his sight had not been affected. He was lying in order to gain sympathy.

'The last time you were in trouble with the police for any instance was in 1933, was it?'

'Yes'.

'Seventeen years ago?'

'Yes'.

'In this last war, in spite of your disabilities, you served in the War Reserve Police for many years; is that right?'

'Yes, I did, and I was commended on two occasions'.

Christie came across as an upright man who had gone down in the world. He made a good and seemingly reliable witness.[11]

Ethel was then asked about hearing the loud bump on 8 November and about meeting Evans earlier that night. Morris asked her about her husband's medical knowledge, but she said that he only knew first aid. When asked about the latter, she replied, 'I do not know. I have never looked at them. I am not interested in such things'. She said she did not see either Beryl or Geraldine after 8 November. She said her husband could not have fed Geraldine.[12]

Mrs Lynch was the next witness. She confirmed Evans had been with them, and had told them that his wife had walked out on them and people from Newport were looking after Geraldine. The letter from Evans's mother was read out in court. DC Evans recounted Evans's arrival at the police station. Evans's first two confessions were read aloud. Jennings was called next and he told of the discovery of the bodies. Evans's next two confessions were also read out. Jennings was asked about the scene at Notting Hill Police Station, as was Black. They said that Evans was shown the clothing which had been worn by Beryl and Geraldine, but that they did not tell Evans how Geraldine had been killed. It will be remembered that Evans confessed to killing Geraldine with a tie. Black stated that Evans had been told exactly where and with what the corpses had been hidden, but in this he was wrong, as the statement read to Evans (see Chapter 5) did not give such details. Thus concluded the case for the prosecution.[13]

The evidence for the defence was then given. There was only the one witness called, and that was Evans himself. Morris began examining him and he denied all responsibility for both murders and said that he was fond of Geraldine.[14]

Morris then took Evans through the various statements he had previously made, beginning with those at Merthyr Tydfil. Evans said that he made the first statement, which he said was mostly untrue 'in order to protect a man called Christie'. He said this in the first place, so he said, because he believed that Christie had put his wife's body down a manhole – that being what he said that Christie had told him that he was going to do. Morris then took Evans through his second statement, which he declared to be true, and that Christie promised to try and abort Beryl, but on Evans's return, he found her dead. Evans said that Christie had taken Beryl's corpse down to Kitchener's rooms, and that he (Evans) had helped him; 'I heard Mr Christie huffing and blowing on the staircase ... I helped him carry my wife's body into the kitchen'.[15]

Evans related how Christie looked after the baby on the following day and that he had made arrangements to give her to a childless couple in East Acton. He then said that Christie recommended he sell his furniture and gave him Hookway's details, who bought it. Evans also said that Christie advised him to tell people that his wife and baby were on holiday if anyone asked about their absence. Evans told how he had gone to Merthyr Vale and stayed with his aunt and uncle, returning to London to ask Christie how his daughter was. Then the account of Evans going to the police station and being brought to Notting Hill police station was given. Until then, Evans claimed, he had no idea that his daughter was dead.[16]

Morris then asked about the two statements made at Notting Hill police station; Evans denied that either was true. Morris asked why he confessed to the murders and Evans replied, 'I was upset and I was afraid the police would take me downstairs ... I was upset pretty bad; Sir; I had been believing my daughter was still alive'.[17]

Humphreys now cross-examined Evans:

'Is it true that on five different occasions at different places and to different persons you have confessed to the murder of your wife, and to the murder of your wife and child?'
'I have confessed, sir, but it is not true'.
  ...
'Are you saying on each of those occasions you were upset?'
'The biggest part of them, Sir. Well, I was not upset on the five, but the last one I was'.
'If you were not upset on the five, why did you sometimes confess to wilful murder if you were not upset – unless it were true?'
'Well, I knew my wife was dead; but I did not know my daughter was dead'.

Humphreys then went through with Evans the confessions he had made and why he had made them. Evans did not deny he had confessed to murder, but stressed these confessions were untrue. Humphreys then asked: 'And therefore you make an allegation in terms through your counsel against a perfectly innocent man that he caused the murder –'

Morris interrupted thus: 'My learned friend has no right to say that'.

The judge intervened, too, though against Morris: 'They have listened to your cross-examination of Christie, and if they think that is not a suggestion that Mr Christie murdered the wife and the daughter I do not know what is'.[18]

Humphreys then asked:

'And you were asking for that charge of murder to be made against you in order to protect a man who you now say is the murderer, is that right?'

'Yes.'

'Why?'

No answer was given. Humphreys now decided to show Evans as a liar. He began thus:

'Now we will come back to the series of statements, and I am putting to you the general proposition that you are a man who is prepared to lie, if necessary upon oath, for your own convenience?'

'Not for my own convenience'.

Humphreys then went through a number of statements which Evans had previously made and he had to admit that most of them were untrue. He asked further questions:

'Let us look a little further at what I suggest is your habit of lying to suit your convenience. You lied to the Christies, did you not, that your wife was away, and all the rest of it, did you not?'

'I lied to Mrs Christie, yes'.

'All right, you lied to Mrs Christie. You lied to your aunt down in Wales, Mrs Lynch, did you not?'

'Yes, Sir'.

. . .

'So you lied to Mrs Christie, your aunt, the police and to your boss?'

'Yes; I did it all on the advice of Mr Christie'.

'All on the advice of Mr Christie. That is a new one'.

. . .

'Now, you are the person who alleges that Mr Christie is the murderer in this case; can you suggest why he should have strangled your wife?'

'Well, he was home all day.'

'Can you suggest why he should have strangled your wife?'

'No, I cannot.'

'Can you suggest why he should have strangled your daughter two days later?'

'No.'

This now concluded the case for the defence. Evans's credibility was in shreds.[19]

It was now the turn of Humphreys, who made the closing speech for the prosecution. He emphasized Christie's good character again, 'fought through the First World War, suffered wounds, and was badly gassed ... in the last war, served in the police force, apparently with distinction'. And his criminal record was seventeen years old. He added:

Do you believe that at that time, as he told you, and went out of his way to tell you, he was so ill that most of the time in his pyjamas ... that that man could undertake the carting of a fully grown woman down stairs ... But still more important – why? Why should Christie strangle the wife and strangle the child? ... It does not make sense. It is bosh! ... Even this fluent liar, who will lie as and when he pleases, cannot invent an answer to that question.[20]

The closing speech for the defence was rather longer. Morris stressed that the jury had to be absolutely sure that Evans could not be innocent before condemning him. He also added 'it is not your duty to say, "Is it Evans or is it Christie?"'. He introduced the following supposition:

if the threat which is mentioned by Evans in one of his statements as being made by his wife was carried out, and whatever it was that was done to her failed, she might, I suppose, although there is no evidence of it, have killed the child, which she threatened to do, and thereafter have been killed, perhaps by Evans.[21]

Morris then made a number of points in Evans's favour. Firstly, he said, 'The man is a perfectly peaceful man' who had no history of violence. Secondly he argued that his second confession was true, because Evans was not an intelligent man and 'there are limits to those things of which anyone's imagination is capable of'. He said that Evans had been able to recall this statement, which he had made six weeks ago, without any written prompts. He also drew attention to the alleged conversation between Evans and Christie about the latter's 'medical' books. Morris said:

A man who cannot read … would never pick up a book … would never find out if there are any diagrams in a book unless he was shown it; and if he was shown that book by Christie – and Christie says he never showed it to him at all – perhaps you think that book was shown to him on the occasion of which he speaks. If that is so, that he, Evans, may be – and I do not have to put it any higher than that – may be telling the truth about that interview with Christie.[22]

Morris then cast doubt on Christie, 'someone who is not a man of good character'. He said that Christie's record in both world wars might have 'nothing to do with this case, nothing at all'. He concluded, 'So do be careful – I know you will – do be careful about Christie'.[23]

Morris then spoke sympathetically about Evans, especially about his relationship with his daughter. He argued that Evans was frightened by the police questioning him at Notting Hill. He said that the second confession at Merthyr Tydfil was true, and referred to the story about the childless couple at East Acton wanting to adopt, 'Just think about that for a moment and imagine what are the chances of this sort of man having made up a story like that … Is he likely to have been able to make that up?' He urged the jury to give Evans the benefit of the doubt: 'you will begin to say to yourselves "Well, the case is black against him, but we are not absolutely happy, we are not absolutely certain in this case that the witness, the main witness … Christie was telling the truth, we just don't know"'. Thus ended the speech for the defence and also the second day of the trial. Clifford Spurling, a colleague of Christie's, recalled that Christie spoke to him on either this day or the next, 'He was very upset and told me that Evans had accused him of the murder and he was afraid he would be charged'.[24]

The third and final day of the trial was on Friday 13 January 1950. It was now time for the judge's charge to the jury. He began by telling them, 'Now, members of the jury, we are entering upon the last stages of this trial ... it is essential that a guilty man be found guilty, and as equally important that an innocent man be found innocent'. Suspicion alone was not enough: 'it is necessary before a man can be found guilty that the Prosecution should have proved to a jury beyond all reasonable doubt he is guilty'.[25]

It was then that the judge recounted the main facts of the case. He emphasized that the point at issue was merely 'the murder of his child ... and that is the only question which you have to consider'. He reminded them that the definition of murder was that of unlawful killing. With the victim being a child, there could not be provocation, which could reduce the offence to one of manslaughter. The jury were shown plans of the house and reminded that Beryl and Geraldine were last seen alive on 8 November. Evans told the Christies his wife and child had gone away and he left on 14 November to go to Wales. It was there that he went to a police station and made his first two confessions, which the judge read out. He read out the next two, and reminded the jury that Evans later said the first, third and fourth were untrue. He said that the fourth confession was 'that which the Prosecution base their case on'.[26]

The judge then cast doubt on the suggestion that Christie was the killer, 'assuming that the latter was an abortionist, 'You will ask yourselves what conceivable reason Christie had for murdering the baby. Indeed, you might ask yourselves the same question with regard to the wife, because that woman ... did not die from the result of an operation ... to procure abortion'. He also cast doubt on Christie's being physically able to commit murder. He then said that if Christie was guilty, 'it would have been easy for Mr Christie to have told you "I know nothing whatever of the wife's condition. That story is a complete lie. I never said I was practising for a medical man"', but instead he admitted to knowing about Beryl's pregnancy and her wish for an abortion. Although there was much contradiction, it was for the jury to decide which version was more likely.[27]

The judge added further weight to Christie's character, 'It would be a terrible thing if a person who has been in trouble with the police ... but has lived straight after that ... that he cannot be believed on his oath'. He also suggested, 'Evans is a person who does not hesitate to lie, on his own confession'. Because Evans, by his own statements, knew that his wife was dead since 8 November, but concealed it from everybody for three weeks, the judge said that this showed he was not a man whose word could be trusted. All the time the judge empha-sized that it was up to the jury to make up their own minds.[28]

Finally, he stated that everything one man had said had been con-tradicted by the other. Which of the two was the more reliable, then? It was evident what the judge thought. His final words were, 'Members of the jury, I have no more to say to you. You will go out now, if you will, and consider your verdict and tell me how you find, whether the accused man is guilty or not of the murder of his child, Geraldine Evans'.[29]

They retired at 2.10pm and returned to Court forty minutes later. The verdict was read:

> 'Do you find the prisoner, Timothy John Evans, guilty or not guilty of the murder of Geraldine Evans?'
> 'Guilty'.
> 'You find him guilty, and that is the verdict of you all?'
> 'It is'.
> 'Timothy John Evans, you stand convicted of murder. Have you anything to say why the Court shall not give you judgement of death according to law?'
> 'No, sir'.

The death sentence was then passed.[30]

According to the local newspaper, 'Whilst Evans was being sen-tenced, the sobs of a man sitting at the back of the court punctuated the judge's words. The sobs came from John Reginald Christie who had given information during the trial'. Christie was affected by the trial and slept badly afterwards, 'I was lost then', he later admitted. Three years later Christie explained that he was tearful because, as an opponent of capital punishment, he had been instrumental in send-ing a man to his death by such a method. However, it should be noted that Christie had also been under a great deal of stress; firstly con-cerned that the police might have found the remains of his two victims buried on the premises; secondly that Evans was accusing him of murder, and these grave worries, being dissipated, resulted in him crying tears of relief. Outside the court, he was confronted by Evans's mother, who called him a murderer to his face. According to Procter, Christie said of Evans, 'What a wicked man he is'. However, on the following day, he went to the offices of *The Kensington Post* and offered to sell them photographs he had taken of Evans. They refused.[31]

Michael Evelyn, an employee of the Department of Public Prosecutions, attended the trial and made the following notes about Christie. He believed he 'looked just that . . . a fine example of a truthful witness, being unable to be confounded in cross examination and he bore the very stamp of respectability'. It 'must have been a sickening experience for him. Christie was obviously a very sick man. The trial must have been an intolerable strain on the unfortunate Christie, although there was never really any doubt as to who would be believed'.[32]

An appeal was made on 15 January, on the grounds that the judge had misdirected the jury to bring a guilty verdict, and the prosecution case was flimsy, based as it was on lies. According to Evans, 'The whole case was built wholly around the evidence of one witness, Mr Christie, who has previous convictions, one being for malicious wounding, therefore how could his evidence be taken except for what it is worth.'[33]

The Court of Criminal Appeal heard the case on Monday, 20 February, before the Lord Chief Justice, Lord Goddard, who announced at the onset:

> A variety of grounds have been urged by Mr Malcolm Morris on his [Evans's] behalf, objecting to evidence and various other matters in the course of the case, but there is really only one point in this case which has any substance, or with which it is necessary to deal at in any length, and that is whether or not evidence with regard to statements which this man made with regard to the death of his wife and an admission on his part that he had caused the death of his wife was admissible in this case.[34]

Goddard judged that the two murders could not be dealt with in strict isolation, and recounted the facts of the case. He also noted that Morris had objected previously to evidence for the first murder being included with that of the second, stating that Morris thought that the two crimes were not part of the same system. Goddard believed that 'it is impossible to say that the evidence was not relevant, indeed it is highly relevant here where two bodies . . . were found together'. The judge in the trial was therefore deemed to have been correct in his judgement that evidence be used from both crimes.[35]

The court also believed that it was correct for the prosecution to outline Christie's character as chief witness for the prosecution. 'We can see no reason at all in those circumstances . . . why the Prosecution should not ask a question to show the class and character of man he had been for a good many years, and that during the war he had been in the responsible position of a War Reserve Constable'. They also believed that the Prosecution stating that Christie was 'a perfectly innocent man' was an unfortunate turn of phrase, for that was for the jury to decide. The appeal was dismissed. James Chuter Ede, the Home Secretary, then wrote the ominous words, 'The law must take its course'.[36]

Evans was also seen by Dr Patrick Joseph Gerard Quinn at Pentonville Prison, where he had been moved after the trial. Evans told Quinn his story of innocence, but the doctor was sceptical, later recalling, 'one gets the impression that it has been well rehearsed. He shows no suspicion or antagonism and there is none of the anger and indignation that one might expect if his story was true'. The Senior Medical Officer at the prison, Dr Stephen Coates, also saw Evans there, from 17 February until his execution. A medical report on 5 March stated, 'He adheres to his statement that Christie committed the crimes ... He is not insane and we have no reason to consider that he is suffering from any minor form of mental abnormality. We have no grounds to justify us in making any medical recommendation'.[37]

It will be remembered that Evans was a Catholic, though not a practising one. However, when he was in Pentonville, he was seen by the Catholic chaplain, one Father Joseph Francis, to whom he made his sacramental confession. Several years later, journalists claimed that the priest had said that Evans went to his execution protesting his innocence, though the confessional is inviolate and thus secret to any third party. Father Joseph rebuffed such insinuations and wrote:

> In regard to the guilt or innocence of the condemned man Evans I have never made any public statement. I have consistently refused to see all reporters. When the grief-stricken mother came to me for consolation I did say to her that I always felt that her son was not the sort of person to be a murderer. This was purely my own feeling and did not rest on anything that Evans said.[38]

Although he had no complaints, on 3 March Evans 'still denies the charge and alleges Mr Christie committed the murders'. He was almost daily visited by either his mother and stepfather or his sisters. However, PC Wright claimed that on another occasion, his stepfather said, 'he had no time for him [Evans] and that he was a proper bastard' and on a later occasion said, of Christie, 'he's a harmless old fellow and

Tim himself said he's always liked him'. It is also noteworthy that Evans seemed calm and resigned to his fate in prison (many killers adopt this attitude); an innocent man who had lost both wife and daughter would be more likely to be angry at the injustice of the situation.[39]

On 9 March 1950 Timothy Evans was hanged at Pentonville Prison by Albert Pierrepoint (1905–1992) and Sydney Dernley, his assistant. Pierrepoint later referred to Evans as 'an insignificant little man' and said 'I am absolutely certain that he was guilty'. The inquest recorded a verdict of 'Judicial execution of sentence of death by hanging'. It was not an event which excited much interest in the world at large, and did not make headlines. A double murderer had been hanged for his crimes and that was that. Sordid, yet commonplace.[40]

Chapter 8

The Murder of Ethel Christie
1950–52

*'After she had gone, the way was clear for me
to fulfil my destiny'.*[1]

Changes were afoot at 10 Rillington Place. Kitchener left the house in mid-December (he died in Worthing in 1964). In January 1950, Christie and his wife were briefly alone there. His job at the Post Office came to an end on 4 April. Christie claimed he had been ill, and off work, and that on his return he was escorted from the premises by two investigating officers, being sacked due to 'changes affecting the character (misc.)'. He soon found other work and from 24 April he was a despatch clerk for Messrs Askey's, a biscuit firm, of Kensal Road, leaving on 19 May. On 12 June 1950 he began working as an invoice clerk at the British Road Services, a nationalized industry which ran the country's road haulage services. He worked at the Shepherd's Bush depot at 192 Goldhawk Road and was remembered as being 'bad tempered', although his work was 'quite satisfactory'. He did First Aid and as a colleague later said, 'He always made a terrific fuss over just a scratch. I've gone to him with only a little cut on my thumb and came away with a huge bandage over it'.[2]

Christie also took a limited part in the Road Service's social activities. A colleague later recalled, 'It always seemed to me that he was trying very hard to be popular and not quite making it. When he refereed British Road Service's football matches he would trot about the pitch very much in command of the game'. He once accompanied his colleagues to a Christmas dance in a sergeants' mess in White City and was encouraged to choose a girl to ask to dance, but he failed to do so.[3]

Christie also became heavily involved in trade union matters, which suited his left-wing politics (he also read the left-wing *Daily Mirror*, but on Sundays the right-wing *News of the World*). He was elected chairman of TGWU (Transport and General Workers' Union) Branch 38 in 1950 and was re-elected in 1951 for two years. He was also grade representative of the West London Group. He was chairman of the London Delegates' Conference in 1950 and was re-elected in the next year. He was nominated for the NEC of the TGWU. A doctor later reported that he 'takes great pleasure in telling me of his activities in trade union work'. Ironically, Denis Nilsen was also a staunch trade unionist and Dr Harold Shipman was left-wing too.[4]

On 22 December 1949 there appears to have been the suggestion that Christie take over the tenancy of the whole house himself, while a letter of 26 March 1950 suggested that Christie wanted to move from 'this unpleasant place', to use his words. His attempts to be rehoused led him to meet his local MP, George Rogers, Councillor Gough, and to visit the local headquarters of the Labour Party, all to no avail. This was because prospective buyers were turning up to view the place at odd times and he allegedly found this disconcerting as he had to show them round. He also said that his bad health should give him priority for rehousing. Finally he claimed that people were pointing the finger at him over the recent murders.[5]

The house changed hands. The owner, Mr G.W. Davies, wanted to sell it. At first, one Ernest McNeil, a former undertaker, was considering buying it and made several visits. He thought that Christie was 'a weird bastard' and Ethel was 'very pathetic'. There was some discussion about the corpses in the wash house, but McNeil said that that did not perturb him. He asked 'How on earth did those two bodies manage to stay in that wash house all that time without your dog smelling them?' At this, Christie became 'very annoyed'. However a survey of the property was not very positive and so McNeil declined to buy. Jack Hawkins bought it on 3 April and sub-let it to Charles Brown, aged thirty-five, a 'man of colour' and a boxer, who lived nearby at 26 Silchester Terrace. On 3 August 1950 he bought the house from Hawkins. Instead of there being two 'flats' on the upper floors, he rented the five rooms singly in order to maximise the return on his new investment (charging tenants £2 per week per room; the rent-protected Christie paid 12s 9d per week for his three rooms). In 1951 the new tenants were Beresford Brown (who was also black), Charles and Susan Edwards (who, by 1953, had a baby) and John Peterson. There were others, too: Ivan Williams, Franklin and Lena Stewart; all three from Jamaica. It was thus far more crowded than it had been.[6]

Christie explained what was happening and its effect: 'When Mr Brown took over the house he put some odd bits of furniture which he brought into each room, the four upper rooms, and then let them to coloured people with white girls … It was very unpleasant because one or two were prostitutes'.[7]

At this time, the Christies began to put disinfectant down, both outside and inside the house. Christie later explained:

> There used to be railings on the small area outside the bay window and those railings were taken away. Occasionally people used to bring their dogs down, and they used to prowl around, and there was nothing to stop it. There were frequent complaints in the whole of the street about that over a number of years, and very often other people in the street used to put down disinfectant in the area for that reason.[8]

Brown also wanted possession of half of the garden in order to store building materials and planned to dig up the garden to level it. Christie, with two skeletons buried there, was understandably opposed to this and consulted a solicitor, resulting in Brown backing down. Brown offered money, but again Christie turned him down. He claimed that to surrender the garden would have been to have surrendered all privacy (Nilsen also managed to monopolize a shared house's garden for similar purposes).[9]

As to the situation inside the house, Christie said:

> When the black man bought the house he installed some – they were rather disreputable people, the ones that had the white women living with them and they used to come down into the hall and spit. It used to happen often enough, and eventually we even had to remove the linoleum from the hall, which was my own, because of that, and we frequently put some ash or something down, and then some disinfectant, and my wife, when she was washing the hall, used to put disinfectant into the water. I used it more liberally; I used to just sprinkle it.[10]

Christie asked for help among officialdom towards the end of 1950, and the council's sanitary inspector, Derek Kennedy, visited the premises. He stated:

> Mr Christie complained, however, that a Mr Brown of 43 Silchester Terrace W10 had obtained possession of the rooms and could I endeavour to prevent these coloured people moving in.

On several subsequent occasions, both Mr and Mrs Christie complained of the dirty habits of the coloured people.

Apparently Brown also bought 61 Blenheim Crescent and installed twelve black men there. Kennedy claimed Ethel 'complained frequently of migraines and rheumatism' and 'she was of untidy appearance and held Mr Christie in high esteem'.[11]

Christie complained of the poor sanitary habits of his fellow tenants, whom, he alleged, used the communal toilet six to nine men at a time and then failed to flush it. This resulted in he and Ethel being forced to use public toilets instead. He also claimed that they were very noisy at all hours and made it impossible for Ethel to sleep at nights (white people in nearby Tavistock Road made similar remarks about their black neighbours), and summed it up thus, 'our lives here have been and still are been made intolerable by the persecution of Brown and the coloured people who are certainly doing all possible to make it impossible for us'. He concluded, 'We were persistently persecuted by the niggers'. Complaints to Brown were of no avail, 'he encouraged it in an attempt to make us leave'.[12]

There were frequent quarrels. Christie claimed, 'My wife has also been assaulted twice and threatened many times, as have I'. Two of the others were charged with assault at the West London Magistrates' Court in 1951, resulting in a fine of £1 and a month's probation. Mrs Edwards was one offender and apparently she and Mrs Christie argued over whether the front door be kept open or not on 16 April 1952. Mrs Edwards denied threatening Ethel. Christie and Brown argued over court costs in 1951, which Christie had deducted from the rent owed, and Brown allegedly threatened to assault him over this, 'he keeps coming here creating a disturbance and threatening me'. Brown claimed, 'I have not threatened him at all'. Christie claimed Brown was 'a known bully and often in court'.[13]

Brown seems to have been a slum landlord of the Peter Rachman variety, who attempted to intimidate sitting tenants (whose rent was fixed) into moving in order to install higher-paying tenants, or more tenants by overcrowding. Brown later used the house as an illegal drinking club, so Christie's complaints about his unscrupulous nature may be genuine in part. Christie's sentiments about black people were shared by many poor white people in that locality in the 1950s, especially against slum landlords who appeared to be doing well for themselves in comparison to their own situations.[14]

Naturally, Brown put matters differently, complaining about Christie's behaviour and saying that the coloured people caused no difficulties. In fact, the police often called, as Brown remembered: 'Mr Christie, he always caused the trouble. Every time I went to get the rent he was always making a fuss over it'.[15]

Then there were health worries. Odess recalled he was 'Very depressed, lachrymose, unfit to work, recommend holiday' on 23 January 1950, but in 1951 his health was good. In July he was losing his memory and suffering from insomnia. Perhaps Christie's worst year, health wise, was 1952. He was on his employer's sick list for eight months of the year, up to early September. All these worries were taking their toll. Dr Dinshaw Petit, a psychiatrist, concluded, in 1952, that his symptoms were allegedly due 'to rough and frightening behaviour on the part of some negroes who live upstairs, used it as a brothel and frequently get drunk and disorderly'. Petit thought that 'his life was one of constant tension' and he advised hospital. However, 'he showed no evidence of insanity or irresponsibility'.[16]

Odess concluded that he was:

A nervous type and he had fits of crying, sobbing; he complained of insomnia, and headaches, and giddiness ... he could not concentrate on his job. That is what I describe as a nervous breakdown. On 10th July 1950, in addition to these symptoms, he also complained that he had lost his memory – amnesia. He could not remember recent things. I prescribed rest; he had to stay away from his job. He was not fit, of course, and I gave him tablets for the night and medicine for the day – sedatives. He seemed to have recovered after a few weeks.[17]

Christie knew this too well, saying in 1952, 'I have not been well for a long while, about 18 months. I have been suffering from fibrositis and enteritis. I had a breakdown in hospital'. As ever, he sought treatment. Odess referred him to others. Dr Charles Howell, a psychiatrist of St Charles' Hospital, whom Christie visited in March, reported that Christie, who said he was anxious about the Evans murders, was 'in a highly neurotic state and would have benefitted from the treatment offered but after a week's daily he refused it'. Howell had suggested that Christie attend Springfield Hospital, but though he went in August, he never went again, as advised, apparently because 'I would not go because my wife would have been left at home on her own with those black people there, and she was frightened to death of them because of the assaults she had had from them'. Howell also remembered, 'he took pleasure in showing both to my registrar and myself press cuttings about a murder in which he claimed he was the star witness'. Odess last saw Christie professionally on 6 September 1952.[18]

Ethel also suffered ill health. Dr Odess first saw her in August 1948 and believed she was 'also a nervous type'. Three times in May 1952 she was given medicine containing potassium bromide and phenolbarbitone. This was a sedative, to be taken in the day, and she also had sleeping tablets called soneryl. According to the doctor, 'I should say she improved. The last time I attended her was 28th August 1952. She came to tell me that she had varicose veins, and I advised a form of treatment. She also had a skin eruption on her hands for which I prescribed some ointment'. She may also have had rheumatism.[19]

Although we know more about Christie's final years, his neighbours knew very little about him. A local newspaper offered the following verdict on the man and his innocent pastimes:

> This quiet spoken trilby hatted person, was known to have been obsessed by a sole hobby, photography. He was a keen amateur photographer and delighted in taking pictures of the local festivities in north Kensington. Last summer when this newspaper and its staff went on its annual outing, it was Mr Christie who loaned a member of staff his German made camera. 'He was not a very friendly man' is the comment made by this staff member. 'He was quiet and kept himself to himself, but a friend of mine said he would be willing to lend me a camera for the trip'.

Despite his keen interest in photography, Christie was not expert with the camera: reproductions of his prints were full of dark shadows or were in a dull brown. In any case, he pawned his camera on 9 August 1952 in Battersea. 'Neighbours say that he had stated that he was particularly looking forward to the street celebrations for the Coronation, and had planned to take several pictures then'; in 1945 he had photographed street parties on VE Day. Neighbours took their film to be developed by him. Finally, 'he was not a good mixer, and seemed to spend most of his time with his dog and his all consuming photographic hobby'. Franklin Stewart, a fellow tenant recalled, 'I never had anything to do with them except to say "good morning" or "good night."' Another neighbour said that he was, 'a very polite man who never talks to anyone very much'. 'His wife, a Mrs Ethel Christie, was also of a very reticent character.' Christie was also a QPR fan, talking about attending their home matches and having a badge in his possession. According to a neighbour, William Swan, he was the acme of humdrum respectability, noting, 'He would go off to work, neatly dressed, carrying a rolled up umbrella'. Another saw a different side to him, 'He always looked as if he had just stepped from a cold shower – shivering and weak'. He was also noted as someone who went for solitary walks at nights, and drank alone. Yet to his neighbours and shopkeepers he was polite, 'Gentleman Johnnie', and always raised his hat in the street.[20]

Christie claimed he rarely drank, stating 'I seldom touch the stuff ... perhaps Christmas and an occasional glass of beer about three times a year'. He recalled visiting neighbours with his wife at Christmas 1951 and having a drink of port. After trades union meetings he went for a cup of tea with his fellows.[21]

Odess was sympathetic towards Christie, and in a letter to Dr Howell wrote, 'I am inclined to agree with you about his anxiety state. There is no doubt a functional element present. At the same time, I wish to point out that he is a very decent, quiet living man, hard working and very conscientious. He is anxious to return to his work as soon as possible'. He also thought he was kind towards his wife.[22]

Although the couple seemed to have few friends or visitors (Christie never saw any of his relations after leaving Halifax in 1923, and had no contact with them – except for sending his mother a photograph of himself in police uniform – and never spoke of them), those who knew them seemed to like him. John Clark, of number 13, recalled, 'I have had conversations with both of them and they have been to my flat. They always seemed a nice friendly couple and I never heard of any quarrel'. Pamela Newman, aged thirteen, of the same address, reported, 'he used to talk to me about flowers and cats' and she visited the Christies on occasion. Apparently Christie once sat up for two nights, looking after her sick cat, and told her how to box up plants. He even took an eight-year-old to the Royalty Cinema, Ladbroke Grove. William Swan of number 9 recalled, 'I have seen both of them fairly regularly. I used to see Mr Christie in the garden and we would talk and his wife, Ethel, used to come in sometimes to ours and have a cup of tea with my wife'. Lena Brown, a fellow tenant, claimed, 'I did not know the Christies very well. I used to speak to them sometimes. I never heard them quarrelling'. Ethel corresponded irregularly with her brother, but he recalled that when he saw her in June 1952 she 'appeared quite happy except for black concerns ... Ethel has never complained to me about the conduct of her husband but she was not the type of person who would complain in any case'. Christie himself said, 'We didn't make many friends. We were devoted to one another and always went about together'. He never appeared in group photographs of neighbours. A neighbour noted, 'He was always regarded as a family man whose only interests outside his work was his home'. He was a loner by nature and his hobbies were solitary ones. This could have been the result of a lack of social confidence. He never answered the door except to those few callers who were expected.[23]

Others also spoke of his good nature. Bessie Styles of number 11 later said, 'It's just not true that he was a grumpy man. He just kept himself to himself'. Christie was kind to local children, though only on his terms. He would make them paper kites and took photographs of them at parties. The pictures were badly developed and on cheap paper, but he gave them out: 'There, take this into mummy – that's you'. But on the other hand, he opened the windows if he heard children playing football or cricket in the street and told them to clear off. Councillor Gough related, 'He was a normal kind of man as far as I could see. I talked to him a lot. He could be very happy go lucky and congenial when he wanted to be. Also he had a sense of humour. He used to pull my leg saying he was a Tory. Afterwards he admitted he voted Labour'. Christie said, 'I'll join [the Labour Party] if you get me a flat'. A less sympathetic side to his character was shown when he attended a residents' meeting on September 1952 about funding a children's Coronation party, where he was the only one who refused to contribute three pence, saying 'I'll have to consult my wife'.[24]

Relations between the Christies are often reported as seemingly good. Rosina Swan, of number 9, said they were 'very happy'. Sidney Denyer, an insurance agent, recalled, 'I formed the opinion from the various conversations I had with Mr and Mrs Christie that they were an exceedingly devoted couple'. Louisa Gregg of number 9, whom Ethel often visited on weekdays to watch TV there, said, 'she did not talk about her personal affairs to us ... she has never mentioned any quarrel with her husband'. Christie, unlike many husbands at this time, shared the shopping duties and bought a loaf every day from, ironically, Lancaster Food Products.[25]

Rosina recalled, 'She usually came in on a Thursday for an hour to see the children's television in my home'. Doubtless it provided Ethel with a break from her other woes at number 10.[26]

Yet there is a less rosy view of the Christies' marriage provided by a fellow tenant, one Joan Howard. She recalled, in 1953, that Christie had photographs of Beryl and Geraldine Evans, as well as newspaper cuttings about the murder case, and Ethel showed these to her, but as Christie returned, 'he had told his wife to put them away as he had had and seen enough of it'. On another occasion, 'she said her husband was mean to her and cruel to her but she didn't know why she stayed with him. She did not explain what her husband did to her. She said that her husband treated her badly since he had been in court in connection with the murder ... I thought she was saying it in spite'. Apparently, 'His wife did tell me that he was not sexy'.[27]

Joan and Christie did not get on and, according to her, she saw his sinister side. He asked her if he could take pictures of her in the nude, but she declined. At the time the suggestion was made, Ethel was, bizarrely, with her husband. Later the thwarted Christie called Joan a prostitute who took men to her room, which she denied. Apparently she threatened Ethel and Christie said to her, 'the only place for women like you, is dead. If I had my way, I would do it'. According to Joan, 'He was very excited at the time'. A constable arrived, as did Charles Brown and his 'wife' (actually one Marjorie Evans, with whom he lived). Later Christie said to her, 'Remember what I said, I'll still do you in'. She recalled that when she arrived home late, 'Christie used to peer around the door and as I went up the stairs he used to come out and shine a torch on me'. She recalled that Christie spent a lot of time in making a rockery in the garden. In 1953 there was an interview with a 'Pat Howard', who was the same woman, in a newspaper. She came out with a more dramatic story, with Ethel confiding in her thus, 'I am convinced that my husband had something to do with those two murders', but added 'I couldn't leave him now. I have lived with him too long for that. Whatever he has done, I am still in love with him'. It is uncertain whether this statement is true or not, and if it is, just what did Ethel know? The statement, however, was made with the benefit of hindsight.[28]

Sexual relations ceased, too. Christie recalled 'Just fell away – just didn't bother'. He also said, 'We never spoke of cessation, it just happened'. But it 'made no difference to our affection for each other'. Yet this is not unusual among middle-aged couples, especially for those whose sex drives have never been strong.[29]

Yet Christie's desires and his latent homicidal urges were surfacing again. He needed gratification and so began to hunt for new victims.

Thus he became a frequenter of cafes in search of women. He was a regular at Peter's Snack Bar on Goldhawk Road, where he met Elsie Morris, who came to visit him and Ethel once. In early 1952 he was often seen there with an eighteen-year-old woman from Wimpey's snack bar further down the road. This continued for about six weeks, three or four times a week. In November 1952 he often went to the Seven Stars snack bar, also on Goldhawk Road, as his colleagues also did, and he was often seen with one Rita, another eighteen-year-old; Lilian Campbell, aged twenty, an art student; and one Kay, aged seventeen. He asked about them, paid for their drinks and they talked to him and allowed him to photograph them. At the same time, one Elsie Barltrop met him in a tea shop in Marble Arch and said he showed her photographs, purportedly of his two daughters (the aforementioned Kay and Rita), though he introduced himself as John Halliday of Argyle Street, King's Cross.[30]

Christie even invited one of these girls back to his rooms when his wife was present. This occurred on 5 November, in either 1951 or 1952, ostensibly to watch the fireworks. A neighbour recalled, 'Mrs Christie also told my wife that the same girl had come to their house one Sunday and Mr Christie had tried to get her, Mrs Christie, to go and cook the dinner, and leave him alone with the girl. She told my wife she would not go and they had some words over it'. Ethel's presence in the house was a bar to what Christie wanted to do, and her days were numbered.[31]

It was on 4 July 1952 that Christie again tried to move house. He wrote to the LCC, complaining that his ill health – 'I am registered as a disabled person owing to a damaged right shoulder and nervous disability' – meant that he had to be urgently rehoused. He stated that their present rooms were 'very damp in places'. A sanitary inspector was summoned, but no repairs were carried out. The Christies also discussed whether Ethel's brother could house them in one of his properties in Sheffield, but he said he could not.[32]

Yet Christie's health improved, for he returned to work in the autumn of 1952. He was now assigned to the Cressy Road Depot, Hampstead, and went to work by Tube. Here he was one of thirty-four invoice clerks under the supervision of George Leathley Burrow, Group Accountant, who found Christie 'quite satisfactorily as far as his work was concerned, but he had been a trades union official and he was the type of man who, if there was any dispute regarding working conditions, liked to be involved'. Christie earned about £7–8 per week and claimed he had an independent income, but 'was always taking tablets which he said kept him going'. For once he enjoyed a clean bill of health throughout this period and worked properly. He seems to have enjoyed his time there and said that he liked his boss very much. But he continued his old stories. Eileen Drew recalled his telling her that he had studied to become a doctor and that his father was a famous Edinburgh surgeon, upon whose death Christie abandoned his medical ambitions. Yet Christie was not popular, as James Morley recalled, 'He had no friends in the firm'. Alfred Gattrell said 'he always kept himself to himself' and recalled Christie was always smartly dressed. Christie was responsible for First Aid and said of himself, 'the men had great faith in me and their injuries always got better quickly'. At lunchtimes he went to Joseph Cattini's café on Constantine Road, where he often met a married woman.[33]

Christie left this job on 6 December 1952, allegedly because of ill-health (due to, in his words, 'an incident at work regarding a half caste Indian woman'), though he did not see Odess about this. Burrow recalled, 'He left at his own request, having given proper notice. He said he had obtained a better job, which I understood to be in Sheffield'. A colleague, Horace Maser, said that Christie maintained he left for a job with an engineering firm in Sheffield. However, the real reason for leaving his job was a sinister one.[34]

Charlotte Barton, who worked at the receiving depot at 138 Walmer Road, Kensington, was one of the last people to see Ethel Christie alive. She stated, 'Mrs Christie was a customer and brought her laundry to the depot every fortnight, usually either on a Thursday or a Friday. The last time she called was Friday 12th December, when she left some washing to be done. It was never called for and I have never seen Mrs Christie since'. Mrs Jennie Grimes, a neighbour, remembered last seeing Ethel three weeks before Christmas. Lena Stewart said, 'The last time I saw Mrs Christie was about ten days before the baby was born [18 December]'. James Stewart, another resident of number 10, recalled, 'The last time I saw Mrs Christie was shortly before Christmas. She seemed alright then'. Dr Odess also asked after her, 'he said she had gone away to stay with her sister – in the Midlands, I think.'[35]

Ethel seems to have had no idea about her fate. On 10 October she wrote to her brother, who had visited her in June, telling him that the landlord refused to repair the cracks in the front room, 'so Reg has done it, quite good, too'. She also wrote, 'if we could only get somewhere else to live it would be better for us'. She wrote another letter to her sister on 10 December, but it was never posted.[36]

Perhaps the worst of Christie's murders was of the woman he claimed he loved, as far as that word had any meaning for him. According to Christie, Ethel was suffering from increased mental strain. He stated:

> My wife had been suffering a great deal from persecution and assaults from the black people in the house, No. 10 Rillington Place, and had to undergo treatment at the doctor's for her nerves. In December, she was becoming very frightened from these blacks and was afraid to go about the house when they were about, and she got very depressed.
>
> On December 14 I was awakened at about 8.15am. I think it was my wife moving about in bed. I sat up and saw she appeared to be convulsive. Her face was blue and she was choking. I did what I could to try and restore breathing, but it was hopeless. It appeared too late to call for assistance, that is when I could not bear to see her so. I got a stocking and tied it around her neck to put her to sleep.
>
> Then I got out of bed and saw a small bottle and a cup half full of water on a small table near the bed. I noticed that the bottle contained two pheno-barbitone tablets and it originally contained 25. I then knew she must have taken the remainder. I got them from the hospital because I couldn't sleep. I left her in bed for two or three days and didn't know what to do. Then I remembered some loose floorboards in the front room. I had to move a table and some chairs to roll the lino back about half way.
>
> Those boards had been up previously because of the drainage system. There were several of these depressions in these floorboards. Then I believe I went back and put her in a blanket or sheet or something and tried to carry her. But she was too heavy and so I had to sort of half-carry her and half drag her and put her in that depression and cover her up with earth. I thought that was the best way to lay her to rest. I then put the boards and lino back. I was in a state and didn't know what to do, and after Christmas I sold all my furniture.

Christie later said, 'I did not want to be separated from her. That is why I put her there. She was still in the house'.

In at least two aspects, this account is incorrect. Camps later found no trace of barbiturate in Ethel's body. Also, the murder was almost certainly premeditated, as Christie withheld his wife's letter to his sister-in-law, which was written by her on 10 December, but altered the date to one five days later before posting it. However, there seems little doubt that Christie strangled his wife on about 14 December 1952.[37]

Christie asserted throughout that this was a mercy killing and later said, 'I loved my wife. I hated seeing her suffer. I decided to end her pain forever. My wife died peaceably and with practically no pain'. His words show that he justified the murder to himself by the use of euphemism, 'I put her to sleep'. However, unlike four of his other victims, he did not render her unconscious with gas prior to strangulation: she knew she was being killed. His motive was almost certainly his desire to kill again. Having killed already with impunity, he had the serial killer's addiction to murder and could not resist this aspect of his nature. Christie later said, 'After she had gone, the way was clear for me to fulfil my destiny'.[38]

On the following day, Christie added to the letter written by his wife to her sister, 'We have no envelopes so I posted this for her from work' and dated it 15 December. Henry Waddington, a local government clerk of Sheffield, recalled seeing it and said it was not in his sister's handwriting. Christie later wrote the following message in a Christmas card:

> Dear Lil,
> Ethel has got me to write her cards for her as her rheumatism in her fingers is not so good just now. Doctor says its the weather and she will be O.K. in 2 or 3 days. I am rubbing them for her and it makes them easier. We are in good health now and as soon as Ethel can write (perhaps by Saturday) she is going to send a letter. Hope you like the present. She selected it for you. Reg.

At the top, he wrote, 'DON'T WORRY. SHE IS OK. I SHALL COOK XMAS DINNER. Reg'.[39]

Christie had to account to his neighbours for Ethel's absence. Rosina Swan spoke to him on 19 December. 'He said he had got a job in the north – a transfer – and that his wife had gone on ahead to prepare. He said the place was Sheffield'. Later that day the two had another chat. Mrs Swan stated, 'He spoke to me in the garden, there is a short wall between the two gardens. He had a piece of paper in his hand,

and I think he said it was a telegram from his wife. He said she had arrived safely and "love to Rosie"'. Christie added, ironically, 'I will have to choke her off for sending love to her and not to me'. To Jennie Grimes, he said, just after Christmas, 'she had gone to see her sister, who was having a woman's operation. He said she had gone north, to Birmingham'. Eileen Styles, another neighbour, was told likewise, albeit to visit her sister, 'he said he had not told anyone else as he didn't want it to get around'. To Hookway, he said, 'he was going to Northampton to look for a job up there as he was out of work. I understood him to say that his wife was with her sister in Northampton, and that he was joining her there'. James Stewart reported, 'In February I spoke to Mr Christie and asked him if Mrs Christie was sick, as I was not seeing her. He said that she was not sick, but that she had gone to see her sister who had a shop and who was sick. He did not tell me where the sister was, but somewhere in the country. He said he was expecting her the following week'. Christie also told his butcher that his wife would be coming home soon, which he looked forward to as he was fed up with shopping for food.[40]

Rosina saw Christie again. She said that this was 'Several times whilst I was shopping. I asked him on one occasion how his wife was and he said she was looking rather pale, as they had had a lot of flu in the north, and he was probably going up on the following Sunday to see her on an excursion'.[41]

On Christmas Day itself, John Gregg of number 9 invited Christie over in the evening. They exchanged presents and watched television. He explained that his wife was away for a few days.[42]

Life for Christie was increasingly wretched and squalid, as he described the situation:

> I made a bed on some bedding on the floor in the back room. I had about four blankets there. I kept my kitchen table, two chairs, some crockery, and some cutlery. These were just enough for my immediate needs because I was going away. I wasn't working and had a meagre existence. I was getting money from the employment exchange. This was £2 14s.

He certainly needed money badly. On 17 December, he sold his wife's wedding ring and her gold wristwatch for £2 10s at Barnet Pressman's jewellery shop on 166 Uxbridge Road, Shepherd's Bush, stating 'I took it off her finger as a keepsake, but sold it ... when I was hard up and hadn't enough money to get food'. He sold a three-piece suite, two sideboards, linoleum, three chairs, a bed and a chest of drawers. This transaction, between Christie and Hookway, took place on 8 January 1953. Christie had hoped for £15, but had to admit 'I got £11 [actually £12] for the furniture and £2 for some other bits that I sold'. Hookway left a mattress 'because it was in a rather disreputable state'. Edward Allen of Walter Hildreth Ltd removed the furniture. The great tragedy for the historian is that though the drawers were stuffed full of photographs, papers, diaries and police note books, these were all destroyed by Hookway, though not before he saw there were some letters addressed to Christie from one Edith Hunt, whoever she was. Christie offered to assist Hookway 'in a case between myself and a hire purchase company', but Hookway refused his help. Christie also stopped paying his rent on 5 January, which points to the fact that he thought that his time at 10 Rillington Place was limited. Brown recalled collecting money in December and that on 5 January that Christie put a notice on his door informing him that he could have his cash, but when he arrived for it Christie was not at home. Or perhaps he no longer cared and was succumbing to a sub-conscious self-destructive impulse.[43]

Christie needed more money, however. Remembering that his wife had an account with the Yorkshire Penny Bank, Sheffield, which she had opened on 14 July 1944, he decided to use his new-found skill of forging handwriting. Frederick Snow, the manager of the Haymarket branch, had no doubts. On 27 January he received a letter written on the previous day, allegedly from Ethel Christie of 10 Rillington Place. It ran, 'I wish to close my account. Please forward to me any amount due. Enclosed is my bank book'. Snow recalled, 'I compared the signature on the letter with the specimen signature dated 14th July 1944, and they agreed. I had no reason whatever to believe that signature was otherwise than genuine. We forwarded the balance of that account, £10 15s 2d, by registered post'. An acknowledgement was received shortly afterwards and again it seemed to be in order. On 27 February Christie sold some of his wife's clothing for £3 5s. He also received a cheque for £8 on 7 March from the Bradford Clothing and Supply Co. From 22 January to 18 March he also received a weekly £3 12s in state benefits.[44]

Lily enquired after her sister on 17 January, imploring her to 'Write soon, we get awfully anxious about you in that place. I wish Reg could find another place'. The letter was never answered, but nor was it destroyed. She later recalled, 'I did not hear anything further, I became very worried and about a month ago I wrote to my sister ... I wanted her to come to Sheffield, because I know they were having some trouble with coloured people'. But she took her concerns no further, and so Christie was granted further respite to continue his evil work.[45]

Yet some of Christie's behaviour did attract attention. Lena Stewart returned from hospital at the end of December, after having given birth to her child (Beresford Brown, whom she married in 1953, was the father). In January:

> I noticed that he was disinfecting the place. He was sprinkling disinfectant all over the passage that leads from the front door. I think it was Jeyes. It was strong ... He disinfected the back yard. I saw him pouring it down the drains. I also saw him put it outside under the window of his front room where I used to put my pram. He told me one morning that somebody had thrown dirty water down the drain. He never spoke to me as to why he disinfected the front passage or outside the front room window. He generally did the disinfecting between 8.30 and 9 am when everybody had left the house to go to work.

James Stewart thought that the disinfectant was being laid down as early as October, though he thought this could have been because dirty water was being thrown down by some of the other tenants. He did not think Christie's actions were odd.[46]

Christie had killed again, and was about to enter an even more destructive phase of his murderous career. As before, no one had suspected that a murder had occurred, and thus, undetected, he may have felt invulnerable, and now he had a freer rein. However, he had also unwittingly lit a fuse under himself, for he had now concealed a corpse where he lived, which would smell and would eventually be found. But, as ever, Christie thought only of the short term and disregarded what his intelligence must have known was the beginning of the end.

Chapter 9

Slaughter
1953

'He was always dropping in for a cup of tea. At all times he was very correct in his behaviour and talk ... such a nice man'.[1]

Now that Ethel was dead, Christie had his rooms to himself. Confident that he had got away with at least three murders, he was now ready for even more and prepared his equipment. He 'kept a piece of rope about 18 inches long with a double knot at each end hidden away in a tool box', although he also claimed he had cord handy, too: 'At one time there was a piece hanging down at the back of the deck chair'. The latter was not the conventional one with a canvas seat but one made up of rope and string; covered with cloth.[2]

Christie then had to select his victims. The next was Kathleen Maloney, who was born at 112 King Street in Plymouth on 19 August 1926, the youngest of three daughters born to Daniel Maloney, a mason's labourer (alternatively a rag and bone man), and his wife Lillian, née Champion. Brought up as a Catholic, she had been orphaned when her parents died in 1928 and 1929. At first an aunt, Emily Oldbridge, took the children in, at 110 King Street in Plymouth. They then went to a Catholic Home, St Peter's, at Durnford and also to Nazareth House, Stone House, Plymouth, where their aunt and uncle visited weekly. The latter remarked, 'She was very wild, not in a bad way, but full of pranks'. In 1940 there was concern at her talking to boys, so she was sent to the Convent of the Good Shepherd, Saltash, Cornwall, where she was suspected of the theft of a coat. Two years later she was at another convent, at Bitterne, near Southampton. Here she was 'found to be uncontrollable' and in 1943 she was sent to Plymouth. En route she absconded at Exeter where she fell in with some black American soldiers.[3]

On 19 August 1944 Kathleen was taken into care by the Plymouth Probation Service. By the following year, however, she had gravitated towards London, though she knew no one there. It may have been at this time that she began her career in prostitution, picking up Americans, going to cheap accommodation in Sussex Gardens and charging them £2 per night. At Bow Street Magistrates' court on 19 January 1945 she was said to have been a vagrant and was put on probation. Two months later, when she was described as working as a laundry hand, it was stated that she had broken the terms of her probation, as she was again found wandering the streets, and was sent to Holloway prison for three months, though she was only there from 8 March to 9 May. After that she left the capital, with one Sylvia Sowerby, who was two years her senior and hailed from Burnley, with whom she had walked the streets of Edgware and spent time in gaol, and the two went to Southampton, where Kathleen was in trouble with the law on five occasions. She was homeless and in 1946 was found living in an unoccupied house in Albion Terrace, 'likely to cause infection' and received two gaol sentences, in February and June, each of another three months. She then spent a month in prison for prostitution and was also fined £1 for being drunk and disorderly. Later that year, whilst with Sylvia, she was arrested for 'most foul' language. There was also a charge of unlawful possession of military equipment, but it was dismissed. She was able to evade the law in the following year and in 1948 there was a case of obscene words, but the case was dismissed. Yet in 1949 she received four short terms in prison; drunk and disorderly (24 February, one month), assaulting a policeman (4 April, three months), soliciting in Andrew's Park (4 July, one month) and using obscene language (7 October, 14 days). This was followed by a relatively crime-free year (on 18 September 1950 she received a month for being drunk and disorderly). There were two similar occasions in 1951, with a fine of £1 for each (29 August and 24 October). In 1952 she spread her wings, but did not change her ways. She went to Liverpool and in February was fined £1 and was given a month in prison for having been drunk and disorderly twice. In March she was back in Southampton and back in trouble, with two months in gaol for being drunk and disorderly. Then she went to Reading and was fined and gaoled for drunkenness and assaulting a policeman in June and July. Then it was back to Southampton.[4]

Kathleen drank a lot, often in Above Bar on Southampton's main street. Her attitudes to her drink problem varied. Once she was aggressive, saying, 'It's a free country. I can do what I like' to a police-man. At Reading she said, 'I am happy go lucky and have had a few drinks'. Later that year she told magistrates, 'I had been under treat-ment for drink in Holloway, but I could not help it'. Her drinking was ultimately to prove fatal.[5]

Southampton seems to have been Kathleen's base, for from 1945–1951 she lived for part of her time there with Sylvia Sowerby, de-scribed as a cleaner. Sylvia, who was also known to be drunk and disorderly, recalled, 'Kathleen was never very particular as to the type of men she met. I have known her to go with Lascars and other sea-faring types. She also associated with the Irish navvy type'. Kathleen lived in 33 Russell Street (1946, 1948, 1950 and 1952), 7 Brunswick Square (1949, 1951), and worked as a cleaner and a laundress, as well as suffering spells of unemployment. Physically, she was five feet two inches tall, had dyed blonde hair with dirty streaks, a plump face and brown eyes. She had five children from 1946–50, one of whom was adopted while the remainder were placed in Hollybrook Homes, Southampton. In September 1952, Kathleen hitchhiked to London because she was 'fed up because the police were always chasing her' and she also told friends that she was pregnant, though there is no evidence of this.[6]

Kathleen's few relatives did not want to know her. Lillian Maloney had not seen her sister since about 1944, and she lived with a Pole in Birmingham whom she was about to marry. Her aunt, Ethel Dymond of Bodmin, did not reply when Kathleen wrote to her, asking to stay. Ethel had eight children and no room for her and in any case, thought her niece was trouble. Her uncle, Mr Oldridge of Plymouth, claimed he had not heard of her since she left Holloway some years pre-viously.[7]

Gladys Jordan had known Kathleen in London, and recalled, 'I used to see her frequently in the Cider House, Hammersmith Road, until she got barred'. She was often seen in the Mitre pub in Edgware Road at lunchtimes and in the evenings in October and November, often with American soldiers, before being barred. As Gladys recalled, 'She used to get very drunk' and would sing when in such a state. Her next regular haunt was the Westminster Arms, 10 Praed Street. In December she went to St Mary's Hospital, Paddington, with a cut finger. Gladys thought she was four months pregnant, though there was no sign of this. Catherine Struthers, alias Kitty Foley, told Gladys that Kathleen had returned to Southampton and Gladys never saw her alive again.[8]

Catherine Struthers, whom Kathleen had met in March 1952, drew attention to her plight and said, 'she had no place to live and went home with any man she could find'. The two would often solicit together in and near Praed Street and in December Kathleen was fined £5. She lived near Sussex Gardens. She was clearly one of the lowest of the low, for, along with others of her type, she was sometimes obliged to sleep in a public toilet on the Edgware Road. Mrs Shields, the attendant, recalled her there, washing, and Kathleen said she had met Christie, had been to 10 Rillington Place and had felt sorry for him because his wife had died. Moreover, he had promised her some of his late wife's clothing. A week later, Kathleen had these clothes, and told Mrs Shields that Christie's landlord had found her there and had thrown her out. A postman whom Kathleen had spoken to in a Praed Street pub told how she had met a man who offered her accommodation in Ladbroke Grove.[9]

It seems that one Maureen Briggs and Kathleen first met Christie in October in the Great Western pub, Praed Street. Maureen recalled:

A man was standing at the bar with a raincoat over his arm. He was about 50 years of age, medium height, not very big build, a big nose, I don't mean long, but it stood out. He wore horn rimmed glasses. He had thinnish lips and he was sort of licking his lips when he was talking. He got talking to me.

Maureen also recalled, 'He asked me if I wanted to earn myself some money and I said I would. He asked me if I ever had any photographs done in the nude. I said I had one or two. He said he did that and he knew a place where he could take me to do some'. Nothing immediately came of this, but she saw him in the Fountain Abbey pub, 109–111 Praed Street, in the following month. Then, in early December, the two women saw Christie in the Standard pub, also on Praed Street. This time the three went to a street just off the Marylebone Road and into a building in which one room was set up as a studio. Maureen stated, 'I was naked. Kay sat on a chair and watched. He took about six of me posing in various positions in the nude'. Christie also disrobed and had Kathleen photograph the two of them naked together, though there was no sex. He gave them a pound each but both wanted more. When they saw him later that month, they asked him again and he refused. On 3 November Kathleen was sentenced at Marlborough Street court to two weeks in Holloway or a £2 fine for being drunk and disorderly; on the following day her fine was paid by George Noakes, who remarked that she 'appeared poorly' and 'down and out'. Catherine and Kathleen next saw Christie some weeks after Christmas, in the Westminster Arms, where Kathleen had worked as a cleaner over Christmas. Augustine Murray, who thought it was about 10 January, but was uncertain (other witnesses spoke of 'a good few weeks after Christmas' and 'about two weeks after Christmas'), said the two women had been there since 8.00pm. 'About an hour after that a man came in and went up to Kathleen and Maureen and asked them to have a drink with him. Then he sat down with them and started talking'. Maureen recalled, 'He bought us each two drinks and as he was leaving she asked him to give the price of another drink and he gave her 2s. He and Maloney left together between 9 and 10'. This man was Christie, who drank two half pints of beer. They almost certainly caught the bus to Ladbroke Grove and then walked the last few hundred yards to Rillington Place. Kathleen had earlier told Murray she had nowhere to sleep that night but she had met a man in a cafe that afternoon who told her he would help her. She had had a lot to drink that night; the equivalent of eight pints of beer.[10]

Christie's version of events avoids all reference to him having darkened the door of licensed premises and claims Kathleen propositioned him in the street:

I walked away, but she followed and pushed into my house. I asked her to leave but she went into the kitchen and began to undress. 'Alright' I thought, 'if ever a woman deserved to die, you do'.

Yet in his own unpublished notes, he wrote, once the two were in his rooms:

In [the] struggle [she] lent forward and I grabbed hold of it at the back as it [a white jumper] had rucked up and held it tight from the back as she was falling forward. Doing this was holding her from falling headlong forward and apparently I caused her death at the same time ... In her drunken state she, no doubt, became unconscious quickly indeed.

Christie omitted to mention that he gassed her before having sex with her unconscious body prior to putting a makeshift diaper on her and covering her head before strangulation. He put the corpse into the alcove in the kitchen, and then wallpapered over it. He later contradicted himself by stating 'it was little Kathy I felt sorry for. She was a sweet kid ... I felt sorry for her'. No one, however, reported her missing, so there was no investigation into her disappearance.[11]

A few days later, Christie encountered his next victim. Her name was Rita Elizabeth Nelson, who had been born at a hospital at 51 Lisburn Road, Belfast, on 16 October 1927, to James Nelson, a labourer, and Lily, his wife (née Brown), who had married in 1923 and had three daughters. They lived at 98 Old Park Road, Belfast. Rita attended Castleton Primary School, Belfast, and her education finished at the age of fourteen. Unfortunately, as her mother said of her, she 'was funny in her way of going' and her sister, Sadie, spent time in a mental home. Her parents separated in September 1930 (divorced in 1952), and she never saw her father again after 1943. She had a string of offences dating back to 31 January 1940, when she was before the Belfast Juvenile Court, accused of larceny, though the case was dismissed. Secondly, she was accused of the same offence on 3 December 1942 at Lisburn Magistrates' Court. Again, the case resulted in her being discharged. She was less fortunate in her later criminal career. On 1 May 1946, the Belfast court put her on six months' probation for stealing a coat from a dry cleaners on Wellington Place. At this time she lived at 9 Antrim Street and worked as a doffer (someone who removes full bobbins and replaces them with empty ones on spinning looms) in a textile mill. Later that year she was fined 20s for prostitution. Her final offences that year were to be drunk and disorderly and to assault a policeman. For these she was put on a year's probation. These sentences clearly had no deterrent effect, for on 25 January 1947 she was drunk and disorderly again, though was not violent, and spent a month in prison. For a whole year she managed to keep out of trouble, yet on 26 April 1948 she was given a 40s fine for being drunk and disorderly yet again. She also gave birth to a son in 1949, called George; who was living in Newton Arge House, Antrim, in 1953. She was said to have been very proud of him.[12]

The next few years saw Rita in and out of various employments. She was in special care in Belfast in 1949, in Purdysburn Mental Home, where Dr Weir stated that she had a kink about men, but was let out on licence in 1950; this licence later extended to 1953. Up to April 1951 she worked at the Massanene Hotel in Antrim. Then, for a few weeks, she worked at Malone Place Hospital, Belfast (from 18 July 1951),

Musgrave Park Hospital and at Claremont Hospital from 3–14 September 1951. In the following month she was a domestic at Foster General Hospital. From then on, she was apparently unemployed and was living with her mother in Derriaghy.[13]

Rita later lived with James Boyd, a cousin, at 222 Blythe Road, Belfast, and on 6 October 1952 they went to London for work. On arrival, they paid a brief visit to her married sister, Mrs Mary Langridge, resident at 80 Ladbroke Grove, where they ate. Then, at 5.00pm, they left to try and find lodgings. The two parted at Tottenham Court Road and Boyd eventually found his way to Essex. He was never to see his cousin again. In November, she was living in a Church Army hostel in Edgware. She wanted to live in a room at 46 Collingham Road, but it was unavailable. She called on her sister in November and continued to call on her each week. The sisters last met three weeks before Christmas. The two were not close. Her sister later said, 'I know nothing about any of her friends or what she used to do'. She believed that her sister died when the ship the *Princess Victoria* sank between Scotland and Ireland on 31 January with a large loss of life. Eventually Rita found other accommodation and lived in a furnished room on the top floor of 2 Shepherd's Gardens, W12, from 13 December. Hannah Rees, her landlady, recalled, 'I know nothing at all about her friends', but thought she was pregnant. This was correct; at the time of her death she was six months pregnant. Kathleen Murray, a fellow tenant, only saw Rita once. Very little is known of her character, and we should certainly view her mother's statement with caution: 'a quiet, serious minded girl whose main outside interest was going to the pictures. She always came home early and so far as I know had no boyfriends. When she wrote home from England she never mentioned boys'. An acquaintance said 'She was a strange, quiet girl'. She may have been of a nervous disposition and regularly bit her nails. She is also said to have been at the Benelux Club in Piccadilly and the Welbeck Club in Baker Street, presumably to pick up clients. Standing at five feet three inches, she had blonde hair, blue eyes and a fresh complexion. It was stated she was friends with a girl called Kay, but no more is known of her.[14]

Rita had a variety of jobs. Though she said she was an art student, a photographer's model and a waitress, only the latter was true. Another job was as an orderly at Great Ormond Street Children's Hospital, where she was dismissed for theft. She was reasonably affluent, though, and sent her parents 30s at Christmas. Rita was briefly employed as a counterhand and in the kitchen on £3 11s per week at a Lyons tea shop, 54 Uxbridge Road, Shepherd's Bush, from 6–9 January 1953. She left because she found the work too hard, and collected her wages on 12 January. Then she had another equally brief job, as a kitchenmaid at £3 3s per week, at the Devonshire Arms, probably the one on Notting Hill Gate; lasting from 10–13 January, leaving because she was deemed unsuitable. Her parents last heard of her on 16 January 1953. They began to worry on 28 February. By this time it was too late. On 10 January she paid her landlady her weekly rent. It was not paid on 17 January and two days later she was reported missing at Hammersmith Police Station by her landlady. Yet one of the girls in the place said that they last saw her on Saturday 14 January.[15]

This may have been her date of death. It has been said she frequented transport cafes such as Ems and the Hut on the Goldhawk Road, and that Christie might have met her in one of these. Or perhaps he met her in Piccadilly, as both frequented the district. Helen Sunderland wrote, 'he would walk up and down Piccadilly, staring at the women as he passed by. He would walk up and down Piccadilly so often and so many times in one night that every woman knew him by sight'. Yet according to Christie's ghostwritten published account:

I was sitting in a cafe at Notting Hill Gate [possibly the Lyons' tea house next door to the Devonshire Arms] for a cup of tea and a sandwich. It was fairly full. Two girls sat opposite me at the same table. One offered me a cigarette and they began discussing their attempts to find accommodation. I mentioned that I might be leaving my flat very soon. I would try and get it for them. I arranged that they should call at No. 10 Rillington Place to see the flat and that evening the Nelson girl came on her own.

According to his unpublished notes, on arrival:

[she] suggested staying. Had a drink [Christie had port and whisky for such occasions] and sat in deck chair I think after she started undoing some of her clothes I wanted her to, possibly because she had come by herself and her dark haired friend might come down. She also said she would not be seeing her friend till weekend when they could arrange to move in. This is no doubt the reason why she suggested staying herself. She would see her friend and she would just like her to stay. This would fit in alright. Knowing this I allowed her to undress as much as liked. That is

when I must have been intimate. She got back in deck chair and I gave her another drink and fetched the blanket back to put round her after that. I removed the clip on gas tube and we were both smoking [hard to believe if he was releasing gas at the same time]. I could see her eyes were going a bit strange soon after. I think I got the cord and put my arm round her neck. She would not realise what I was doing. There was no struggle so she must have become unconscious right away. You will no doubt see that in all cases there was … no pain at all.

Of course, as with Kathleen, all we can be certain about is that he inveigled her back to his home, gassed and strangled her, and had sex with her at some point. He put cloth over her head and had a makeshift diaper between her legs to prevent any discharge of fluid. She was then covered in a blanket and put in the alcove in the kitchen. Christie, having two corpses to cram into a small space, had to arrange them in order to fit; he tied them to each other and put Rita at the back. This has led to the supposition that Rita was killed first, but Christie's evidence suggests not and this is supported by Murray's testimony.[16]

Unlike Kathleen, Rita's disappearance was noticed, though without any immediate effect. On 20 January, her room was opened by her landlady and there she found a letter addressed to the Lady Almoner of the Samaritans' Hospital on the Marylebone Road. This was from Dorothy Symes, Medical Officer for Lyons, and was a letter of introduction for Rita to attend the hospital and then to be admitted to a Home for Unmarried Mothers, as Dorothy had examined her and found she was with child. Rita never attended it. A WPC took the details of what seemed to be a missing person's case on 21 January. Rita's mother wrote to her, but her landlady, annoyed at her errant tenant, told her not to worry.[17] Nor did her sister look for her.

Christie's last victim was Hectorina McKay MacLennan (known to her friends as Ina), born in 8 Grove Park Place, Glasgow, on 26 February 1926. Her father was William, a journeyman joiner, and her mother was Marion (married in 1918), described as a hotel charwoman. They had seven children, four boys and three girls. She was five feet six inches tall, with dark hair and a scar on the right side of her abdomen. She had a squint in one eye, wore tweeds and smoked heavily, having nicotine-stained fingers on her right hand. Frank Collyer, a thirty-nine-year-old burglar who was separated from his wife, and known as Ron, recalled, she 'wore no make-up and was generally untidy'. According to someone who knew her, she was 'easily led' and 'easy to take advantage of'. The family moved to Ross-shire when Hectorina was very young and she was brought up by Loch Ewe. During the Second World War, she worked in a laundry with her mother. William MacLennan arrived in the capital in 1944 and the rest of the family came in 1948. They lived together at 153 Warwick Road, Kensington, for the next four years. Her father later said that she was a happy girl who spent most evenings at home with her parents. In 1949, the first of Hectorina's two children, a daughter called Marion, was born. Her family did not know who the father was. Hectorina and her younger sister Benjamina, a factory worker, often went down to Portsmouth to visit their boyfriends in the Burmese Air force who were stationed nearby. She had her second illegitimate child; one Juline Anna Maung Sou Hla, born on 24 January 1951, when the father was in Cardiff. It was rumoured that she had married the father, Khin Muang Sou Hla, a Burmese Air Force man, on 12 October 1950 in Portsmouth. He often visited her at her family home but never lived with her there. He returned to Burma in 1951. However, there is no evidence of any wedding ceremony having taken place (certainly not in England), yet on the electoral register for 1951 and 1952 and on her ration book (which she was always losing) her surname is given as Hla. It was also noticed that she wore a white metal wedding ring, possibly with stones. She was not receiving anything from her alleged husband, but talked about joining him in Burma. However, she also referred to planning to marry Collyer.[18]

It is often said, as it was at the trial in 1953, that Christie's last three victims were prostitutes, but there is no evidence that Hectorina was one. Rita and Kathleen had criminal convictions for soliciting, but Hectorina had none and had never been in trouble with the law. She lived with her family throughout her life in London. We know a little about her working career. One report refers to her being in domestic service. From 17 April to 3 June 1950 she was employed at the Imperial Cinema, Portobello Road, as an usherette, but was dismissed. From June 1951 until December 1952 she looked after the youngest of the five children of Alexander Pomeroy Baker, a lorry driver with a criminal record, and his wife, Dorothy, at 11 Pembroke Place. She was paid £1 per week (compare this to Christie's £7–8). However, Mrs Baker recalled, 'I heard that Hectorina was carrying on with my husband. It came to a head about Christmas time and we had a row'. She told Hectorina never to come there again, but she did.[19]

Ernest John Christie. (Jack Delves' collection)

Mary Hannah Christie, née Halliday, 1917. (Jack Delves' collection)

Ethel (wife of Percy), Percy and Mary Christie. (Jack Delves' collection)

Black Boy House, 2010.

5. All Souls' Church, Halifax, *c*.1900. (Author's collection)

Halifax Post Office, *c*.1920. (Author's collection)

John Reginald Halliday Christie, Postman
9. Brunswick Street. Halifax
Age 22. 5ft 8" Blue Eyes Brn Hair fresh comp.

Before the Magistrates 12-4-21.

Stealing Postal Orders   2 charges
Committed 3 months each charge. Concurrent

Hanged for Mass
Murders ~ Metropolitan

John Christie, 1921. (Wakefield Archives)

RAF Uxbridge.
(Ken Pearce's collection)

Empire Cinema,
Uxbridge.
(Ken Pearce's collection)

Hillingdon School,
1930s.
(Ken Pearce's collection)

Southall Park, 1920s.
(Ken Pearce's collection)

Uxbridge Magistrates' Court.
(Ken Pearce's collection)

Wandsworth Prison, 1980s. (Author's collection)

No. 23 Oxford Gardens,
Notting Hill.
(Author's collection, 2010)

Map of Notting Hill, 1914.
(Kensington Library)

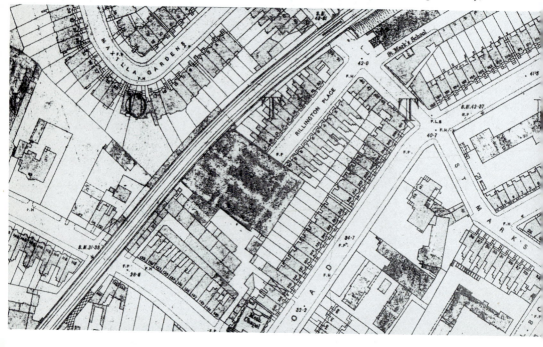

Christie's police record, 1939–1943. (Scotland Yard)

Beryl Evans's birth certificate. (Author's collection)

GPO Savings Bank, Blythe Road.
(Author's collection)

John Christie, *c.*1950.
(R. Maxwell, *The Christie Case*)

Kathleen Maloney. (R. Maxwell, *The Christie Case*)

Maureen Briggs. (R. Maxwell, *The Christie Case*)

Hectorina MacLennan.
(R. Maxwell, *The Christie Case*)

Alexander Pomeroy Baker.
(R. Maxwell, *The Christie Case*)

Mr Beresford Brown.
(R. Maxwell, *The Christie Case*)

Rillington Place, 1953. (National Archives)

Piccadilly Circus, 1953. (Author's collection)

Furniture being removed from the murder house. (R. Maxwell, *The Christie Case*)

Search of the back garden. (R. Maxwell, *The Christie Case*)

Removal of a corpse from the murder house. (R. Maxwell, *The Christie Case*)

Putney Bridge, 2009.
(Author's collection)

Old Bailey.
(Author's collection)

Derek Curtis-Bennett.
(R. Maxwell, *The Christie Case*)

West London Magistrates' Court, 2010. (Author's collection)

Pentonville Prison, 2010. (Author's collection)

HC 760636

CERTIFIED COPY of an
Pursuant to the Births and

ENTRY OF DEATH
Deaths Registration Act 1953

Registration District ISLINGTON

Death in the Sub-district of BARNSBURY   in the Metropolitan Borough of Islington

No.	1 When and where died	2 Name and surname	3 Sex	4 Age	5 Occupation	6 Cause of death	7 Signature, description, and residence of informant	8 When registered	9 Signature of registrar
52	Fifteenth July 1953 H.M. PRISON Pentonville	John Reginald HALLIDAY CHRISTIE	Male	54 55 years	(formerly a Clerk (Road Haulage) 10. Rillington Place Notting HILL	Instanto to central Nervous System following Judicial Hanging on 15.7.1953 P.M Judicial HANGING	Certificate received from R. Ian Milne. Assistant Deputy Coroner for county of London Inquest Held 15.7.53	Sixteenth July 1953	Gladys i.M. file Registrar.

"In No 52 in column 4 for '55 years' read '54 years' corrected on 19th September 2002 by me X.C. Conno Superintendent Registrar, on the Authority of certificate from the Coroner";

Christie's death certificate. (General Registry Office)

Waxwork of Christie at Madame Tussaud's, 2011. (Author's collection)

Hectorina's parents returned to Scotland to live at Rose Cottage, Tignafiline, near Aultbea in Ross, with their two other daughters and the two granddaughters in November 1952. Hectorina saw her daughters off with tears in her eyes. She and her brother Robert, a carpenter, remained at 153 Warwick Road. Baker saw her again at the end of January in Holland Park. He recalled, 'She looked so shabby' and offered to buy her breakfast. They began to live together at 4 Oldham Road, but not for long (two to three weeks), and at this time her brother reported her missing. In any case, she and Baker argued, and Baker returned to his wife. She went back to her brother for two weeks in February, having been returned by the police. There she took money from the gas meter and left, possibly because she had become acquainted with Collyer and come under his influence. The two lived together at Warwick Road. She also pawned her ring at this time, in a shop on the Uxbridge Road, for 8s 6d. Later that month she bought a plain yellow ring from Woolworths in Shepherd's Bush for 2s 6d. She was last seen by her brothers, Robert and Donald, at No. 153 on 15 February. Donald stated, 'I didn't have much to say to her', 'I do not know anything about her private life at all' and 'I do not know what kind of life she led'. Her father believed she was working at St Mary Abbott's Hospital in Kensington and had a young doctor as a boy-friend. It has also been said that she often went to the Blinking Owl, a snack bar on Portobello Road.[20]

On about 18 February (the day Collyer was arrested in Hyde Park in Hectorina's company for a burglary in Acton) Baker and she were reunited in a cafe and the couple stayed briefly with Ivor Elliott, a friend of his for eighteen years, at 35 Hetley Road. She told him she was frightened of a man (never named). On 21, 24 and 27 February they visited Collyer, who was in Brixton prison. Hectorina had a habit of wandering off without informing anyone, as Elliott noted. On 23 February 'She had gone off about 11 o'clock in the morning and he had not seen her since'. She wandered off again on 26 February but they met at the Cunningham pub on the Uxbridge Road the next day. Jobless, Hectorina was in need of money, and Baker may have pressurized her into trying to obtain it from others; certainly he wrote to her 'Maybe you can get some cash off Ron'. On 20 February and 3 March she called on a Methodist minister, the Rev. Bernard Arthur Shaw of Hinde Street, telling him she had been sacked from a job in Kensington for being pregnant. He referred her to the National

Assistance Board. His wife also saw her and thought, incorrectly, that she was pregnant. She also saw Collyer's estranged wife, who gave her money, clothes and advice to return to her parents. Baker and Hectorina flitted from address to address; on 18 February they were at Pembroke Place, on the 19th at 153 Warwick Road, on 21–22 at a house off St Anne's Road, Holland Park, then at Hetley Road until 2 March. Evidently Elliott could not house both of them on a permanent basis. Neither seems to have been working, so their plight was desperate. Hectorina asked for money from a former colleague at the cinema and asked that they be allowed inside for free; both requests were granted.[21]

It is possible that Hectorina had known of Christie for some time, for Collyer recalled being with her in a Notting Hill milk bar and seeing him there. According to him she said 'He's a chap I had some trouble with. He gave me an unpleasant time', but did not elaborate. He also recalled her showing him a piece of paper whilst in prison on 24 February with his name on. Christie had been hanging about boards advertising accommodation in Hammersmith and it was here that he met Hectorina, though another account states that they met outside the Gaumont cinema on Queen Charlotte Street, Hammersmith, on 3 March. She said she needed a flat and he replied that he would help if she would meet him alone at 7.30 that evening at Ladbroke Grove bus station. An hour before the appointed time, Hectorina met Baker in a cafe and told him of the offer.[22]

William MacLennan recalled his final conversation on the telephone with his daughter, which happened at about this time. He had wanted her to return home, but she insisted she stay in London to help her sister with her forthcoming wedding. Eventually she said she would come home if she failed to find accommodation, but had a place to inspect that evening, having seen a postcard in a Paddington shop advertising 10 Rillington Place. Her father told her not to go and offered to pay her rail fare home, but Hectorina laughed.[23]

Christie recounted his version of events:

> Not very long after this I met a man and woman out of a cafe at Hammersmith. If I remember rightly I had been to sign on that day [it was 3 March]. It was in the morning. The man went across the road to talk to a friend and while he was away she said they had to give up their diggings at the week-end. He was out of work.

Baker recalled, 'We were about 10 minutes late getting to Ladbroke Grove Station. The man was waiting outside. I asked him about having a look at the place and he seemed rather reluctant to let us see it'. Christie said 'I told you not to tell anyone, even your husband about this, because I don't want a lot of people making enquiries about the flat'. He said he was being transferred for a new job, and offered to sub-let his rooms at 12s 9d per week.[24]

Christie continued, 'Then I told her that if they didn't find any-where, I could put them up for a few days'. Both, however, left and went to 35 Hetley Road, only to find the door locked on them. It was late at night and their options were now reduced to Rillington Place or nowhere. They both came up together and stayed a few days. They said they had been thrown out of their digs. They stayed there for the nights of the 3–5 March. Baker recalled, 'The first night we all sat up the whole night in chairs [he in an armchair, she on the deck chair and Christie on a bucket]. The second and third night I slept on a bed on the floor of the back room. Ina and Christie sat on the chairs in the kitchen. I asked Ina if Christie had interfered with her and she said he had not'. He also recalled the reason for this strange sleeping arrangement, 'He would not let Ina and I sleep together, as his wife, who was supposed to be living next door, might have come in and if she had found Ina and I there would be trouble'. Baker smelt nothing unusual. Christie said 'I told them they would have to go as he was being very unpleasant'. He also said Baker was moody and Christie resented the fact that he 'had been giving them food all the time they were there out of my own rations – I had given them breakfast'.[25]

Christie continued, 'He told me that police were looking for her for some offence. When they left the man said that if they couldn't find anywhere could they come back for that night'. Christie agreed. They left at 9.30am on 6 March to go to the Hammersmith Labour Exchange on Sulgrave Road and met Christie there. Christie then went to the National Assistance Office. Baker recalled, 'On the way there, Ina said that she had arranged to meet this man at her flat at 12 o'clock. She didn't say what for', but she arrived there, alone. Christie stated in his unpublished notes:

McLennan was not in fact pushed out by me but may have been anxious to go and it was I who was restraining her. She had been sitting in the deck chair and it was possible I used the gas and [she] may have noticed a smell of it and she got up to go. I could then have followed her into the place and got hold of her over her clothes at the neck and that caused her to fall to the ground. I could then have dragged her into the kitchen and used the gas to render her unconscious and been intimate after which I could have put her into the chair again or removed the cupboard and put her quickly into the alcove in case Baker came back.[26]

Christie added that he meant to 'lay her to rest decently' by reclothing her, but claimed he never had the chance, 'Once the bodies of my victims were in the cupboard I forgot about them'. As with the others she was gassed, raped and strangled. Yet she was put into the alcove unwrapped; presumably Christie realised Baker would visit him so speed was essential. By now the alcove was full with three corpses.[27]

At three that afternoon, Baker was waiting for Hectorina in a cafe on the Uxbridge Road. She did not arrive. So he went to 10 Rillington Place at about 5.00pm and saw Christie. Baker recalled, 'I then went to the flat and there saw the man. He said she had not been there. He asked me in and gave me some tea. He showed me round the rooms so that I could make sure for myself that she wasn't there. He then came with me to Shepherd's Bush to look for her, but we could not find her. He left me at about nine o'clock'. Baker later recalled, 'I did not notice anything unusual about the flat at all'. He did not report her absence; he was used to it.[28]

Christie later made another confession as to how he really killed these three women. Once he had been informed that a high level of carbon monoxide gas (34, 40 and 36 per cent respectively) had been found inside them, according to him:

I gassed the three women whose bodies were found in the alcove, by getting them to sit in the deckchair in the kitchen between the table and the door. There is a gas pipe on the wall next to the window that at one time had been used as a gas bracket. The pipe had been plugged. I took the plug out and pushed a piece of rubber tubing over the pipe and let it hang down nearly to the floor. There was no tap on it so I put a kink in the tube with a bulldog clip to stop the gas escaping. When they sat in the deckchair with the tube behind them, I just took the clip off and let the fumes rise from the back of the deckchair. When they started getting overcome that's when I must have strangled them.[29]

There has been much doubt cast over the veracity of this murder technique. It is difficult to understand how the women were gassed and why they did not smell and hear the gas and attempt to escape. Possibly Kathleen may not have done because she was drunk, but the others were not. It would take several minutes for them to fall unconscious. Secondly, Christie himself could hardly have escaped the effect of gas, because the kitchen was a small room, only nine feet seven inches by eight and a half feet. He could have stood by an open window to escape it, but this seemed doubtful. If they were rendered unconscious by gas, then so must he have been, too. Professor Camps and Mr Smith of the Gas Institute were both of this opinion.[30]

Shortly after this, Christie wrote to his brother-in-law about Ethel, 'She's coming home next week, and I'll be very glad as I am fed up with this shopping'. On 14 March, Gregg recalled giving Christie some cigarettes and remarking, 'he was feeling a bit restless and wanted a smoke'.[31]

Christie also spent some of his time in cafes. The Panda cafe at 232 Westbourne Park Road was one. He usually had morning tea, lunch and afternoon tea there, the latter being at 4.30pm. Edward Smith said, 'Mr Christie never spoke of any relatives'. Ada Robertson recalled, 'He never seemed short of cash ... He never said anything out of place to me. He always seemed very nervous ... He also told me he had once been a doctor and that he had been struck off the register for helping a girl out of trouble'. He showed Ada photographs of Ethel. Christie was last seen in this cafe in early March 1953.[32]

Frank Nicolle, a local artist, sketched him in a café in Ladbroke Grove and hung it on the wall. He recalled:

I was fascinated by the high dome of his head and sketched as he sat on a high stool by the counter. He came over and asked me to show the portrait. He seemed delighted with the result and we had a long conversation about art and photography.[33]

One purpose of haunting cafes was, of course, to meet women. He was seen by some as a suspicious character, and Jane Hodson, waitress at the Rainbow cafe, St Mark's Road, remembered, 'The man just sat and stared at me. His eyes were most peculiar and he would burst out laughing at nothing at all'. Mrs Robinson, a waitress at the café, was told by him he could cure her overstrain by a bottle of pills he offered. Once he met Margaret Forrest in the Panda cafe at the beginning of March 1953. It was lunchtime and he approached her with the following opening: 'Excuse me, have you got a bad cold? Do you suffer from migraine?'

When she said she did, he said he could cure her, being a doctor struck off for performing an abortion. He said that his father had been a specialist from Scotland, and arranged to meet her at his home on Saturday afternoon. However, Mrs Forrest recalled later, 'I thought the matter over and did not keep the appointment'. She did meet Christie in the cafe on a further occasion and he was angry that she had not kept the appointment. He said she should come but she told him she was no longer interested, so he replied, 'Well, if you would rather suffer, I can't help you'.[34]

Another woman encountered by Christie was Mary O'Neill/ Ballingall, a twenty-year-old from Ireland, who had once been a prostitute and had a three-week-old baby. She lived at 248 Westbourne Park with Leonard Ballingall, a thirty-five-year-old welder. She met Christie by chance at Ladbroke Grove railway station. He lit her cigarette for her, helped her onto a train, and then to the National Assistance offices at Hammersmith. He then gave her what must surely have been one of his few pound notes, bought her cigarettes and took her to a cafe for a cup of tea. Christie then put forward a proposition to her, saying, 'Come along just after dark, I don't want anyone to see you. And don't tell anyone you are coming'.[35]

Mary did so, on four occasions. Christie tried to gain her sympathy by telling her of his sadness following his wife's death, and also tried to impress her with stories of his war service in the police. Once he tried to kiss her, but she screamed and he gave her £1. He also tried to ply her with alcohol, but never allowed her into the garden or anywhere near the kitchen cupboard. Mary received £10 in total from him and spoke well of him. She said, 'He usually behaved like a gentleman. He spoke well and seemed to be very generous. He always seemed kind and gentle and rather sad and I felt sorry for him'. Yet her husband thought that she was scared of Christie and that he had threatened her. She saved her own life by telling Christie that Ballingall knew where she had gone. Christie 'got up and muttered to himself' and let her leave.[36]

There was perhaps another female visitor. This was Helen Sunderland. She had met Christie in Piccadilly and he offered her a cigarette – 'he seemed so nice' – explaining he was lonely and would she want to drink tea with him. They went back to Rillington Place one night in a taxi. There, 'He kept putting his clammy hands about my face and neck'. He then asked her to remove her clothes whilst he went into another room. She refused to disrobe, and then explained:

> When he came back into the room he had over his arm a heavy-looking dark rug or a blanket. I asked him what he was going to do. He told me to wait and see. I pulled it off his arm and found he had a piece of cord about three or four yards long. It looked like a sash cord. I became really frightened. I banged on the door and kicked it. Then he took the piece of rope off his arm and took both ends in his hand, so I knew at that moment he intended to murder me. I could see it in his dreadful eyes.

She kicked him, knocking off his glasses and hat and then climbed out of a window, thus effecting her escape.[37]

Christie approached others. On 9 March he met Esther Smith in Portobello Road, offering accommodation and saying, 'If you were pregnant, I know how to get rid of it for you'. She was not. Kathleen McAllum met Christie at Ladbroke Grove on 13 March, and he asked her about accommodation. She later said, 'I walked away as I did not like his looks'. Another potential victim was Anne Clarke, three days later: 'he was obviously trying to induce me to go to his house. I was suspicious of him'.[38]

However, Mary O'Neill was not alone in being sympathetic to Christie. Lilly Taylor recalled, 'I felt rather sorry for him after the other trouble [the Evans murders] and he always seemed as if he wanted to stop and speak to people. He was always polite'. Jean Middleton, a cafe owner, recalled, 'He was always dropping in for a cup of tea. At all times he was very correct in his behaviour and talk ... such a nice man'.[39]

Other people enquired about his rooms. One was Ronald Court, a labourer, and his wife, who met him on 16 March in the Rainbow cafe. Christie asked for 12s 3d per week, in advance. The Samuels also visited on 16 March and were told that Christie had been a policeman. Mrs Samuel recalled, 'Mr Christie seemed disappointed that I had come accompanied, so it appeared to me'. She also noticed that he peered around the curtain before allowing her in. She added, 'My friend and I did not like Christie'.[40]

Suspicion of Christie was limited, even though some people detected an unusual odour. Cyril Edwards, a fellow tenant, noted, 'For several weeks now there has been a nasty smell about the house'. Visitors noticed it too. Phyllis Crocker, who came along with a friend, recalled, 'I noticed a peculiar smell in the room'. Beatrice Short said, 'I asked Mr Christie if there were coloured men in the house and he said there were and I put the smell down to this'.[41]

Christie did take some precautions against being caught. A fellow tenant stated, 'Christie used to keep the back door locked and would not allow anyone out there'. James Hardy said, 'He locked and unlocked the inside doors as we went from room to room'.[42]

Routine matters began to unravel in Ethel's absence, though Christie tried to keep up appearances. In March 1951 they had taken out life insurance, and paid monthly premiums of 1s 3d to the Co-operative Insurance Society. The last payment was made on 17 January 1953. He last paid the milk bill on 20 February, though it continued to be delivered until 21 March, as was the newspaper.[43]

It is worth analysing Christie's technique. He chose his victims among the transient population of London; from among the vulnerable whose disappearance would not be likely to create a stir. As with some serial killers, he chose mostly prostitutes, who are willing to accompany a strange man to an isolated place as a matter of course. Again, as with many killers of this type, he sought his prey close to where he lived; all three were located less than a mile from Rillington Place. This was probably due to the ease of having them accompany him home. There was nothing personal in any of these murders. He killed to satisfy lusts which he could not satisfy in any other way, rendering his victims unconscious, then raping them and finally strangling them. The corpses were then hidden so he could continue in this way. He was also a reasonably organized killer; selecting his victims and becoming acquainted with them in order to gain their confidence before persuading them to return with him to their deaths. Yet he was becoming far less cautious and more confident that he could kill frequently and with impunity; not unlike other serial killers once they have killed several times. However, Christie was playing with fire. All his victims had relations or friends in west London; though he was lucky in that none of their suspicions were fully aroused (Baker was accustomed to Hectorina's unexplained absences). Christie was also on a path of self-destruction; after he left the house someone would eventually uncover the corpses he had concealed – either by sight or smell – and once they did, the police would come looking for him.

Christie recalled, 'Had I not been caught I would have gone on killing'. He later claimed he had a mental picture of his next victim.

She was a smartly dressed woman that he had seen in a car in Ladbroke Grove one day and 'the strange dark force in my mind' meant that 'She would have been my next victim if I had not been arrested'.[44]

Readers might wonder how Christie managed these murders whilst the house was crowded with other people. Basically people minded their own business and did not investigate. Emily Lawrence of number 8 stated that she 'never had anything to do with them and I know nothing about their private affairs'. John Clark saw Christie carrying rolls of wallpaper back home, and asked how his wife was. Presumably the same wallpaper covered up the bodies in the alcove. Ivan Williams of number 10 noted, 'I have only seen Christie on one occasion, and have no idea who may have visited him, or who was supposed to live with him. I have never heard any suspicious noises from the flat or anything to cause suspicion'. Franklin Stewart said, 'I have not heard any knockings or unusual noises in the house', and though another resident later heard knockings in the kitchen, they took it no further.[45]

Realising that he could not stay at home much longer – he lacked money if nothing else – Christie decided to have his fourteen-year-old-dog put down. In February he told Franklin Stewart that the dog was too old and would have to be put down. He went to Ernest Jacobs, 'The Animal First Aid Man' at 132 Clarendon Road. Jacobs was not a qualified vet, but he took the 5s and destroyed the fawn-coated Irish terrier. He did not ask why the dog had to die, but presumably it was partly due to old age. Christie's cat was later found running wild; despite offers of adoption, the RSPCA put it down.[46]

Christie finally found someone to let his rooms to. This was Mrs Mary Margaret Reilly. She met Christie while out shopping in Ladbroke Grove on 13 March. She was looking at a noticeboard for accommodation and he asked if she was seeking a flat. When she said yes, he told her, 'I have the lease, and the lease will last 16 years more. I am ready to move out, I have a transfer to Birmingham. My wife is living up in Birmingham in a new flat. She has been up there three months'. Mary and her husband, John, went to see the flat the following day and agreed to rent it for 12s 8d per week and to pay a deposit of £7 13s 0d. They also gave Christie £1 for some odd fittings. He told them of his service in the police during the war. They made the deal on the day that Christie left and the latter gave them a receipt, and a meaningless declaration, 'I declare that I shall, during the tenancy of

Mr Reilly shall accept full responsibility for any damage'. Christie left 10 Rillington Place on 20 March 1953 for the last time, taking a case borrowed from Reilly. Amongst other items he put in there was some of Kathleen's clothing – presumably a souvenir, though as we shall note, he left behind others. Mrs Reilly later recalled, 'I noticed a very unpleasant smell in the kitchen ... I thought it was the dog, as he used to have a dog there. It was a very noticeable smell'. Charles Brown was surprised to find them ('I found two strange people living there') and so they had to leave the next day, but only after Brown had called the police.[47]

One of the last people to see Christie in Notting Hill was his doctor. 'I met him accidentally in the street at the beginning of March this year. I inquired after his health. He said he was feeling better, but that he had several attacks of pain, but he did not see me'. Another man seen by Christie on 21 March was a photographic shop assistant, to whom Christie inexplicably said, 'You'd better get a lot of stock in. I shall be doing a lot of photography from now on'.[48]

Christie later recalled that he had always been a gambler. Yet this was sheer recklessness. He stated, '... leaving that kitchen. It might have been discovered, or it mightn't'. On 21 March Beresford Brown moved into Christie's old rooms. He had been born in 1909 and had taken the ship *Colombie* from Kingston, Jamaica to Plymouth, arriving there on 29 December 1950, and was described as a musician. On 22 March, he and Charles Brown cleared all the debris from the ground floor rooms and put it in the garden. He wanted to find a place where he could fix brackets on a wall so he could install a wireless. On 24 March, he chose the kitchen and found that one of the so-called walls was actually hollow. He pulled aside the covering wallpaper and made a terrible discovery.[49]

He later recalled:

I was going to fix some shelves in the kitchen and knocked the wall first above what appears to be a door and then just at the top of it it appeared to be hollow. I then took a torch and tore the top corner of the paper away ... I shone my torch through the hole I made and saw the back of somebody's body. I called another tenant [Ivan Williams] and we fetched the police.

It was at about 5.00pm that Williams telephoned the police from the corner telephone box on the junction of Lancaster Road and then went back to number 10 to await their arrival.[50]

PC Leslie Siseman was one of the constables who arrived first and he stated, 'I could see the body of a woman in a sitting position back to the opening with her head and shoulders hunched'.[51]

A more detailed account of the discovery by Dr Francis Camps, a leading pathologist, who 'had great enthusiasm for his job, and very considerable ability' was as follows:

One [of the corpses] was on its back with the legs vertical against the back of the cupboard. It was wrapped in a blanket, tied round the ankles with a piece of wire, and the torso covered with earth and ashes.

Another body, also wrapped in a blanket and tied round the ankles with a sock, was lying on top of the other in a similar position and also covered with earth and ashes.

The third body was sitting in an upright position and kept in that position by her brassiere, to the back of which was tied the end of the blanket from the feet of the middle body.

A police officer recalled, 'Over the years I have seen some shocking sights, but never one so un-nerving as that which greeted ourselves'. It should be stated that the alcove containing the three bodies was packed indeed, as it only measured four feet high and was five feet six inches deep.

Yet there was worse to come, as Camps wrote, 'Later that night I examined the front room on the ground floor and noticed some loose boards in the middle of the room. I lifted the boards and completely buried in earth and rubble was another body wrapped up in a blanket'. All four corpses were removed to Kensington Mortuary the next day.[52]

The shocking news was reported in the daily newspapers on the following day. The police stated that they wanted to trace Christie and issued the following description of him:

Aged 55, height 5 ft. 9 in., slim build, dark hair thin on top, clean shaven. Sallow complexion, long nose, wearing horn rimmed spectacles, dentures, top and bottom, walks with military bearing. Wearing a dark blue herring bone suit, brown leather shoes, fawn belted raincoat, and brown trilby hat.[53]

The hunt was now on and Christie's days of freedom were surely limited. He never explained why he left 10 Rillington Place, knowing that his victims' corpses must soon be found. One reason was that he needed the money. Having disposed of most of his furniture, his wife's belongings, her savings and ring, he was desperate for cash and the National Assistance payments were insufficient for his needs. His rooms were his last asset, so they had to be sold. But he must surely have reasoned that his days as a free man – and in fact his life – would be short; perhaps, after three murders in two months, he was past rational thought and had become careless. It was also the following day that Christie emerged from total obscurity to become a national figure in the media.

Chapter 10

Christie's Nemesis
1953

'I saw a man leaning over the embankment with his arms resting on the wall itself. He was unkempt'.[1]

It was only now that the full and shocking extent of Christie's murderous career became known. The police investigation was two-fold. Firstly there was the examination of the house and garden of 10 Rillington Place. Secondly they had to locate Christie. The corpse under the floorboards of the living room was soon identified as Ethel and the others were soon identified too. Several days later bones were found in the garden, though their identification took a little longer. Other gruesome finds were a femur (leg bone) holding up the garden fence and, amongst the rubbish in the garden, a square glass jar with tubing attached.

Evidence of Christie's collecting habits was also found. Dr Lewis Nickolls examined a pastilles tin containing four lots of pubic hair, which had been found under a piece of linoleum in the garden. He said that none could have belonged to any of the women found in the alcove, despite Christie later saying they were. He thought that one might have belonged to Ethel, though not necessarily, because they were a very common type of hair. Furthermore, the hair found had been cut and there was no evidence of hair cut from her at the time of her death. Possibly it could have been cut off some months previously. Two sets of hair might have belonged to the skeletons in the garden, judging by the sample of hair found in the garden and by the description of one of the victims. But 'the final and fourth one is like no pubic hair I have received in this case at all, or any of the persons described to me'. It is unknown to whom this belonged. Dr Keith Simpson later wrote, 'One piece of evidence suggests he had at least one other victim; perhaps four'. Yet if this were the case, where were the bodies? Christie's method of murder was to kill on his home territory, so it is more likely that he snipped hair from prostitutes he had business with than that he committed further murders. The saving of 'souvenirs' is another classic trait of the serial killer.[2]

Christie's clothes were later examined. Semen was found on his plimsolls, trousers, vest and shirt. Clearly he had worn these items when he had killed his last three victims.[3]

At the same time, Christie's whereabouts were unknown. The police requested that people letting rooms and cafe proprietors inform them if they saw him and enquiries were made at these places. One sighting was of him sleeping in a van in Powis Mews, Portobello Road, a mile from Rillington Place. When the police arrived, the van was empty. Nationwide enquiries were made and Christie's relatives were contacted; Winifred Delves made a plea for him to give himself up.[4]

Lurid headlines featured in the press. Those for *The Daily Mirror* included, 'Three Women dead in house of murder' and 'Race against time to trap horror killer'. *The Sunday Pictorial* led with 'Another body is found' and 'House of Death yields new secret'. The former newspaper commented 'the sex strangler of Notting Hill may strike again' and said that Christie was 'one of the most dangerous of modern time murderers'. *The News of the World* referred to him as 'the Ripper of Rillington Place' and said he was worse than Haigh or Gordon Cummins ('the Black Out Ripper' of 1942). There were theories that his murders coincided with the phases of the moon and that he must be taken before the next full moon on 30 March. It was also initially thought that the murders might have been committed for the money the victims possessed.[5]

People claimed they had seen him and wrote to the police. One Arthur Turner claimed to have seen him on a bus from Notting Hill to the Albert Hall. Henry Willcox thought he had seen him at 2.00pm on 25 March, walking from Fulham Broadway towards North End Road, and that 'he looked smarter than usual'. Robert Denver claimed to have been in his company for nearly two hours at the Eastern Hotel in Docklands and 'talked of general matters'. He was also seen in a doorway of a shop by a man on the 607 bus travelling towards Ealing. On 27 March he was seen eating lunch in an Italian restaurant on Moscow Road. A woman said a man 'staring at me' at Bethnal Green on 22 March was the wanted man. There were also a reputed sightings throughout the country and overseas. Balding middle-aged men found themselves being brought in for police questioning.[6]

In fact, Christie had gone from Rillington Place to a lodging house called Rowton House, King's Cross Road. It housed about 1,000 men each night. He claimed not to know why he went, later stating:

I was not intending to go there. I really went out and I had it in my mind to come back ... I do not know whether I walked, or went by train, or anything, but next I was in King's Cross, in the street. I met a man and asked him, because I felt rather exhausted; I felt tired out; I asked him if he knew any accommodation where I could stay for that one night, so that I could go back to Rillington Place, you see, the next morning.[7]

Harold Cooper, booking clerk there, recalled, 'On 20th March, 1953, a man came to Rowton House and booked in for the night, to whom I made out a registration card signed "Christie" ... The address given was 10 Rillington Place. I gave him a seven-nights ticket for bed 610'. He arrived in the evening and was given a locker ticket for his case and a key rental ticket, and Christie showed him his identity card.[8]

Christie was apparently careless with money whilst at Rowton House. He gave 2s 6d for a breakfast costing 1s 4d, and told the server to keep the change. Alfred Arrowsmith, an unemployed man who was also staying there, later gave the following statement:

A man got talking to me there. He was talking a lot about Birmingham. He told me he lived in London and he had got a job, but he had just come out of hospital and said he had been suffering from a chest complaint, said to be catarrh. I spent some time with him in Rowton House on the Sunday and Monday. We had some tea together and I later saw him playing snooker in the games room. He seemed to be pretty well educated, he spoke nicely and was quietly spoken. He also said that he had domestic trouble which caused him to live in Rowton House. He said that he had never lived in this kind of place before.[9]

Arrowsmith added 'He was worried about something. He seemed on edge'. He sold his overcoat to Christie for 25s. Christie did not have much money on him. He had a few pound notes, and was concerned that he should not reveal his wealth at Rowton House, 'because I had heard about Rowton House and some people living there – peculiar people'.[10]

During this period, he approached one Margaret Wilson at the Starlight Cafe, Pentonville Road. She was twenty-four and pregnant.

He said he was Scottish, that his father was an Edinburgh surgeon and asked, 'Do you want to keep it or get rid of it? ... You can come to my place if you want to get rid of it'. She refused. He may have met another woman at this time, too. Helen Sunderland told that she saw him walking up and down Piccadilly and was approached by him. Asking her if she wanted to smoke and come back to his home, she recalled, 'he seemed so nice when he spoke to me, although I felt a cold feeling come over me when talking with him'. She briefly went with him, but soon left. He had paid up to the 27th, but when the news first broke about the three bodies being found in Rillington Place he left, leaving his suitcase there, recalling, 'I just walked out, and I had no reason not to go back. I just started walking then'.[11]

He was next seen at Paddington Station at four in the morning on 26 March, then at the Great Western Royal Hotel on Praed Street. The police called at Rowton House on 27 March, but only found his abandoned suitcase.[12]

Christie recalled, when asked about his later wanderings:

Well, I don't recollect, really, what I was doing. I must have been walking round and round all the time. I know that when I reached a cross roads at one time I saw a sign which was strange, it said 'Barking Road,' and then I asked where I was and somebody said I was at East Ham. I asked if they could direct me back to Kensington, and they told me what to do.

However, he ended up in Aldgate.[13]

He also made other comments about this period: 'One thing I remember at that time when I was walking about, is that when I went into a cafe and sat down at a table to eat, I heard people talking about it. They were discussing – well, I did not know it was me they were talking about'. However, he did not immediately rise and leave when they began talking about him, but 'I just finished in the ordinary way, got up and went out. He did not follow the case about himself in the newspapers, but admitted, 'I did see one large headline. I do not know what paper it was, it was all folded up. I just saw something about "Will the Killer Strike again?" I just happened to see it, as it was in very large print. I saw it as I walked past, and I did not bother about it'. Christie's reaction to his new-found infamy was thus: 'not moved emotionally – just interested. There was no feeling of remorse – just interest'. Nor did he try to avoid the police, as he noted: 'On one particular occasion on my way back to Kensington from East Ham I stood at a crossroad, and all of a sudden I realized a policeman had held the traffic and beckoned me to go across. I did not want to go across, but I went, and thanked him as I passed'. Apparently he rested in cafes and cinemas. He was certainly running out of cash, for on 28 March he pawned his watch for 10s at William Fayley's, 5 Plough Road, Battersea. His state was pitiable, as he wrote, 'I wandered about for days, not sleeping anywhere [one account states he slept rough in wasteland Hammersmith and in half-built flats in Putney, 28–30 March]. My feet and ankles were swollen up, I hadn't eaten from Friday till Tuesday afternoon'. On his last day of freedom he tried unsuccessfully to scrounge two pence for a cup of tea from a man in Putney. There is no evidence that he arranged to meet veteran *News of the World* journalist Norman Rae near Wood Green Town Hall in this period, in order to trade his story for a hot breakfast (he did not turn up).[14]

The denouement of the manhunt was something of an anti-climax. On 31 March, at 9.10am, PC Thomas Ledger was on his beat and saw a man, unshaven, obviously hungry and down and out, near Putney Bridge, on the junction of Lower Richmond Road and the Putney embankment. Christie recalled, 'There was a barge there and what struck me at the time was that a vehicle was being loaded down there, and I was just watching and noting how that vehicle had got down towards the water'. Ledger recalled, 'I saw a man leaning over the embankment with his arms resting on the wall itself. He was unkempt. I first noticed he was wearing glasses and from a side view thought he resembled the man Christie'. He then challenged the man:

'What are you doing, looking for work?'
'Yes, but my unemployment cards haven't come through yet'.
'Where do you come from?'
'Paddington'.
'What is your name and address?'
'John Waddington, 35 Westbourne Gardens.'
'Have you anything on you to prove your identity?'
'Nothing at all'.

Ledger then asked the man to remove his hat, to which he replied, 'Certainly'. Ledger said, 'I recognised him quite easily'. Two other officers joined Ledger and they took Christie to Putney Police Station, where he produced his identity card and threw it at Ledger. They arrived at 9.15am. Christie was 'physically tired and exhausted', emotional and tearful, and was given bacon to eat, the first food he had eaten for four days. Detective Inspector Edward Kelly asked him, 'Are you John Reginald Halliday Christie?' Christie replied 'Yes'. Kelly then announced, 'I am going to take you to Notting Hill Police Station, where you will be charged with the murder of your wife'. He made no reply. Kelly searched him at 9.25am. On his person were a wallet, his identity card, a rent book, his marriage certificate, National Insurance papers, a St John's Ambulance card, his union card, his ration book, that of his wife and a newspaper cutting about Evans being remanded. His only money was a half penny, a three penny and a bent florin. Christie stated, 'I wish to state that I am grateful to the police in charge for the kindly way in which I have been treated in Putney police station. There has been no act of any kind to force me to say or do anything'.[15]

Once he was arrested, the machinery of the law began to grind into motion. Chief Inspector Albert Griffin recalled, 'I told him who we were and asked him if he were John Reginald Halliday Christie. He said he was. I told him I found the body of a woman, later identified as his wife, buried under the floor of the front room, and asked him if he wished to say anything about it'. Christie began to cry when told of his wife's death. He then confessed to the murder (and to those he committed in 1953), was cautioned and then signed a statement. Christie distanced himself from the murders, claiming he killed his wife as a mercy killing and the others in self-defence, neglecting to state he gassed and assaulted them. For instance, part of the confession read as follows:

> in Ladbroke Grove a drunken woman stood in front of me and demanded £1 for me to take her 'round the corner'. I said, 'I am not interested' . . . I walked away . . . She came along, and she came right to the door, still demanding 30s. When I opened the door she forced her way in . . . I tried to get her out, and she picked up a frying pan and hit me. I closed with her and there was a struggle . . . I must have gone haywire.

In reality he had met her in a pub. Another of the victims 'started fighting. I am very quiet and avoid fighting'. Christie was taken to Notting Hill Police Station, where a large crowd, including Evans's sister, watched his arrival. At 3.30pm Griffin officially charged him with his wife's murder.

Christie appeared at the West London Magistrates' Court at 10.00am on 1 April, when he was charged with his wife's murder. He shuffled into the court, with head bowed and eyes staring at the floor. After ten minutes, he was remanded for another week. He made two more appearances there (on 8 [his 54th birthday, when he said to a detective, 'Don't wish me many happy returns'] and 15 April). At the final hearing charges were preferred alleging he also killed Rita, Kathleen and Hectorina. On 22 April he was brought before Mr Clyde Wilson, but this time at the Clerkenwell Magistrates' Court, charged with these four murders. When he entered the court he covered his face with his hands. The prosecution detailed the discovery of the corpses, and read a statement made by Christie, in which he admitted to these four killings. He appeared before the court again on 29 April and on 6 May was formally committed for trial at the Old Bailey.[16]

Christie was a figure of great interest both to the public and the press in a way that Evans never was. When he arrived at the court for the first time, he was watched by the people living in the houses adjoining the court house. Fourteen people were allowed into the small court room.[17]

His legal defence was paid for by the proprietors of *The Sunday Pictorial*, a bestselling illustrated tabloid newspaper, though *The Sunday Despatch* also bid for the rights to Christie's story. Christie said, 'I want the Sunday Pictorial to have my story'. Procter, who had met Christie in 1949, saw him again and took a dislike to him. Mr Derek Curtis-Bennett, QC, was briefed as Counsel and concluded that the only possible defence was insanity. It was also decided that he should confess to the murder of Beryl Evans, too, if this was true, in order to strengthen the case in favour of insanity. Christie was made aware of all this.[18]

On 4 April Christie began to make jottings about his life, which the newspaper would use for their story in July. This was a twenty-nine page document which continued to be written until 11 June. It is not a chronological autobiography, but is a collection of reminiscences about his childhood and later life. In it Christie stresses his liking for animals and children and his love for his wife, as well as his illnesses and persecution by his landlord and fellow tenants. Christie discussed his dreams, 'For many years I have had dreams at night and am nearly always mixed up with some form of violence. Sometimes I have helped to check it but mainly I have just been looking on'. He wrote of his opposition to capital punishment, and his murders. Yet in the latter he stressed his humanity, 'in all of the cases my intention was to avoid hurting them at all. They were rendered semi-conscious first and that in each case would eliminate the possibility of hurting them and causing pain'. He hinted at other murders, 'I have tried to think hard about whether there were other bodies but seem to think it is possible. Those hairs in the tin lead me to think that but I have no clear recollection'. He also talked about the deaths of Beryl and Geraldine Evans, though he changed his story as he went along – from being wholly innocent, to having killed Beryl and having had sex with her at least once, to killing Beryl but not having sex with her.[19]

As noted, Christie confessed to his murders of 1952–53, but he was less forthcoming about earlier victims, until irrefutable proof was available. On 22 April, Christie was told of the two skeletons in the back garden, so he admitted that he was responsible. On 5 June he confessed to killing Ruth Fuerst and Muriel Eady, which helped the police identify the two skeletons. Ruth's mother had believed hitherto that her daughter had married a wealthy man in London. The police had to trawl through the index cards of 8,000 employees of Ultra until they found Muriel's.[20]

Christie initially denied any connection with the Evans murders, claiming, when the suggestion was made, that he was physically incapable. When Dr Hobson spoke to him on 20 April, he denounced Morris's 'monstrous suggestion' of three years ago. There were more interviews on 22 and 23 April with Hobson. Hobson recollected 'Christie enjoyed being interviewed, and he liked talking and would keep the interview going as long as possible ... in order to do this Christie had a habit of saying something provocative at the end of an interview to prolong it'. It was here that he concluded, 'There is something about Mrs Evans which I can't quite remember'.[21]

It was not until 27 April that Christie said that he had killed Beryl. He was asked, 'Are you saying this on the basis of the more the madder?' It is probably right to assume that Christie was employing this gambit as an attempt to try and save his neck. In an interview with Professor Desmond Curran, a psychiatrist at St George's Hospital, a month later, Christie made a remark about Broadmoor, 'I have heard people are very happy there and that is what I want'.[22]

Christie made a lengthy statement on 8 June confessing to the murder of Beryl Evans and this is often taken as truthful by those who believe Christie was guilty, yet as we shall see it does not match the facts and is inherently improbable in other ways. He said:

That evening Evans went out with the blonde and he was carrying a suitcase. He came back alone later. The next day Mrs Evans told my wife that she was going down to the police court to get a separation from her husband. My wife and I had a chat and we agreed between us that if they did separate we should adopt the baby, but Mrs Evans told my wife that if they did separate his mother would take the baby. At a later period, Mrs Evans told me that her husband was knocking her about and that she was going to make an end of it, meaning that she was going to commit suicide.

One morning shortly after this, it would be early in November, I went upstairs and found Mrs Evans lying on a quilt in front of the fireplace in the kitchen. She had made an attempt to gas herself, and I opened the door and window wide because there was a lot of gas in the room. There was a gas-pipe on the left hand side of the fire-place with a tap about two feet six inches from the floor about the level of the top of the kitchen fireplace. There was a piece of rubber tubing from the tap to near her head. She was lying with her head towards the window. She was fully dressed and was not covered over with anything. When I opened the door and window she started coming round. I gave her a drink of water. I do not know what she said, but a little while after she complained of a headache, and I made her a cup of tea. My wife was downstairs, but I did not call her or tell her. Mrs Evans asked me not to tell anyone. Mr Evans was out and I don't know if there was anyone else in the house. I had a cup of tea, too, because my head was thumping as I had got the effect of it too. After a while, I went downstairs.

The next day I went upstairs again, I couldn't say if it was the morning or afternoon. I think it was about lunchtime. She still said she intended to do away with herself. I am certain that there was a small fire in the grate in the kitchen when I found Mrs Evans the day before, and that's why I rushed to open the window.

When I went up to Mrs Evans at lunch-time the next day she begged of me to help her go through with it, meaning to help her to commit suicide. She said she would do anything if I would help her. I think she was referring to letting me be intimate with her. She brought the quilt from the front room and put it down in front of the fireplace. I am not sure whether there was a fire in the grate. She lay on the quilt. She was fully dressed. I got on my knees but found I was not physically capable of having intercourse with her owing to the fact that I had fibrositis in my back and had enteritis. We were both fully dressed. I turned the gas tap on as near as I can make out I held it close to her face. When she became unconscious I turned the tap off. I was going to try again to have intercourse with her but it was impossible, I couldn't bend over. I think that's when I strangled her. I think it was with a stocking I found in the room. The gas wasn't on very long, not much more than a minute, I think. Perhaps one or two minutes. I then left her where she was and went downstairs. I think my wife was downstairs. She didn't know anything about it.

Christie then described his meeting with Evans:

Evans came home in the evening about six o'clock. It was dark when I heard him come in. I went to my kitchen door and called him. I spoke to him in the passage and told him that his wife had committed suicide, that she had gassed herself. I went upstairs with him. We went into the kitchen, and Evans touched his wife's hand, then picked her up and carried her into the bedroom and put her on the bed. It was dark, and there were no lights on in the kitchen or the bedroom ... After Evans lay his wife on the bed, he fetched the quilt from the kitchen and put it over her ... I told Evans that no doubt he would be suspected of having done this because of the rows and fights he had had with his wife. He seemed to think the same. He said he would bring the van down that he was driving and take her away and leave her somewhere. I left him and went downstairs ... I was under the impression that he had taken his wife away in his van ... When I left Evans in the bedroom in that Tuesday evening he did not know that his wife had been strangled. He thought that she had gassed herself ... I never mentioned it to him. I never had sexual intercourse with Mrs Evans at any time. We were just friendly acquaintances ... I feel certain I strangled Mrs Evans and I think it was with a stocking. I did it because she appealed to me to help her commit suicide. I have got it in the back of my mind that there was some other motive, but I am not clear about that. I don't know anything about what happened to the Evans' baby. I don't recollect seeing the baby on Tuesday or at any time afterwards ... The pubic hairs found in the tin at 10 Rillington Place came from the three women in the alcove and from my wife. I feel certain about this, but I can't remember when or how I took it.[23]

However, to further muddy the waters, on another occasion Christie claimed that he had had sex with Beryl: 'I think she knew I felt like making love to her ... This I did ... I believe I made love to her again just then ... I am not certain but think I did'. Furthermore, there are at least four important problems with taking this confession as being truthful. Firstly there is no reference to the bruises found on Beryl's face which indicate an assault about twenty minutes prior to her death. Secondly, Beryl cannot have been gassed because, as already noted, Teare found no traces of gas when he examined her corpse. Camps noted that Christie's story was 'Highly improbable if not impossible' and 'it is possible it could have happened as he said, but improbable', partly because the high level of gas would have risked an explosion. Thirdly, he concluded that she had probably been strangled by a rope, not a stocking. Finally, Christie was almost certainly not in the house when Evans returned. We could also add that the hairs in the tin did not belong to any of his three last victims, nor does his story about meeting Evans tie in with Evans's account.[24]

It was necessary to try and verify Christie's confession. To do so, an order was made for the exhumation of Beryl and Geraldine. They had been buried in Gunnersbury Cemetery. The exhumation occurred at 5.30am on 18 May 1953. Among those who stood around the grave were Drs Teare, Camps and Simpson. They reassembled at Kensington Mortuary at 8.15am. Nickolls was also there, as was Jennings.[25]

Jennings identified the corpses and Camps lifted them out. What they were looking for was whether there were any signs of cherry pink colouring, indicative of carbon monoxide poisoning. Both sides of Beryl's thighs and teeth were this colour. However, the colour faded once the corpse was exposed to air. This was merely 'post-mortem pink' to use Simpson's words. Beryl had been strangled, not gassed. Simpson wrote, 'there was nothing in Teare's original autopsy that appeared to have been overlooked' and 'No one could reasonably suggest that a pathologist of Dr Teare's ability and experience could possibly have overlooked coal gas poisoning in a case of such a nature'. Simpson thought, 'I am obliged to say that ... exhumation proved unrewarding'. If Christie did kill Beryl, he did not do it in the way he said he did. His confession thus looks extremely shaky.[26]

Meanwhile, Christie was placed in Brixton prison. He played dominoes and chess with his fellow prisoners and was known as 'Chris the chess champion'. He was well behaved in gaol and co-operative with staff. Daniel Heaney reported some eccentric behaviour, however. Once Christie said to him, 'I have just drunk my urine and enjoyed it'. On another he was having a bath and once naked, pointed at his penis and said to Heaney that that was the reason why crowds were visiting Rillington Place.[27]

Christie wrote a letter, describing his experiences in prison: 'The officers here seem very considerate and do what they can to make me feel more settled'. He said he would like more cigarettes, a few sweets and an apple, as these 'would make me much happier and settled'. However, 'At present I occupy a small room and am really glad to be alone to settle a bit as I am still somewhat fuddled and dazed. My head is aching rather badly'.[28]

Christie also liked talking about himself to other prisoners, and tried to present the best possible image he could of himself. He portrayed himself as a ladies' man, due to his polite manners, 'I had a gentlemanly uprooting, you see, and know how to behave myself'. He was also convinced that he was attractive to women, 'It wasn't me who did the chasing. Girls were attracted to me'. Christie added, 'I'm not like Boris Karloff ... more like Charles Boyer'. He liked to think himself merciful, 'I gave them a merciful end, the mob should remember that'. Yet, as ever, Jekyll could not conceal Hyde, 'You can't help feeling that women who give you the come on wouldn't be so smug if helpless, or dead'. Finally he said, 'Cats should be cuddled, not throttled. Animals and birds are my friends ... women, well, that's different'. Nor did he entirely deceive his fellow prisoners, one of whom noticed he read thrillers while claiming he read non-fiction, and that, for all his intellectual airs, 'he wasn't much of a scholar'.[29]

As with all prisoners facing a murder trial, doctors were called in to interview them. Matheson was one. Psychiatrists were also summoned; one being Hobson, who first visited Christie on 4 April and then again on the 20th. Another was Curran, acting for the prosecution, who saw Christie there on 20 and 25 May.

Curran later made this summary of his time there:

Christie was somewhat emotional, tremulous and tearful on admission, but soon settled down. He has been meticulously clean and tidy in his person and habits; he has always kept himself well occupied; he has mixed freely with the other patients. He has been noticeably egocentric and conceited. He keeps a photograph of himself in the cell. He has been a great talker and has seemed to enjoy discussing his case, bringing the conversation round to it. He has been cheerful and boastful; he has compared himself to Haigh; he has admitted in conversation that he 'did some of them in'. He appeared to be above average intelligence – he has always been polite and well behaved; he has never said or done anything to suggest he was not in his right mind. He has slept well, his appetite has been good and he gained 11 lb. in weight between 1.4.53 and 29.5.53.

Dr Matheson noted that Christie 'showed signs of emotion' when talking about Ethel's death and 'he wept for the first time'. No 'evidence [was] found of the presence of insane delusions nor hallucinations' and he had a detached attitude. Christie was above average intelligence and tests found he had an IQ of 128. He was considered sane and so fit to plead in court.[30]

Christie was examined by Stephen Coates, a criminal psychologist, and he made the following report on his subject on 19 June. After all, he had to be proved to be sane if he was to stand trial:

Mr Christie is not insane. He suffers from acute anxiety hysteria: the anxiety being mostly centred on sex fears. He would probably be unable to approach normal sexual intercourse at all; and if at all then only with considerable fears. He would appear to have a dread of women ... A sad, unhappy, rather inadequate anxiety ridden man [with] a considerable amount of repression, especially of aggression ... [there is] little to explain Mr Christie's criminal acts: except for the suggestion that they were committed to ward off acute feelings of fear produced in him by women.[31]

Dr Matheson's verdict was thus:

Christie has a very weak sex instinct and to complete the sexual act he needs considerable stimulation by adopting perverse practices. He has, I think, to render the woman with whom he was going to have intercourse, unconscious before he began, lest he prove impotent and again subject to jeers and have it revealed once more that sexually he was not a normal man. Having done it [murder] once and not been found out it tempted him to repeat the act.[32]

Curran interviewed Christie on 20 and 25 May, and later wrote a summary of his findings at these two sessions:

Christie was alert and attentive, obsequiously polite and quick in grasp, except occasionally when asked an awkward question. He was apt to be circumstantial, often adding irrelevant details; this apparently being motivated by a desire to show himself in as good a light as possible or to play for time when uncertain what lie to tell. He prided himself on his abstemious habits and I could find no reason to associate his crimes with alcoholic intoxication. Physical examinations and investigations have been negative and he is not epileptic. He showed some transient evidence of emotional upset when discussing his wife's death and wept; but in general he seemed happy rather than depressed, his usual attitude being one of would be co-operative interest in an intriguing problem. When discussing neutral topics his emotional response seems quite normal. His memory is good on general and neutral topics. As regards the crisis, however, he explained apologetically that his memory was apt to come and go and his story varied from one minute to the next in response to suggestions made. I could find no evidence of delusions, hallucinations or misinterpretations. There can be no doubt that Christie is a highly abnormal individual ... I could find no evidence that Christie did show such symptoms before, during or after the murders, and he does not show such symptoms now. I would regard Christie as the possessor of a highly abnormal character rather than as a victim of disease. Nor am I completely satisfied that the murders were necessarily sadistic. There is nothing, for example, to suggest that a sadistic motive entered in the murder of his wife. Christie himself repudiated any sadistic motive, emphasising that to hurt anybody was the last thing he ever wished to do or had done.[33]

Personally I do not believe Christie's alleged loss of memory is genuine. It is in my opinion too inconsistent, variable, patchy and selective to be genuine. It is striking how Christie remembers what he regards as being in his own favour and forgets, or can only remember transiently, what is not. His lies seemed to me to be purposive if not convincing. Christie has, however, like many other criminals and murderers, a remarkable capacity for dismissing the unpleasant from his mind. This capacity helps to explain that common finding in murderers as in the case of Christie, namely, lack of remorse. How can one regret what one cannot recall? Christie is well aware of and interested in his lack of remorse. As he put it to me, 'It must have been planned on each occasion, but if I did plan it, I never gave it another thought. I must have remembered putting the bodies in the alcove, but I do not remember doing so and I never thought about them'. This amounts to saying 'out of sight, out of mind' but, be it noted, not out of mind all the time, for Christie used disinfectant to reduce the unpleasant smell ... I could find no evidence that Christie at the time of the murder of his wife was suffering from any defect of reason due to disease of the mind, nor that he is suffering now. His behaviour both before and after the murder of his wife and of the three prostitutes forms a sequence that seems to me to show that he knew what he was doing and knew it was wrong. I do not think Christie is medically insane and he is certainly not mentally defective. On the contrary, he is above average intelligence. I regard Christie as being the possessor of a highly abnormal character rather than as the victim of mental illness or disease. Christie is in my opinion fit to plead and to stand his trial. He fully realises his position and indeed discussed with me the various possibilities the future might hold for him. He told me that on principle he had always been opposed to the death penalty.[34]

Ironically, Curran referred to Christie as being an 'inadequate psychopath', just as Matheson described Evans in 1949.[35]

Christie was only visited by his defence team, newspaper representatives and one single friend, Frank Ross, whom he had not seen since 1946. Ross visited him several times, and added 'he has not got a friend at all'.[36]

This, then, was the man who was about to stand trial for murder. The consensus of opinion that was emerging was that he was bad, rather than mad.

Chapter 11

The Trial of Christie 1953

*'I am not asking you to say he [Christie] is a nice man –
if I did you would soon tell me to shut up'.*[1]

The trial of Christie was a major media event and journalists and the public, including celebrities, flocked to attend. This was not only the trial of a wife killer, although of course it was that too, but was also the trial of a mass murderer. A total of thirty-eight newspapers, eleven of which were from abroad, sent journalists and the trial was constantly on the front pages, unlike that of Evans.

Proceedings took place at the Old Bailey and began on Monday 22 June 1953. The judge was Mr Justice Finnemore. The Counsel for the Crown, instructed by the Director of Public Prosecutions, was Sir Lionel Heald, QC, the Attorney General, and he was opposed by Derek Curtis-Bennett, QC.[2]

The Clerk of the Court read out the indictment: 'John Reginald Halliday Christie, you are charged with the murder of Ethel Christie on or about the 14th day of December 1952. Are you guilty or not guilty?'

Christie replied, 'Not guilty'.

The Clerk continued: 'Members of the jury, the prisoner at the bar, John Reginald Halliday Christie, is charged with the murder of Ethel Christie on or about the 14th of December, 1952. To this indictment he has pleaded not guilty, and it is your charge to say, having heard the evidence, whether he is guilty or not.'[3]

Heald then began the opening speech for the prosecution. He reminded the jury why they were there: 'the issue you have to try is whether or not Christie is guilty of the wilful murder of his wife. That is the charge against him, and it is the only charge upon which he is being tried here today'. He told the jury that they must try to forget all that they had previously read on the case, as 'every single one of us in this Court, almost without exception, must have read something in the press about No. 10 Rillington Place'. He aimed to show, of course, that 'you give no alternative but to find Christie guilty'.[4]

The facts of the case were then laid out. The Christies had lived in the ground floor rooms of 10 Rillington Place. Ethel was last seen alive on 12 December 1952 when she took clothes to a nearby laundry. On 24 March 1953 her corpse was found by the police and then identified by her brother. She had been strangled, so had died shortly after the laundry trip. Christie had left his job on 6 December, and then sold his wife's wedding ring on 17 December. He then told different people different stories as to why his wife was absent. He told his in-laws that she was still alive and forged her signature to gain access to the money in her savings account. He was also seen putting disinfectant in the house on a daily basis. In March 1953 Christie sub-let his rooms to Mr and Mrs Reilly and left, staying first at Rowton House, then wandering until his arrest near Putney Bridge on 31 March.[5]

Heald then concluded the summary with these words of analysis:

> Now, if we just pause there to take stock for a moment to consider what it amounts to so far, here is a man whose wife disappears while they are living alone in the flat, and her body is found three and a half months later hidden under the floor in the place where they were living alone together, in a condition which is consistent with strangulation, and there is the clearest evidence that the husband had been engaged in an elaborate series of deceptions clearly intended to conceal her death and to suggest that she had gone on ahead in preparation for a move from London by both of them. If there were nothing else at all in this case except that against Christie, you might well think that it looks very black indeed ... there is much more serious evidence here.[6]

This 'more serious evidence' lay principally in that not only did Christie not deny the charge, but he also admitted to it. Heald then read out part of Christie's confession of 31 March, but Heald was careful to include only that part of the statement which referred to the murder of Ethel. He pointed out that the pills Christie referred to as being taken by his wife had not been. Apart from that, though, 'It is entirely consistent with the medical evidence both as regards the approximate date of death and as regards the cause of death'. He added, 'can you have any possible doubt that Christie deliberately killed his wife on the morning of 14th December?' The jury was also reminded that there was no such thing as a 'mercy killing', which was what Christie said was the reason for the murder of his wife. There was also no need for the jury to find a motive for murder; the establishment of intent was enough.[7]

Finally, Heald tried to pre-empt what the defence might say: 'they have to show, as a matter of reasonable probability, to your satisfaction that at the time the murder was committed the accused man was suffering from such a disease or disorder of the mind that either he did not know what he was doing or that he did not know what he was doing was an illegal act.'[8]

A number of witnesses were then called for the prosecution. PC Watson explained the geography of the house and Chief Inspector Law showed photographs of the corpse and where it had been found. Law was asked by Curtis-Bennett about the discovery of the other bodies in the kitchen cupboard, because the defence argued that the other killings were important in understanding that of Ethel. He did so. Photographs of the skeletons found in the garden were also exhibited.[9]

Christie's last employer, Mr Burrows, was called and gave him a good reference and confirmed his date of leaving. Rosina Swan recalled last seeing Ethel in early December and Christie's excuses for her absence afterwards. Charlotte Barton reported last seeing her at the laundry on 12 December and her brother spoke of identifying her corpse on 26 March. Lily Bartle identified Christie's handwriting on the Christmas card of 15 December. Judith Green recounted buying a wedding ring from Christie on 17 December and Robert Hookway of purchasing the furniture in the following month. Frederick Snow told how he had received a letter purporting to be from Ethel asking to close her account with the bank. Evidence was given that Christie put disinfectant in the passageway. The Reillys spoke of subletting the rooms from Christie in March 1953. Finally, evidence was given of Christie booking into Rowton House.[10]

Various policemen then gave statements. PC Ledger told how he arrested Christie. Detective Inspector William Baker related how Christie arrived at Putney Police Station on 31 March. Griffin spoke of finding Ethel's corpse and then attending Putney Police Station to take a statement from Christie. This statement was then read out in court, when Christie spoke of killing his wife and his last three victims. Griffin was then asked about the discovery of the corpses in the kitchen cupboard, about the murder of Beryl and Geraldine Evans and Christie's alleged involvement. The final question of that day in court was, 'When the trial of Evans was going on in this very Court, there were lying, in all probability, in the garden of 10 Rillington Place, two skeletons?' To which Griffin answered, 'Probably'.[11]

On this day and the next Christie was placed on special watch, presumably because suicide was feared, but these concerns proved needless.

The second day of the trial took place on the following day. Griffin once more stood in the witness box, to be cross-examined by Curtis-Bennett, who resumed on the topic of the Evans murders. He quickly moved on to the skeletons of Ruth Fuerst and Muriel Eady. The Clerk of the Court read out Christie's statement of 5 June about his killing them. Griffin was asked about the discovery of the glass jar with the two tubes which Christie had used, along with gas, to render Muriel unconscious. Then the Clerk read out Christie's statement of 7 June relating to his murder of Beryl Evans. There was then some discussion between the judge and Curtis-Bennett over who had killed Beryl and Geraldine. The latter said, 'If my learned friend is asking me to make plain that Christie did not kill Mrs Evans, I am going to try and make plain the reverse'.[12]

Medical evidence was then called for, beginning with that of Dr Odess. He referred to Christie's ailments in the late 1940s and early 1950s, including enteritis, fibrositis and nervous debility. He had been prescribed tablets for insomnia. The doctor summed up his patient as 'a nervous type and he had fits of crying, sobbing; he complained of insomnia, and headaches and giddiness'. In 1950 he had attacks of amnesia and was unable to work. He mentioned that Ethel was also 'a nervous type' and had been given sedatives. He also said that Christie was recommended to go for psychiatric interrogation in 1952, but refused to go to the hospital.[13]

Dr Camps spoke next. He gave evidence of the discovery of Ethel's corpse on 24 March. Curtis-Bennett asked about the three other victims, and Camps spoke of their having been gassed and strangled, and there being evidence of intercourse. He was also asked about the two skeletons found in the garden. Nickolls was then asked about the victims. He spoke of the four tufts of hair from the tin, stating that one tuft might have come from the skeletons in the garden, but that the others were not from any of the four most recent corpses, nor from Beryl Evans (certainly not at the time of her death).[14]

The last witness to be called was Alexander Baker. He was asked by Curtis-Bennett about his meeting with Christie in the company of Hectorina MacLennan. He said that he had smelt nothing untoward during his stay at 10 Rillington Place.[15]

Curtis-Bennett then began the opening speech for the defence thus:

> Members of the jury, it now becomes my duty to address you for the first time in the defence of the accused man, who (as I have already made quite plain, I hope) is not asking at your hands a verdict of not guilty. That has never been the position here at all. He is asking at your hands, under the direction of his lordship when you have heard all the evidence, to return what is called a special verdict of guilty of the act as charged, but insane at the time; in other words, guilty but insane, as it is called.[16]

What insanity meant was then discussed. Only a certain type of insanity was recognised by law, not the everyday use of the word used when someone does something odd or uncharacteristic. Christie had been gassed in the First World War, 'I do not suppose you will think that did him much good'. Curtis-Bennett said that when considering his sanity, all his victims must be taken into account. 'This is a man who for years now has had periods of insanity ... which takes the form of killing women'. There had been seven women killed over a period of ten years, 1943–53 and so, 'on the face of it, without any medical evidence whatever, he must be, in my submission, a maniac and a madman'.[17]

The McNaghten Rules of 1843 were still the basic standard by which the law recognised insanity. If a man could prove that he acted without knowing what he was doing, or without knowing that what he was doing was wrong, he was classified as insane. Curtis-Bennett pointed out that Christie's actions were definitely without reason. He illustrated this by referring to his having tried to conceal so many corpses in such a small space of ground and then letting the place when the new tenants might have easily discovered them. Then he went to Rowton House, registering himself under his own name and address where anyone might find and apprehend him. Dr Odess had recommended Christie psychiatric treatment. The Evans case was also recalled, with the implication that Christie killed Beryl as he had said he had. Curtis-Bennett also indicated the unlikely coincidence of two killers in the same house, 'there were two stranglers in this tiny house

... where there is not enough room to swing a cat in the kitchen. That may seem to you to be extraordinary'. Curtis-Bennett then introduced Christie himself into the witness box, with the following remarks, 'Now this man at this moment will go into the witness box and tell his terrifying story ... I suggest to you now that by the time he has finished although you may think he is sane now, you can have no doubt ... that at the time he did each of these killings, including that of his wife, he was mad in the eyes of the law.'[18]

The man in the dock was variously described by two journalists. One said that he entered the court 'briskly and without trepidation'. He added that he detected a slight pride in his voice when he described, after he left 10 Rillington Place, seeing a newspaper headline about him. According to him, Christie seemed 'a weird character'. Another journalist thought he was 'a worried looking, insignificant little mouse of a man ... a sad little monster'. He added that Christie's voice was quiet and had a slight Scottish accent. Another said he was hesitant, nervous and mumbled quietly. He spoke for three hours.[19]

Christie gave a brief account of his life. However, once he reached the questions about his first murder, he began to be vague. On asked about his meeting Ruth, he answered, 'I just don't recollect. It has gone out of my mind'. When asked about sex with her, he said, 'I am not sure' and about her intentions, 'I just cannot recollect'. He was asked about strangling her and replied, 'I do not know whether I was doing it'. Was she his first victim? 'I think so. I don't know'.[20]

He was then asked questions about the murder of Muriel Eady and the device he used to gas her. He was then asked about any murders he might have committed between 1944 and 1949 and he replied, 'I don't know' and when asked what he meant he said, 'I might have done. I don't know whether I did or not'. Christie continued in this vague way, 'At times I have got something in my mind and I cannot get it out. I have had that for years'. Christie was asked about the Evanses. He alleged that he found Beryl trying to commit suicide using gas. He said he revived her, but on the following day she pleaded with him to help her end her own life by that same method. He said he agreed. Apparently when she lay down on the quilt:

> When she laid down there was a piece of gas tubing that I put to her face, a piece of gas piping going down the side of the fireplace with a tap that had been used, I think, for a gas stove at one time, and I attached this piece of tube and then brought it down near

her face ... When she was unconscious, I believe – I think I strangled her then.[21]

When Evans returned, Christie explained that his wife had committed suicide, but that he would be suspected of murder because of the well-known quarrels between them. They took the body to Kitchener's rooms and that was the last he saw of the body. Apparently Evans suggested he could dispose of the corpse in his van. Christie was asked if he killed Geraldine, but he denied this. His statement at the previous trial, denying responsibility for both murders, was mentioned and Christie merely answered by saying that he had not killed Geraldine. He was asked why he had not mentioned the murder of Ruth, Muriel and Beryl in his initial statement of 31 March and he replied that he had simply forgotten all about them.[22]

Christie was then taken through the arrival of the new tenants after 1950, then his murder of his wife. He was quizzed about the tablets he claimed his wife had taken, as there was no evidence that she had done so. He was asked about writing and signing the letter and card to Ethel's sister, which purported to show that she was still alive, and Christie admitted he had done all he was accused of. The judge asked, 'Why were you doing that?' Christie replied, 'I do not think at the time I was realizing that she had gone'. So ended the second day of the trial.[23]

The third day of the trial was Wednesday 24 June 1953. Christie took his place in the witness box and Curtis-Bennett's examination continued. He was asked about the last three murders, and he gave the same version that he had on 31 March. As on the previous day, when pressed on a number of points he was vague and apparently forgetful. When asked if he had sex with Kathleen, he replied, 'Well, I am not quite certain. I don't remember, really'. He was asked why he had killed her, but all he could say was, 'I do not think I know', and this applied to all these three women. 'No, there was no reason. There is no sense'.[24]

Rita Nelson's case was then discussed, and again he claimed to be uncertain about what he had done or why. When asked about motive, he replied, 'I did not want to hurt her. I have never hurt anybody'. He was asked about how he had disposed of the body and answered thus, 'Well, I just do not know'. When pressed about the body being found with the others in the cupboard, the answer was 'Yes, I was told later that it was, but I do not remember it'. When asked whether he murdered Hectorina, he said, 'Well, I don't know, but I must have done'. Again, he forgot about putting her into the cupboard, so he said, and about the return of Baker.[25]

Christie was then asked about the period since he sub-let his rooms to the Reillys. He was vague about what he did in these weeks and said he did not consciously think about leaving them in a house with four corpses. He recalled his visit to Rowton House, wandering about London and his arrest and arrival at Putney Police Station. He was asked about the statements he had subsequently made and whether he had killed anyone other than the seven he had admitted to and again he was unhelpful: 'I do not remember. If somebody said I did, well, I must have done'.[26]

He was then asked about his last job and his leaving of it. He was questioned about his attempts to conceal from the neighbours and Lily the fact of Ethel's death (about which he wept openly). He admitted to writing what he had and what he had said. But when asked why he had acted thus, he was characteristically evasive, with phrases such as 'I do not remember' and 'I may have said anything'. He eventually agreed that he had killed his wife 'to put her out of her misery'. When asked if he must have known he was doing wrong by trying to conceal the death, he replied, 'Well, I did not look at it that I had done anything wrong; I never gave it a thought that way'. The Attorney General then asked: 'Christie, if on 14th December when you killed your wife in the bedroom there had been a policeman there, you would not have done it, would you?'

Christie replied 'I don't suppose so. That's obvious'.[27]

Curtis-Bennett then took Christie through his putting disinfectant down. He asked him about whether he thought the murders were wrong and answered 'Definitely I did not'. Did he know that he had killed people when he was doing so? 'No, I do not think that I did. I am certain that I did not'. The Attorney General intervened to ask about the fact that in the previous trial he had denied killing Beryl but now he admitted it.

'You have sworn two things which are opposed to another about it?'

'Yes'.

'How do you expect the jury to believe you?'

There was no answer and that was the end of Christie's appearance as witness.[28]

Curtis-Bennett's second witness was called. This was Dr Hobson. He was first asked about Christie's medical history. His war wounds, his traffic accidents and then the state of his mental health in 1950–52 were discussed. Hobson stated that Christie was suffering from hysteria. According to him:

> I feel that throughout he has been unable to remember things. He has falsely remembered things. I feel that most of the time this falsification of memory or this forgetting resulted from this hysteria, from his disease of the mind. I think that most of the time he did indeed forget and did not know that there was some purpose in his forgetting. At other times, of course, he has also lied.[29]

Hobson was asked about Christie's feelings towards pubs:

> There is little doubt that at times Christie has been in public houses, but he himself is very indignant at this suggestion. He was more upset at this piece of evidence in the lower court than by the suggestions of his killing. He feels that going into public houses is something very disgusting, and very morally wrong, and he strongly denies that he has been in public houses. He still denies that it was in a public house that he met Maloney.[30]

Hobson told of his conversations with Christie, which he described as rambling, but he added that contradictions and lies were only 'to preserve his own self respect, to preserve this fictitious aura which he has of himself, rather than to avoid incriminating himself'. When asked if Christie was truthful in saying he did not know what he was doing was illegal, Hobson replied, 'I think it is very possible. I think it is probable ... it is most likely that at this time the possibility of it being wrong would be blotted from his mind'. He was asked in more detail about Christie's murder of his wife:

> I feel that most of this forgetting is an unconscious mechanism, and is more to prevent himself feeling ashamed rather than to avoid incriminating himself. This seems to be true, in that, as much as Christie can love anyone, he loved his wife and it would be intolerable to him if he were to realize that his killing of her was similar to the killing of these other women, and it is, therefore, likely to be more difficult to get him to remember the true facts

about his wife than about the women with whom he had no emotional link-up.[31]

Christie's mental disease may have stemmed from his being gassed, and his 'abnormal feeling of fascination in seeing bodies' originated from seeing his maternal grandfather's body at an early age and the corpses he saw in wartime. 'I think he got some feeling of satisfaction in continuing to live in Rillington Place with the dead bodies'. Christie's youthful sexual humiliation and his collection of pubic hairs were also mentioned. The Attorney General asked whether it would be correct to simply say that Christie was mad, and Hobson agreed. However, Hobson could not explain what drove Christie to kill, although he rejected the view that Christie had killed his wife as a 'mercy killing'. The Attorney General concluded his cross examination thus:

> 'When you say he tells a convenient story, or forgets conveniently, do you mean he really does forget or not?'
> 'Yes, he really does forget'.
> 'And in that way, in your view it is very probable that he did not know that what he was doing was wrong at the time that he did it?'
> 'Yes'.

That concluded the case for the defence.[32] The Attorney General was allowed to call medical evidence which attempted to rebut that given for the defence. First on the stand was Dr Matheson. He was asked about Christie's medical history and said that Christie was an intelligent man, and that he suffered from anxiety, not insanity. He said 'He is a man of weak character; he is immature – certainly in his sex life he is immature; he is a man who, in difficult times and in face of problems, tends to exaggerate in an hysterical fashion'.[33]

There was discussion of Ethel's death and Matheson was asked whether Christie had shown emotion at this, and he said, 'He did; his voice fell, and his eyes were filled with tears which overflowed'. Matheson was asked about Christie's memory:

> I found at my interviews that his memory of general topics and topics which do not affect him as regards the alleged charges was quite good, the volume and tone of his voice was quite good and he could speak quite fluently and rationally, but when it came to the circumstances of the alleged offences I found that at first, for

the first part of the story, his memory was quite good and he spoke quite freely, but when it came to what might be incriminating facts as to the actual circumstances of the killing he became vague and started saying: 'Well, it must have been so,' 'I think it must have been that,' 'I can't be certain,' 'I can't remember'.[34]

Matheson put Christie's lack of memory down to his not wanting to say anything which would damage his case, adding that this was not uncommon in criminals. He thought Christie was perfectly sane, though hysterical, 'I think he knew the nature and quality of his acts. In my opinion he knew at the time he was doing those acts that it was against the law'. His behaviour in the witness box was consistent with how he had been during the interviews in prison.[35]

Curtis-Bennett then cross examined Matheson, who agreed that Christie displayed hysterical symptoms, but that he was not a 'gross hysteric' as Hobson suggested. This was an important distinction because the latter is a disease of the mind and the former is not. They agreed that Christie was abnormal (to kill seven people and have sex with some of them when unconscious), but not that he was necessarily insane. Matheson argued that Christie knew what he was doing.[36]

Dr Curran was the next medical witness called by the prosecution, who concluded thus:

> I would classify him certainly as an inadequate personality with hysterical features, and a very extraordinary and abnormal man. I cannot myself see evidence that he was a gross hysteric; but rather that he is the possessor of an unstable personality, certainly, and that he was liable, in the past at least, to develop hysterical symptoms.[37]

Curran thought that Christie was a very abnormal character, but not one who was insane. He thought that he was a liar when it suited his case. He was an intelligent man who knew what he was doing. As with Matheson he disagreed with Hobson that Christie was hysterical. He wanted other evidence that Christie was mentally ill. 'I do not think he is suffering. I think his present reaction, abnormal as it may seem, is usual in the case of a murderer – the absence of shame and remorse at the crime'. Curran also believed the murders were planned. When asked about Hobson's differing views, Curran tended to discount them, but added that the other man might be correct in his conclusion, 'I think we make a fundamental disagreement about whether he is a gross hysteric or not'. He was asked why Christie seemed to suggest that he was not responsible for murder and Curran put it down to a capacity for self-deception. Finally the judge asked him for a motive for the murders and Curran stated: 'Again, this is speculation: I think it might be it was sadistic, but I do not think it was; I think it was because he wanted to have unconscious people to have relations with, possibly because he did not want them to know he was impotent'. The third day of the trial was now at an end. Dr Matheson noted, 'Christie appeared always alert and appeared to be well in touch with his position'.[38]

On that day Christie did not eat his dinner, claiming he disliked sandwiches, but was talkative and seemed emotional when in the witness box.

The fourth day of the trial commenced on Thursday 25 June. Curtis-Bennett gave the closing speech for the defence, 'Members of the jury, it now becomes my duty to address you for the last time at the end of this very long and exhausting case'. He began with some mild complaints he had of the prosecution and their witnesses. He stressed that the murder of Ethel could not be seen as an isolated event, but as part of a chain beginning with Christie's being gassed in 1918, and considering his ill health in more recent years. Curtis-Bennett stated, 'I am not asking you to say he [Christie] is a nice man – if I did you would soon tell me to shut up'. He also referred to the murder of Beryl and said that if Christie were not responsible for it, 'One wonders about the possibilities of there being two stranglers living in the same tiny premises in Notting Hill Gate'. Yet he also reminded the jury that they did not have to deal with the question of whether Evans had been rightly hanged or not.[39]

Curtis-Bennett then returned to the question of why Christie should murder his wife, who was apparently living happily with him. He put it thus: 'No evidence that Mrs Christie did or could have known anything. What was his motive? A woman he loves ... It is absolutely motiveless. What is the clue to it? Insanity'. He said that Christie's efforts to cover up the murder were due to the 'instinct of self-preservation'. An instance of insanity was when Baker and Hectorina stayed with him, 'The man is crazy, is he not, if he allows two decent people to sleep in the kitchen next door to two bodies and the other body in the front room?' Likewise his sub-letting of corpse-filled rooms and his arriving at Rowton House under his real name and address were also mentioned as evidence of a man who was insane.

He ridiculed the idea that Christie was sane, 'There is this man living day by day with these dead people in the garden slowly rotting away, rotting away to skeletons; the bodies in the cupboard becoming more and more rotten ... and it is said that this man is sane within the meaning of the law'.[40]

There was some discussion of the doctors' evidence. Naturally that of Hobson was said to have proved that Christie was insane. Curtis-Bennett said that Matheson could not be certain about Christie's mental state, using words such as 'possibly' and 'probably'. He stated that Matheson and Hobson virtually agreed with one another. He was dismissive of Curran because the latter claimed he had not seen enough of Christie to come to a definitive verdict.[41]

The final appeal to the jury was formed of a series of rhetorical questions:

> what man who is not mad goes about strangling women and having intercourse with them after death? What man keeps collections of pubic hairs who is not mad? What man who in fact has gone through a period of three and a half years when he is unable to speak is not starting on the road to insanity? What man could leave the bodies in that house and let the premises to people who ought to have smelt it in five minutes who is not an insane man? What man goes around afterwards covered in identification marks who is not mad? ... I ask from you at the end of this case that you should find this man guilty of the act but insane at the time.[42]

It was now time for the closing speech for the prosecution. The Attorney General stressed that to find Christie guilty they must rely on the proof offered by the prosecution. He also referred to the disagreements by the doctors, though, of course, he urged the jury to prefer the evidence of Matheson and Curran over that of Hobson. He reminded them that the two former insisted that Christie knew that he was doing wrong when he committed murder. He also pointed out that Christie gave 'his evidence yesterday in thoroughly intelligent and intelligible way' and admitted that had there been a policeman in sight when he killed his wife he would not have done it.[43]

Reference was made to the trial of Neville Heath, who had killed two women in 1946 for sadistic sexual reasons and whose defence was insanity. This was rejected and there was no appeal. The Attorney General noted, 'sexual perversion is not necessarily insanity'. He added that it was not necessary to find a motive, 'It was a deliberate killing, and in the absence of insanity, it is murder'. He did suggest that there might be many reasons between a married couple which were unknown to anyone else which might lead to murder. Insanity was thus not the only possible answer. He added that the case of the murder of Beryl was not relevant at this point.[44]

Finally, he urged the jury to remember the McNaghten Rules about whether the accused was aware of what he was doing and whether he knew it was wrong. He concluded: 'it is my duty to submit to you that the Defence has not established as a reasonable probability that Christie was insane within the meaning of the McNaghten Rules at the time when he killed his wife'.[45]

It was now time for the judge to make his charge to the jury. He told them that their decision must be unanimous in this 'difficult task and an unpleasant task'. He said that the onus was for the Crown to show that the accused was guilty. In this case it was easy, because the defence did not dispute that he had killed his wife. The judge recounted the events leading up to the murder of Ethel and the events following it. He then reminded the jury, 'the Defence do not challenge that at all, they accept all that. They say the answer to this charge is a plea of insanity'. The judge tried to define insanity, pointing out that it was not used legally in the same way of common parlance, nor did it equate with abnormality, perversion or sadism. Rather adherence to the McNaghten Rules was the key. These assumed that everyone was sane unless proved otherwise. The criminal must be proved to have been suffering from a mental disease.[46]

'Reasonable probability' one way or the other was the jury's task. They had to study the witness evidence and decide for themselves. No one else could do that for them. The prosecution argued, he said, that Christie was odd, forgot matters dangerous to himself and planned his murders, whereas the defence argued the murder was motiveless, rationally speaking, and that Christie was an ill man. The judge took the jury through Christie's crimes from 1921–53. The judge suggested that Christie seemed to have been aware of his actions and that his covering them up was not due to a horror of what he had done. Just because his actions were cruel and wicked did not mean he was insane.[47]

The judge discussed the conflicting medical evidence about Christie's mental state, reminding the jury that all three doctors were experienced and respected members of their profession:

You are not bound to accept Dr Curran's view, you are not bound to accept Dr Matheson's view, you are not bound to accept Dr Hobson's view; you will consider them all and then consider the whole of the circumstances of this case, the whole of the evidence we have had, the evidence of the man himself and the history of the crimes, and then consider the one question you have to ask yourselves: is it reasonably probable that when he killed his wife, Mrs Christie, he was suffering from the disease of the mind producing a defect of reason so that if he knew what he was doing he did not know that it was wrong? ... Hold the scales of justice equally and decide solely on the view you have formed on the evidence that has been given before you over the last few days in the witness box.[48]

The jury of nine women and three men retired at five past four (Christie asked about the Test match scores in the interval) and returned eighty minutes later.

The Clerk of the Court asked:

'Do you find the prisoner at the Bar, John Reginald Halliday Christie, guilty or not guilty?'

'We find him guilty'

'You find him guilty, and that is the verdict of you all?'

'It is the verdict of us all.'

'Prisoner at the Bar, you stand convicted of murder; have you anything to say before judgement of death is passed according to law?'

Christie said nothing, but shook his head. The formal sentence of death was then passed.[49]

At this, it was noted, 'Christie received the verdict and sentence without any display of emotion' and he later said, 'The newspapers cannot say that I fainted or made a scene in the dock'. However, his knuckles were white as he gripped the edge of the bar before him, he compressed his lips and gave a slight shudder. Dr Matheson observed, 'He was affable and polite and showed no anxiety nor distress'. This is in contrast to his anger at Heaney, who tapped Christie on the shoulder during an adjournment in the trial, 'Downstairs, please'. Christie shouted, 'Take your bloody hands off me'. He later repented, 'I'm sorry, sir, I just had an outbreak of temper'. Nothing unusual occurred in the rest of the day and Christie showed no further sign of emotion.[50]

After the trial, Christie made a remark to Joseph Roberts, a hospital officer. It was potentially very significant, because all throughout the last few months, he had denied any involvement in Geraldine's murder, telling one Walter Williams, 'I haven't killed Mrs Evans' child and I would like to know who spread the rumour around'. He said to Roberts, 'If the police only knew they could also charge me with the murder of Evans' baby girl'. When pressed on the truth of the matter, he continued, 'more or less as far as I can remember, but they can't do anything about it now'. He suggested Roberts sell the story to the press and make a little money out of it.[51]

No appeal was made, so Christie's days were numbered, but it was not quite the end.

Chapter 12

Execution and Enquiries
1953–66

'I hanged John Reginald Christie, the monster of
Rillington Place, in less time than it took the ash
to fall off a cigar'.[1]

Christie did not have long to live. But now a new question loomed. Christie was a murderer of women by strangulation. It seemed hard to believe that there could be two stranglers of women living under the same roof. Had an innocent man been sent to the gallows? This was a question on the lips of some in politics, the legal and journalistic professions, to say nothing of the Evans family themselves.

After the trial, Christie was sent to Pentonville. Joseph Roberts was amongst those accompanying him and he recalled, 'there was a slight public demonstration against Christie, people booing him and calling him foul names. This shook him up a little and he remarked, "How disgusting some people are"'. From then on two prison warders maintained a daily vigil on his cell.[2]

In prison, a reporter stated, 'Christie is calm, talks cheerfully to his guards and sometimes plays cards with them. He is eating and sleeping well'. He often read books from the prison library, mostly on technical subjects. He recalled his murderous career:

I have flagrantly broken one of God's foremost laws ... I have always succumbed to a dark sinister force which has never allowed me to be at peace. Thou shalt not kill is the commandment that has haunted me all my life. I have broken this commandment so many times that I cannot be sure how many women have died at my hands.

He also wrote:

All my life I never experienced fear or horror at the sight of a corpse. On the contrary, I have seen many and they hold an interest, a fascination over me ... That for years I had to kill just twelve women and then my work would be finished and I would continue for a further period. There was just some unknown urging me to do it and compelling me to go on ... after she [Ethel] had gone the whole business seemed to come to the fore again. How and under what circumstances didn't enter the picture after number five, six ... It did occur to me as I looked on my gruesome handiwork, that I was gradually reaching the twelve mark. It would then be all I was expected to do ... to me there was nothing gruesome about it. It still does not strike me that way.

Yet he also affected modesty, 'I am a quiet humble man who hates rows or trouble. I love animals. I am fond of children ... I am the sort of chap you would never look twice at on a bus'.[3]

Christie's time in gaol was not at all bad. In his cell was a bed, a table, a chair, a shelf for his books, and he was allowed an hour's exercise each day. He was guarded day and night, but looked on his end with calm, 'I am not afraid' he claimed. He wrote, 'The food is good and all possible facilities are given'. There was a 'liberal allowance of cigarettes and the food is good ... really well cooked and plentiful. I am even putting on weight'. All his life he had been a heavy smoker.[4]

Christie also saw extracts from his autobiographical writings published in *The Sunday Pictorial* in several editions in July 1953. The accounts of his murders differed a little from some of his earlier statements, but he wrote 'This is the correct version'. Such writings are common among notorious criminals. They write them in order to portray themselves to the public in the way they want to be remembered, and as a means of justifying their actions. Christie portrayed himself as a victim of his father and of cruel fellows, as a friend to animals and children and as a model husband, but showed no shred of sympathy for his victims.[5]

Meanwhile, in the real world, Sir David Maxwell-Fyfe, Home Secretary, appointed John Scott-Henderson, QC, to examine the case and to report on whether there were any grounds for thinking there might have been a miscarriage of justice. He was assisted in his work by George Blackburn, Assistant Chief Constable of the West Riding of Yorkshire. Neither had been involved in the case up to this point.[6]

From 8–10 July Scott-Henderson heard evidence from twenty-three people, including Christie.[7]

The enquiry then went through the evidence that Evans did indeed kill his wife, considering the confessions he had made at Notting Hill, evidence of mounting debts and problems within the marriage as well as physical evidence and reports by doctors and psychiatrists. Scott-Henderson noted, 'I am therefore satisfied that there was a great deal of evidence to support Evans' account of his confession'. He also thought that the method of disposal was similar to that used by Donald Hume. Both had bundled up their victims' corpses with cloth tied with cord.[8]

Perhaps the most important part of this investigation was the interview with Christie. This took place on 9 July at Pentonville. Christie seemed agreeable to talk, as it made him feel important. He said that many people had been 'trying to help' him remember about the people he had killed. He was as non-committal in his responses as ever; when asked about Hobson's visits to him, he replied, 'He just called, and I was asked if I wished to see him, and I was not compelled to see him. I said that if it was in the interests of the case I would certainly see him'.[9]

Christie tried to show that his memory had been problematic:

I was very fogged about everything and I asked him for his assistance. I asked him to help me, and anything which he said or he mentioned that had happened at times was just for the benefit of trying to get me to recollect for the purposes of the defence, because as I stood at the time I could not have remembered anything practically, and I had to be helped ... Inspector Griffin ... told me that some bodies had been found, and I did not even know then about the case until he said, 'You must have been responsible for it, because they were found in the kitchen in an alcove' and so he said 'There is no doubt about it that you have done it'. So I turned round and said 'Well, if that is the case I must have done it' but I did not know whether I had or I had not. From what he said it was very obvious that I must have done it.[10]

Christie claimed not to recall the murders, but said that he would accept that he had done them if people told them that he had, 'They said I must have done it'. He carried on in this vein for some time, even talking about 'the moment I get out of here'. He was also asked about other murders:

'I think that you said something about them asking you to think about a case at Windsor [the murder of Christine Butcher in July

1952]; was that one of the cases that they asked you to think about?'

'The question they asked me was, had I visited Windsor recently. I said emphatically that I had not been to Windsor for years. At that interview it was not mentioned to me at all why that question was asked, not until the following interview. In the meantime I think it had dawned on me about the Sugar Ray Robinson business, and then it just struck me: "Well, that is why I was asked about Windsor."'

'That was a murder case, was it?'

'It was a little girl, but anyhow I had not been to Windsor. I advised them to make investigations as to where I was at the time, and it would obviously have been proved that I could not have been at Windsor'.

Christie also said, 'Mine were all adults'. The conversation continued:

'In regard to Windsor it was not a question of thinking hard and then you might remember but you knew enough to know that you could not possibly have been there?'

'Well, as far as I know, that is correct'.

'Were there other cases – we need not go into details – but did they mention other deaths, and want to know whether you could remember anything about them?'

'I cannot remember that'.[11]

Christie was then asked about whether he was responsible for the deaths of Beryl and Geraldine. He was equivocal about the former, stating, 'Well, I am not sure' and 'Well, I cannot say whether I was or not'. When pressed, he replied, with the same apparent lack of memory as before: 'It is not a case of whether I am prepared to or not. I just cannot unless I was telling some lie or other about them. It is still fogged, but if someone said: "Well, it is obvious you did, and there is enough proof about it" then I accept that I did'.

Christie was asked again about other murders, and replied, 'Well, I could not say that I did. I should accept that I did'. Without proof brought before him, however, he was 'not prepared to swear either way'. However, he also said that if there were any other murders committed by him 'It would not surprise me'. When asked about the hairs in the tin, he replied, 'I have tried hard to think whether there were other bodies but seem to think that it is possible. Those hairs in the tin lead me to think that, but I have no clear recollection'.[12]

Scott-Henderson considered that Christie's confession about Beryl was incorrect, partly because it was uncorroborated and because he changed his mind as to whether he had killed her or not. He related a conversation with the prison chaplain, who stated that Christie used the phrase, 'The more, the merrier'. 'I am satisfied that Christie gradually came to the conclusion that it would be helpful in his defence if he confessed to the murder of Mrs Evans'. Therefore, as to his confession, 'I am satisfied that they are not only not reliable but that they are untrue'.[13]

On 13 July, Scott-Henderson summarised his findings thus:

(1) The case for the Prosecution against Evans as presented to the jury at his trial was an overwhelming one.
(2) Having considered all material now available relating to the deaths of Mrs Evans and Geraldine Evans I am satisfied that there can be no doubt that Evans was responsible for both.
(3) Christie's statements that he was responsible for the death of Mrs Evans were not only unreliable but were untrue.[14]

Reference has been made to Christie's possible killing of Christine Vivian Butcher, a young girl (never solved), largely based on a photograph taken at Windsor on the day of the murder of a bald-headed man in a crowd, but also because he was deemed 'a sexual pervert' and the girl had been raped. Yet it was concluded, 'Enquiries have been made into all the known information obtained about Christie, but no evidence has been disclosed which might associate him and the deaths of any persons other than those already referred to'. In fact, the bald-headed man was traced and it was not Christie. Furthermore, Christie's description did not match that of the man last seen with the girl, nor was there any evidence he had been to Windsor, nor that he molested children.[15]

In some ways, Christie was unchanged. Dr Matheson noted, 'He has not shown any alteration in his behaviour from what he has shown throughout the period in which he has been under observation at Brixton Prison'.[16]

A board of doctors had to examine Christie and determine whether he was sane enough to be hanged. The statement included the following conclusions that he was:

cool, calculating and plausible. No reliance could be put upon his statements and he was an intentional liar ... He showed no remorse and had spoken of no one in terms of affection ... conceited, cool, cunning, alert, bad tempered and vicious criminal ... We have no reason to believe that he is a necrophiliac and he denies the suggestion that he is a sadist ... We do however incline to the view that sadism is a part of his mental make up and may be connected with some of the murders but this is little more than an assumption.[17]

Dennis Hague, his old wartime comrade, wrote to him, asking if he was the same Christie he had known four decades ago. Hague was hoping that Christie would be given a reprieve, 'in which case I shall always be pleased as an old comrade of the Sherwood Foresters to pay you a visit'. Christie wrote, 'I was very happy to receive your pleasant letter. It was a surprise and just demonstrates that one begins to know one's friends in times of adversity'. Hague asked permission to see his old comrade, and this was granted. Before the visit he wrote to Christie on 3 July, 'I was very pleased to hear that you still have the smile which I always knew you to wear in the days gone by'. The two were reunited on 13 July, for half an hour, and spent much of it reminiscing about the war. Hague later said, 'I saw a lonely, broken man. Christie is dejected, utterly dejected. I don't think he realises what he has done'. Christie said, 'I don't care what happens now. I have nothing left to live for'. Towards the end of this time, Hague asked him if he had killed Geraldine and Christie was suitably vague, 'I don't know, I can't remember'. He then gave a sly look and blinked. Apparently this was signalling code for 'yes'. 'I consider Christie killed the Evans baby' concluded Hague, but there was some doubt over the exact meaning of the blinking. Apart from Hague, only Phyllis Clarke visited him in prison. She did so on the eve of his execution and found her brother in good spirits. He explained, 'Don't worry about the morning. They won't hurt me. They'll take my glasses off before they hang me so I won't see much'. George Rogers requested to see him alone, but Christie refused.[18]

A less sympathetic correspondent was Evans's mother. She wrote on 2 July and urged him to confess all, 'it may save your soul from Hell and it will give me the peace of mind I have not had for three years past'. The press, too, were harsh in their references, 'the bald headed bigot', 'the most ghoulish murderer of all time', 'just a nobody with a twisted mind' and 'he had no conscience about much at all'.[19]

In the meantime, Christie was preparing to meet his maker. Ever since the First World War he had not been a particularly religious man. Now he took a fresh interest in the faith of his youth. The Anglican chaplain at the prison since 1948 was the Reverend William George Morgan. He had two conversations with Christie. Christie denied killing Geraldine and was pretty certain that he had not killed Beryl either. Christie used the phrase 'the more, the merrier' at one of these interviews. In late June he attended a church service, with two warders, and sat in an alcove near to the altar.[20]

As with Evans, there was to be no reprieve and on 13 July the Commissioner of Police received a letter containing the ominous phrase, that the Home Secretary had 'failed to discover any sufficient ground to justify him in advising Her Majesty to interfere with the due course of law'. On the following day, Christie made a will. He left almost everything to Phyllis Clarke. The photographs of his wife were willed to her sister, along with the marriage certificate. He ended the will with the following understatement, '... and an apology for any trouble I may have brought about'. On the 14th the governor visited him in case there were any last words; apparently there were not.[21]

The next day was Christie's last. Despite his aversion to alcohol, he had a drink before his death. The execution took place at 9.00am on 15 July 1953. Pierrepoint described the scene:

Christie had his back to the door when I went in. He was listening with a tight lipped little sneer to the low consoling words of the chaplain ... I hanged John Reginald Christie, the monster of Rillington Place, in less time than it took the ash to fall off a cigar. I had left my room at Pentonville. As I motioned towards (the execution chamber) all Christie's face seemed to melt. It was more than terror. I think it was not that he was afraid of the act of execution. He had lived with and gloated upon corpses. But I knew in that moment that John Reginald Christie would have given anything in his power to postpone the moment of detail. My assistant and I had his skimpy wrists pinioned before he knew fully what was happening, and then he rose to his feet, a little taller than I was, so that I had to reach up to remove his spectacles. In that instant I met his eyes and quite slowly pulled off his glasses, laying them carefully upon the scrubbed bone table besides me. This was his last moment to speak. He blinked bewilderingly, screwing up his eyes. Then he focussed them on the door that stood open between the condemned cell and the execution chamber.

I had watched him in the prison yard the evening before and he had not seemed downcast there. He had come striding between his two death watch officers ... His eyes glinted sharply behind spectacles, the big domed head with his carefully combed wisps of hair were so familiar. But his hair was uncombed now, and he was paying no heed to vanity ... Faltering pitifully, his movements were not so much a walk, as a drifting forward, his legs stumbling. I thought he was going to faint.

There was only a half stride to reach the trapdoor. Pierrepoint pulled the lever to open it and pushed Christie forward and to his death. The death certificate gave cause of death thus, 'injuries to central nervous system following judicial hanging.' He was the last serial killer to be executed in England.[22]

Christie was buried within the prison, as Evans had been in 1950. On death, Christie was 5 feet 8 inches tall and weighed 148lbs. He was aged fifty-four years, three months and one week. He was stated as being well nourished. Appropriately, perhaps, Camps carried out the autopsy. There was also an inquest. About 200–300 people, including women, schoolchildren and babies, 'laughing and jeering', came to read the notice of his execution, which was posted on the prison gates at six minutes past nine. Meanwhile, people visited 10 Rillington Place to gape. Sightseers continued for months, to the annoyance of residents. Madame Tussauds had a wax figure of Christie alongside Heath and Haigh even before Christie was dead to capitalize on this morbid curiosity, and one can still be seen there to this day, though he now stands alone, a besuited middle-aged man with hands behind his back. Some people, though, had a grudging respect for the man who had killed and had eluded the police for a decade.[23]

The inquests on Christie's victims were not complete until 27 August when that for Ruth Fuerst and Muriel Eady was finally dealt with. Both Camps and Griffin attended the inquest, where the coroner, Mr Neville Stafford, stated that although the victims were identified, no cause of death could be established, such was the lack of data provided by the skeletons. Their final resting place is unknown. Meanwhile, the bodies of Rita Nelson and Kathleen Maloney had been buried in unmarked graves at Gunnersbury Cemetery on 18 April, with a Rev. Davies officiating, and Ethel was cremated. Hectorina, whose inquest was on 9 July (as were those of Ethel, Rita and Kathleen), was buried in Gunnersbury Cemetery too, in a marked grave.[24]

Later that year, three books were published which concerned the case to varying degrees. Ronald Maxwell wrote *The Christie Case*, described as 'the only complete story of the most startling crimes of our times'. It was an account of the case from the discovery of the bodies to the passing of the death sentence, by a journalist who covered the case and attended all the court hearings. Dr Camps wrote *Medical and Scientific Aspects of the Christie Case*, which was a coolly factual forensic analysis of the corpses and skeletons found at 10 Rillington Place. Finally there was *Hanged and Innocent?* by Paget and Henry Silverman, an MP who passionately opposed capital punishment. One of the three cases examined was that of Evans. Paget concluded, 'I would say that Evans was not guilty as charged, and that this is about as certain as one can be certain of anything in human affairs'.[25] All subsequent books on this case concentrated on this issue.

After 1953 there was additional controversy. Michael Eddowes, in *The Man on your Conscience*, published in 1955, makes the case for Evans's innocence, largely based on the number of coincidences which it would be necessary to believe if Evans was indeed guilty. He concluded, 'We have come to the conclusion that ... the unpalatable truth is that Evans was innocent and because his accusation against the real killer was not believed, four more women were later to be strangled by Christie'. Eddowes thought that a number of legal reforms should be brought about; independent witnesses being present at police interviews with suspects, all evidence being given to the defence and trial transcripts being given to the public afterwards.[26]

In the lengthy introduction to the valuable book that is a transcript of the trials of Evans and Christie, Miss Fryniwyd Tennyson-Jesse, a journalist and criminologist, discusses the controversy. She is not very sympathetic towards Evans, referring to him as 'weak ... unfaithful, insensitive, quarrelsome and given to violent impulses ... a low form of life'. However, she was not certain he was a murderer as well, concluding:

> it seems to me more likely that, in the pursuit of his lust and under the guise of performing an abortion, Christie murdered Beryl

Evans, and that he murdered the baby … There are objections to this conclusion; it does not satisfy all the conditions or resolve all doubts. No explanation that I have thought of does this; each one leaves something unaccountable. I have arrived at it because it offers less obstruction to my mind than do the others, but I am fully conscious that it is not the only one.[27]

Another book, which was published in the following year, discussed both Haigh and Christie and came to a different conclusion, stating 'I think Evans killed Beryl' and 'I incline to the view that it is very probable indeed that Evans killed his baby'. She had no time for Christie, of course, who, she claimed, had a 'marked resemblance to a slice of yesterday's filleted plaice'.[28]

Heald waded into the controversy thus:

I was Attorney General at that time and I prosecuted Christie. I knew all about the case and I think Evans was guilty … My own view is that both Christie and Evans were concerned in that matter and if there was a miscarriage of justice it was this technical one that Christie was not hanged at that time. However, we put that right later.[29]

Similarly Harold Scott, the Commissioner of the Metropolitan Police, commented:

If, for a short time, it seemed to indicate a possible miscarriage of justice, in the case of Evans, this was cleared up by the searching enquiry conducted by Mr Scott-Henderson. It is still safe to say that the risk of an innocent man being executed is so remote that it can be disregarded.[30]

James Chuter Ede thought otherwise, noting about the Evans case:

the apparently cast iron case was unquestionably a false one … [had Christie been revealed as a double murderer before 1950] they might have found Evans guilty of murder in conjunction with Christie; I doubt whether they would have found Evans guilty of murder in any other circumstance … I think Evans' case shows, in spite of all that has been done since, that a mistake was made.[31]

However, it was in 1961 that the most well known and most frequently quoted book on the subject was published, and on being republished and as the source of the film later to be discussed here, it has achieved its aim of being seen as the definitive and authoritative one on the topic, but it was highly partial. This was Ludovic Kennedy's *Ten Rillington Place*. Kennedy had read Eddowes's book and was convinced by his argument. Because his book is prefaced with an open letter to the Home Secretary – stating 'I myself am wholly convinced of Evans' innocence' – with an appeal for another judicial review of the whole affair, with a view to leading to Evans's pardon, he endeavours to excuse every instance where evidence might indicate his guilt. Thus the arguments between the Evanses are merely stated as being commonplace between working-class couples. Kennedy argues that the confessions made by Evans were made under great emotional strain by a man of limited intellect, and that he was brainwashed by Christie and the police. Every benefit of the doubt is used in Evans's case, while no such benefit is offered to Christie. Kennedy admitted, 'My book was to put the case against Christie'.[32]

Kennedy's argument is that Christie offered to abort Beryl; but instead strangled her and convinced Evans that she died as a result of a botched operation, and then convinced Evans that he should not say anything to his family nor the police for he would be implicated in murder. Christie then convinced him that he would give Geraldine to a family in East Acton, but in reality strangled her, too. Because he had his wife under his thumb, she backed him up in everything he said. Because Evans was of low intelligence, he swallowed Christie's arguments and so paved the way for his own fate. It basically assumes that Evans's second confession at Merthyr Tydfil is true and that the others are fabrications. The Scott-Henderson report is taken apart by Kennedy point by point. This argument has been hugely influential.[33]

It must be emphasized that Kennedy was not aiming to write an impartial history of the murders. Rather, as he admitted during the Brabin proceedings, he was writing the case against Christie, and looked for evidence which would incriminate him.[34]

Not all were favourable. Maurice Crump, who dealt with Kennedy during his researches, commented, 'I regret to have to record that I found Mr Kennedy only interested in things which could somehow or other be construed as consistent with Evans' innocence to the exclusion of anything tending to prove guilt'. Sir Theobald Matthew, Director of Public Prosecutions, read the book and stated, 'it is a very readable reconstruction, I think, of how the crime could have been committed on the assumption that Evans was innocent; but it does not help much to determine whether he was innocent or not'. He added that Kennedy's criticisms of the Scott-Henderson Report were 'puerile and intemperate'. An even more intemperate comment came from Hume, writing in 1965 of Kennedy, 'I know him from experience to be a phoney who has used the Evans case for nothing else than to further his literary ambitions and make money out of it'. However, Kennedy did interview some of the people involved in the case and spent rather more time on Christie's life prior to 1949, but much of this was inaccurate. He portrayed Christie as a weak and inadequate man who sought power over others. In fact the book is a catalogue of factual errors and assumptions.[35]

One of Kennedy's chief contentions was that Teare had not taken a vaginal swab from Beryl, for, 'Had he done so, he would almost certainly have found traces of Christie's spermatozoa ... Here, so to speak, were Christie's fingerprints ... in the light of what we now know, it pins the crime fairly and squarely on Christie'. Teare denied that this would have been the case. Professor Simpson was scathing in his autobiography about this, and as a professional pathologist as compared to the amateur sleuth, his verdict is worth noting as to Kennedy's assumptions, 'I doubt if a more reckless overstatement can be found in all the millions of words written about the Evans-Christie case'. As to this non-evidence providing the missing link, as Simpson stated, 'It does nothing of the kind'.[36]

Kennedy's book was not the only one on to appear that year. A less well-known book, *The Two Stranglers of Rillington Place*, was published, written by one Rupert Furneaux. He had initially collaborated with Eddowes, but had disagreed with him on the book's conclusion, so each man wrote his own. His argument was the novel one that Christie and Evans worked in tandem. Evans killed Beryl and then Christie killed Geraldine. There seems little evidence for such a theory, though it was one which the Brabin report later supported. John Newton Chance, a writer of fiction, also brought out in this year (clearly a bumper year for Christie aficionados), an even more forgotten book, *The Crimes at Rillington Place: A Novelist's Reconstruction*. Here, Christie suggests that Evans 'scares' Beryl by putting a rope around her neck and tightens it, but stopping short of murder. Later Evans kills both his wife and daughter. Christie helps him to dispose of the bodies and gives him suggestions as to what he should do next.

It was in 1965 that a new independent inquiry was set up, to be conducted by Mr Justice Daniel James Brabin, a Judge of the High Court. The terms of reference were as follows:

> To examine the evidence given in the case of Rex vs Evans and that of Rex vs Christie relating to the deaths of Mrs Beryl Evans and of Geraldine Evans; to hear any witnesses and to consider any other information which is in his view relevant to these deaths; and to report such concerns as he may find it possible to form as whether Evans did or did not kill either or both.

Not everyone welcomed it. Former police sergeant Trevellian observed, 'I consider all this a waste of time because in my own mind I have every confidence from what he [Evans] told me that he was guilty'. Likewise Basil Thorley, who said in 1965, 'Why can't they leave us alone? ... I am convinced Evans was involved in my sister's death'. He based this on Evans's words to him on the day of the trial, 'I'm sorry, Baz'.[37]

The independent review took two months and seventy-nine witnesses were called. These included most of those associated with the case. A million words on 2,000 foolscap pages, in thirty-two bound volumes, were written and after January 1966 Brabin began to write the report, which was published on 12 October 1966. He concluded that Evans probably killed his wife after a quarrel over debts. He was uncertain about Christie's knowledge of this, writing, 'It is not possible to know how Christie became aware of the killing of Beryl Evans. Whether he discovered it after hearing yet another row, or whether Evans sought his help after he killed his wife, cannot be known ... Christie knew everything which went on in that small house'. He concluded that Christie would not have wanted the corpse to have been found in the house, for that would have meant the police, and as there were two skeletons of his victims in the garden, he would want to have avoided their being found. But Evans losing his job, and thus access to the van, made disposal elsewhere impossible.[38]

As to the other murder, Brabin concluded:

> I find the evidence in respect to the death of Geraldine more perplexing. I do not believe that he who killed Beryl Evans must have necessarily killed Geraldine. They were separate killings, done I think for different reasons ... I think it was more probable

than not that Christie did it. It was a killing in cold blood that Christie would be more likely to do.[39]

Brabin remarked on the coincidence:

But can one accept that to this small house in their turn there came two men, each to become a killer, each a strangler, each strangling women, always by a ligature … and neither aware that his housemate was like himself? Some claim that to suggest that this coincidence could come about is to stretch credulity too far.

As to the coincidence, it did not surprise some. Trevellian remarked, 'that point has never struck me, because Notting Dale, that part of Notting Dale, is the home of many murderers, and in those days I could very seldom find a house which was not the house of a criminal with a record'. Simpson thought likewise, remarking that 'it never seemed to me very far-fetched. Coincidences are far more common in real life than in fiction'.[40]

The enquiry had been a difficult one, as Brabin observed:

They [the Evanses and the Christies], or some of them, are the only ones who know for certain what happened in that house … The two women have been murdered and the two men executed … One fact which is not in dispute and which has hampered all efforts to find the truth is that both Evans and Christie were liars. They lied about each other, they lied about themselves.

Despite this, Brabin gave his verdict: 'I have come to the conclusion that it is more probable than not that Evans killed Beryl Evans. I have come to the conclusion that it is more probable than not that Evans did not kill Geraldine.[41]

Therefore, Evans was given a posthumous free pardon (in the previous year his remains had been reburied at the Leytonstone Cemetery). Yet had Evans been tried and hanged for Beryl's murder, the verdict would have been upheld. The Brabin report, after all, concluded that he was probably guilty of that murder, but suggested that Christie's grim tally was seven. Yet if Christie did not kill Beryl, there seems little reason for him to have killed Geraldine.

Chapter 13

Further Controversy
1966 to date

Following the Brabin Report and the rehabilitation of Evans, there were a number of semi-fictional accounts of the case, though few full-length factual studies.

In 1969, Howard Brenton brought out a short play, *Christie in Love*. It was first performed at the Portable and the parts were those of Christie and two police officers. It is entirely set in the back garden of 10 Rillington Place.[1]

Christie is portrayed as sinister but also pathetic. We first see him wearing a paper-maché mask and pulling out rubber tubing from his trousers. He tries for the sympathy of the audience, referring to being gassed in the First World War and being mute for three years there-after. An inflatable doll is then introduced by the constable and Christie shows his contempt for women, saying, 'Bloody tarts' and 'Women bring out the nastiness in me'.[2]

The doll is then introduced as 'Ruth Fuerst'. Christie embraces the doll, makes her a cup of tea. He then tells his audience that he can't remember what happened next, but states, 'I must have gone haywire'. The doll is then strangled with a rope, before being buried in news-paper. Christie announces, 'I was in love with her'. The police have nothing but disgust for this 'Bloody pervert' and hang him, before burying the corpse in the garden.[3]

Even less well-known was a TV programme, *The Dreams of Timothy Evans* by Clive Exton, starring Don Hawkins as Evans, screened by London Weekend TV in September 1970. This was a drama which portrayed the encounter between Christie and Evans on the evening of the murder of Beryl Evans, and was based on the assumption that Christie was responsible. It also tried to explain Evans's subsequent behaviour.[4]

However, the best known and easily most influential work about Christie is the film, made in 1970 and shown at cinemas in early 1971, entitled *10 Rillington Place* (Clive Exton wrote the screenplay and Kennedy advised). The medium of cinema, especially with the advent of video and DVD, can reach a far wider audience than the printed word. In an interview, Lord Attenborough, who starred as Christie, explained that the film was made as a riposte to a Private Member's Bill to reintroduce capital punishment. This is how the film must be seen, rather than taken as a factual account of the murders.

The film was partially shot in Ruston Close (as the street was renamed in 1954), from 18 May until early October 1970 (when the house was demolished), though the interiors were filmed in studios and in houses further down the street. One resident said that it was as if she was seeing people 'risen from the grave'. The film opens during the Second World War, with Christie in his policeman's uniform receiving Muriel at his house before murdering her. The timeframe then leaps forward to 1949 and the arrival of all three Evanses at Rillington Place. Christie is shown to murder Beryl and Geraldine. Evans confesses, is arrested and put on trial. He is sentenced to death, whilst he pleads his innocence. Later we are shown Ethel refusing to sleep with her husband and hinting that she knows rather more about him than the police. He then kills her and we are shown Christie in a cafe, inveigling another victim back to his rooms. After the bodies are discovered by black tenants, Christie is apprehended and justice is done. The film ends with the message that Evans was given a posthumous pardon. The film is widely seen as a strong indictment of capital punishment, with errors leading to an innocent man being hanged. It certainly is an emotionally powerful work, and is also claimed to be a true story.

Reviews of the film were overwhelmingly favourable. *The Times* said 'we should be grateful for a film as good, truthful and thoroughly decent as we have been given'. 'Nothing is glamorised, nothing sensationalised' and as much as possible of the recorded dialogue had been used, 'with a fine sense of period and character'. Another newspaper, *The Middlesex County Times*, was also congratulatory, praising the acting of John Hurt: 'an incredibly moving portrayal of an innocent dupe', and that of Attenborough: 'a fine performance of the creepy Christie'. As with *The Times*, there is praise for the factual nature of the film and no doubt is raised that Evans was innocent. More recent reviews of the film, such as those on the Amazon website, have continued to be favourable, with most reviewers awarding the film the maximum five stars and praising its authenticity and its message.[5]

However, despite the excellent acting and the film's evocative portrayal of the seedy milieu of post-war Notting Hill, we should not accept this film as uncritically as did the reviewers, who probably only had a perfunctory knowledge of the case. Although the film claims to be factual, this, sadly, is not the case. There are very many errors of fact – the Evanses arrived at Rillington Place in 1948, not 1949; Christie was no longer a policeman when he killed Muriel; in the film there is a female character – Alice – who is a friend of Beryl's, but she is an invention, although loosely based on Joan Vincent and, to a lesser extent, Lucy Endecott. Other factual errors include the arrival of the builders on 8 November, and Christie suddenly deciding to take that day as sick leave and then asking his wife to take documents to his workplace for him to get her out of the way. Then we have Evans leaving the house for Wales on the night of 8 November and Ethel being aware of both murders on that day (Geraldine's murder occurs on that day, too). At Merthyr Vale, the Lynches do not receive a letter from Evans's mother, but a telegram from William Thorley. Mrs Lynch, not Evans's mother, visits him in prison. Ethel states, in 1952, that the house is empty save for themselves and that Christie gave up his job a long time ago. Christie's in-laws are misnamed. When Christie departs, we see Brown arriving for the first time. The woman Christie lures back appears to be based on Mrs Forrest. Readers of this book will note these departures from the known facts (and there are others). Perhaps the film's biggest problem is that we are shown Christie gassing Beryl, which is indeed what he once confessed to. Yet, as noted, Teare found no evidence of gas; thus exploding both Kennedy's theory and that of the film.

Christie is portrayed as a manipulative monster, a Jekyll and Hyde, a one-dimensional figure of evil. There is no attempt at any depth or effort to explain his motivations. There are hints of his outward respectability and later of his pathetic nature, but they are brief. Nor are we shown what he actually did to his victims.

Most viewers will not be very knowledgeable about the Christie case and so will be unaware that what they are seeing is just one inter-pretation of what happened at Rillington Place, largely based on the assumption that Evans's second confession was truthful. They are not shown the brutal side of Evans's character, which was discussed in

Chapter 4. Instead Evans is portrayed as an innocent victim of the cruel and deceitful Christie. Nor are we told at the end that the Brabin report, which led to the pardoning of Evans, also stated that he probably did kill his wife. The film is propaganda dressed up as factual documentary and is only loosely based on fact. The film makers did a disservice to history, but they were not aiming at impartiality, only making a political point.

More recently there has been a novel which deals with aspects of the case, although there is barely any reference to the Evanses. This is *Thirteen Steps Down* (2005) by Ruth Rendell, set in 2004. The plot concerns Mix Cellini, a young technician who lives in Notting Hill because of his fascination with a supermodel living there and his obsession with Christie. Cellini is largely unsympathetic, as is his landlady, the elderly Gwendolin Chawcer, who has lived in Notting Hill all her life and once met Christie. Both characters have obsessions and, as the plot unfolds, we see how these develop and one result is murder. It is an engrossing novel and well-paced, as one would expect of a novelist of Rendell's calibre.

From the point of view of this book, however, it is the portrayal of Christie that matters. Cellini has a small library of books about Christie, though Kennedy's apart, the remainder are all fictitious titles (Christie's Victims, John Reginald Halliday Christie *et al.*). Cellini admires Christie, whom he almost always refers to as 'Reg'. He likes him for being a basically upright man, a man of power who commands respect, and has no time for the killer's victims, whom Cellini dismisses as being merely prostitutes. Cellini likes the film, too, which he has on DVD, but doesn't think Attenborough, fine actor that he is, gets the part right. He bemoans the demolition of Rillington Place, points out where Ruth Fuerst lived, complains how writers about Christie have made 'feeble' comments about his wickedness when they should have praised his skill as an artist, and bemoans the lack of interest his landlady shows in Christie. Cellini likes to drink in the Kensington Park Hotel, which he states was Christie's haunt. He regards himself as the greatest living expert on Christie. Yet at the same time he is worried about having seen Christie's ghost and even consults an alleged medium about it.

As said, this works well as a novel. However it is curious that the author does not mention actual books about Christie and opts for fictional titles. Furthermore, it was Evans, not Christie, who frequented the Kensington Park Hotel. As important to the plot as it is, it is far from certain whether Christie was an abortionist.

Although there was a novel about the Christie case in 1961, it was not until 2010 that the matter was novelized again. In her book *A Capital Crime* Laura Wilson decided to focus on the police investigation rather than on Evans or Christie, and also chose to avoid real names. Thus it is John Davies who is the Welshman who confesses to killing his wife and child in 1949 before retracting, but is found guilty and executed. Norman Backhouse, a fellow tenant, was accused by Davies, and in the following year he goes missing. He is described thus, 'a bald-pated, feeble looking middle aged man in a cardigan, blinking through pebble glasses'. In the meantime, corpses of women who have been gassed, raped and strangled are found in the garden. Detective Inspector Stratton investigates and the book strays from known fact by having him arrest Backhouse in a café with his next would-be victim. Despite numerous sub-plots, the book mostly sticks to the facts and reaches a refreshingly open verdict about the killer of Davies's wife and child.

Meanwhile, as far as non-fiction books were concerned, no full-length studies were published for three decades after 1961. It seemed there was little new to say and little new material available. Kennedy's book was reprinted at least twice, and the version he put forward became the 'authorized version'. The Marshall Cavendish *Murder Case Book* series had the Rillington Place murders as its fourth issue in 1990, and this well-illustrated magazine followed Kennedy's thesis. Martin Fido made an audio book on the topic, again with the same line of argument, shortly afterwards. There was a programme about the Christie murders on television in 2011, which was chiefly a rehash of the Kennedy thesis.

It was not until over three decades after Kennedy's account appeared that a fresh approach to the case was taken, ironically enough by John Eddowes, son of the aforementioned Michael. This had the advantage of access to many hitherto inaccessible files. It also had the radically opposite interpretation to Kennedy, and indeed spent much time attacking Kennedy's arguments step by step. Eddowes argued that Kennedy had ignored evidence which had not suited his case in order to exonerate Evans from any guilt.

Eddowes stated that Evans was a young psychopath, prone to drink and violence, who threatened those who crossed him, including Beryl.

He produced the statement of a builder's labourer, who saw Beryl leave the house on the morning of the day of the murder, not returning until the evening. Evans then killed her, as stated in his third and fourth confessions. Eddowes then argues that Evans later killed Geraldine as he said and planned to dispose of the bodies at sea, following the example set by Donald Hume. Because he lost his job, he failed to get rid of the bodies as he had planned. Eddowes also argues that Ethel was not her husband's dupe and did not cover up for him at the trial of Evans. He makes many excellent points, but does so in a way which makes the book almost a personal attack on Kennedy.

This book, published in the year following his father's death, did not go unnoticed by its principal target. Kennedy, described in *The Times* as 'the writer and justice campaigner', was outraged, as anyone who has read his autobiography would expect him to be. He sued Eddowes and was given a public apology and won substantial damages over the allegations that he had distorted evidence. Kennedy had been happy to ridicule the Scott-Henderson Report, but when it came to his own work he did not brook such criticism. The book had to be amended. In 2002, Kennedy wrote a book which included a chapter on the case, but he only restated his earlier proposition even more firmly, writing 'Today we know that Evans did not murder his wife and child, but that his fellow lodger Christie did'.[6]

A decade later, Edward Marston wrote a book about the murders entitled *John Christie*. The book followed Kennedy's interpretation, adding very little that was new, despite the fact that there was a mass of new evidence available for consultation at the National Archives. There were also numerous errors of fact. Nor did Marston accept the challenge of Eddowes's revisionist thesis. As with all these books, it is the Evans controversy which dominates, with the rest of Christie's life and crimes being treated only briefly. Another reappraisal appeared in 2011, this time by Edna Gammon, *A House to Remember*, though this took the view that Evans was guilty. There was little original therein, either, and many fallacies.

Books about crime have often included a chapter or a few pages about Christie, but these were inevitably only summaries of what had already been published, and often repeated errors which had already established themselves in these earlier books. The Evans murders are still seen as a crucial element of the case, if not the most important feature of it. Neil Root's *Frenzy* (2011) had much to say about the

Christie case in a study of the tabloid press and three infamous post-war killers, but there was little that was new and much that was factually incorrect. Judicial investigations post-Brabin have also inferred Evans's utter innocence, have awarded his relatives substantial sums, and also inferred Christie's guilt of the Evans murders.

Although long dead, Christie has not been forgotten.

Conclusion

Most readers will, by now, have added to their knowledge of John Christie, the mild-mannered man who made a mortuary of the house in which he lived. There is, however, much that we will never know for certain. Why did Christie commit relatively minor crimes? How many victims did he claim? Why did he leave 10 Rillington Place when he did? Speculation can be offered, but there are few hard facts.

However, it seems fairly certain that he can be cleared of the murders of Beryl and Geraldine Evans. The evidence against Evans is strong indeed; that against Christie is flimsy and rests on little more than the coincidence that the two men lived in the same house at the time of the murders. Anyone believing in Christie's guilt must accept a far greater number of improbabilities than this.

Although Christie did not leave corpses scattered about on public view and create a reign of terror, as did Jack the Ripper in 1888 or Jack the Stripper in 1964–65, he shares many characteristics with other well-known serial killers. As with Haigh, Nilsen and the Wests, he concealed his corpses and so it was only after the dreadful discovery of these that his murderous nature was known. He selected his victims carefully (as did those just mentioned), choosing people for whom enquiry would be minimal. He was able to appear normal and trustworthy enough in order to persuade them, preying on their needs, whether it be money (Fuerst), a cure for ill health (Eady) or accommodation (Maloney, Nelson and MacLennan) to return to his 'killing zone'. He was motivated, probably, partly by power and also by the fact that he could not gain satisfaction unless having sex with an unconscious woman. Power and sex are the drives of most, although not all, serial killers. His first murder was not pre-meditated, but finding he enjoyed it, he continued to kill. He became a serial killer by accident. As with others of this ilk, he did not particularly stand out from his fellows ('I'm the sort of man you don't look twice at on the bus', as he said) and had few obvious worldly achievements, yet he wanted that self-esteem which he could only obtain by murder. Similarly, he was also somewhat of a loner, cut off from family, and had no close friends. He began cautiously and carefully, but became less so as the years passed and he remained unsuspected. He felt no remorse or regret for his victims, except for his wife. Like many serial killers, he left a written testament behind him, designed to create a favourable image for posterity. However, unlike most killers, he began his murders when middle-aged. To many, he is a monster. Apart from those he killed, there were families and friends left behind them, including small children in four cases, as well as an unborn baby in one or possibly two victims.

But we should also remember that he was a human being; capable of acts of murderous violence and a fit choice for the rope, but a man for all that. He was not all bad. Christie was a good scholar and volunteered when under-age for the army in the First World War, where he had a good character, as he did whilst in the RAF. He was a friend to animals and children. Before the murder of his wife, he was a good husband, inspiring love in his wife, shopping for food as well as undertaking repairs at home. At work he undertook First Aid duties and was an active trades union representative. His police work was commended. To his neighbours he was a quiet, well-dressed and respectable man, one to exchange greetings with and even to invite around at Christmas. His behaviour in public was not bizarre or threatening. In many ways he was incredibly ordinary. It is easy to point to all this as being the facade behind which Mr Hyde lurked, for a mass murderer can hardly advertise the fact. He was also prudish and puritanical concerning sex and drink. He was a boaster and a man who consorted with prostitutes. He suffered from many physical and mental ailments in the latter years of his life. Despite his intelligence, he never rose very high in the world. He suffered, too, whether from his stern father, war wounds (though he exaggerated these, they were real enough), and difficult fellow tenants in later years. Perhaps above all he was a shy man, lacking in social confidence, who lacked deep human friendships. This is not an attempt to build up sympathy for Christie, but to demonstrate that he was human.

Christie was not evil, though he was capable of evil deeds. Nor was he a sadist, as were Brady and Hindley and the Wests. Perhaps his very ordinariness makes him seem all the worse. He was, in many ways, the ordinary man, on the surface, similar to our neighbours and colleagues, who was nevertheless a mass murderer. As with all such, he was not a devil, but a man. To label him as a monster is simplistic and emotive, for Christie was just a sexual inadequate who murdered to sate his lusts. Although serial murder was an important facet of his character, it was not the whole of him.

The reader may wish to conclude with the following assessment of Christie, made by Dr Hobson (no friend of Christie), who stated:

I have never succeeded in conveying to anyone a glimmer of my 'understanding' of the man. I have described him to many people, including Mr Ludovic Kennedy, but journalists tend to emphasise selectively, and pay comparatively little heed to observations which fit uncomfortably into their main thesis. Black and white prints more dramatic pictures than shades of grey.

I have known many 'bad' men, but no one wholly bad. Evans and Christie alike were inadequate, insignificant little men, misfits in society, liars and boasters. Unlike Evans, Christie in addition was a self righteous prude, a moralizer, and a killer of women (perhaps more than we yet know).

He was gentle in voice and manner, and probably essentially gentle and kind in his nature. He hated cruelty in any form: there was nothing whatever of the sadist in his make up; he went to extraordinary trouble to ensure that the killings of his victims should be painless. On at least one occasion he interrupted his routine when his intended victim became frightened, and he allowed her to leave.

He was completely inadequate sexually, and I doubt whether he was ever capable of sexual relationships with women, living, dying or dead. I believe his motive for killing women was more anti-sexual than sexual, and I remain unconvinced by the evidence put forward suggesting necrophilia. He feared women and their criticism, and hated their sexuality.

He cared little for men either, though he courted their esteem, and readily excused himself on grounds of imaginary illness for falling short of the conceited image he held of himself.

Above all he was a self deceiver. Right to the end of his trial it was not he who might be hanged, and it was impossible for him to imagine that anyone could possibly entertain the idea that he might be insane.

He was an unpleasant bore, but not a monster; a man I found impossible to like, and very difficult to love; a man sick in mind; a man we hanged. In the 'Christie-Evans' case we should have not one, but two men on our conscience.[1]

However, we must remember that ultimately Christie was not a victim of anything except his depraved desires; he chose his own fate and did not permit his victims a similar choice.

Notes

Introduction
1. P. Rogers, ed., *Defoe's Tour around the Whole Island* (1971), p. 498.
2. F. Tennyson-Jesse, *The Trials of Evans and Christie* (1957), p. 122.

Chapter 1
1. TNA, HO291/227.
2. Ancestry.co.uk, 1871–1901 censuses; *Halifax Evening Courier*, 11 September 1990, 11 May 2000; *Halifax Courier*, 27 March 1880, 5 January 1918.
3. Census 1911, *The Halifax Evening Courier*, 4 June 2002; TNA, PCOM2/1668, Calderdale Archives, DC/1540.
4. *The Halifax Daily Courier and Guardian*, 13 February 1928, 26 March 1953; *The Halifax Daily Guardian*, 17 October 1911 and 25 July 1912.
5. Calderdale Archives, All Souls' parish registers; *Halifax Daily Guardian*, October 1911, 26 December 1923.
6. Jesse, *Trials*, p. xliii.
7. *The Sunday Pictorial*, 5 July 1953; Jesse, *Trials*, p. 223; TNA, DPP2/1927; PCOM2/1668; TS58/856.
8. *The Sunday Pictorial*, 12 July 1953; *The Halifax Courier*, 25 March 1911; Jesse, *Trials*, p. 186; L. Kennedy, *Ten Rillington Place* (1961), p. 25; TNA, CAB143/21.
9. *The Sunday Pictorial*, 12 July 1953; Jack Delves' information; Jesse, *Trials*, p. 216; TNA, PCOM2/1668; H. Proctor, *Street of Disillusion* (1958), pp. 176–7.
10. *The Sunday Pictorial*, 12 July 1953; *The Times*, 25 June 1953.
11. *The Sunday Pictorial*, 5 July 1953; Jack Delves' information; Kennedy, *Ten Rillington Place*, p. 24; TNA, HO291/227; TS58/856; CRIM1/2326; DPP2/1927; *Murder Case Book, 4: The Rillington Place Murders* (1990), p. 120.
12. *The Sunday Pictorial*, 28 June 1953, 5 July 1953; *The Sheffield Star*, 9 July 1953.
13. TNA, HO291/227; *Halifax Daily Courier and Guardian*, 26 March 1953.
14. TNA, DPP2/1927.
15. *The Sheffield Star*, 9 July 1953; *The Sheffield Telegraph*, 13 July 1953; TNA, PCOM2/1668.
16. TNA, PIN26/16679.
17. *The Times*, 26 June 1953; *The Sunday Pictorial*, 12 July 1953; TNA, PIN26/16679, DPP2/1927.
18. TNA, Medal card, DPP2/1927, CAB143/17; *The Sunday Pictorial*, 19 July 1953; Kennedy, *Ten Rillington Place*, p. 27.
19. *The Times*, 23 June 1953; TNA, DPP2/1927 MEPO2/9535.
20. Census 1901 and 1911; TNA, DPP2/1927.

21. Ancestry.co.uk; *The Sunday Pictorial*, 12, 26 July 1953.
22. TNA, MEPO2/9535; PCOM2/1668; HO291/227; TS58/856.
23. *The Sunday Pictorial*, 5 July 1953; TNA, PCOM2/1668; CAB143/21.
24. F. Camps, *Medical and Scientific Investigations of the Christie Case* (1953), p. 179.

Chapter 2

1. *The South Western Star*, 17 May 1929.
2. GPO POST58/117, TNA, CAB143/21; *The Halifax Courier*, 9, 16 April 1921; *The Halifax Guardian*, 16 April 1921.
3. *The Halifax Courier*, 16 April 1921; *The Halifax Guardian*, 16 April 1921.
4. *The Halifax Courier*, 16 April 1921; *The Halifax Guardian*, 16 April 1921; TNA, PIN26/16679.
5. TNA, PIN26/16679, CAB143/21; *The Daily Telegraph*, 26 June 1953.
6. TNA, CRIM1/2326; *The Halifax Daily Courier and Guardian*, 15 January 1923.
7. Ibid.
8. *The Sunday Pictorial*, 26 July, 28 June 1953; *The West Middlesex Gazette*, 27 September 1924; TNA, TS58/856.
9. *The West Middlesex Gazette*, 27 September 1924; *The Middlesex Advertiser*, 3 November 1933; TNA, TS58/856.
10. TNA, DPP2/1927, CAB143/21; Jesse, *Trials*, p. 153.
11. Ministry of Defence, RAF Service Record; *The West Middlesex Gazette*, 27 September 1924.
12. *The West Middlesex Gazette*, 27 September 1924.
13. *The Middlesex Advertiser*, 20 September 1924; *The West Middlesex Gazette*, 27 September 1924; TNA, MEPO2/9535; CRIM1/2326.
14. *The West Middlesex Gazette*, 27 September 1924; *The Middlesex Advertiser*, 20 September 1924.
15. *The West Middlesex Gazette*, 27 September 1924.
16. Ibid.
17. LMA, PS/U/1/35; Acc.3444/PR/01/192.
18. TNA, DPP2/2246.
19. *The Halifax Daily Courier and Guardian*, 18 February 1928; Calderdale Archives, DC/1540; Will of Ernest Christie, Ancestry.co.uk; *The Halifax Evening Courier*, 4 June 2002; TNA, TS58/565.
20. TNA, DPP2/2246; HO291/227.
21. Ibid, MEPO2/9535.
22. Ibid.
23. Ibid.
24. *The South Western Star*, 17 May 1929.
25. Ibid.
26. Ibid.
27. Ibid.
28. Ibid.
29. Ibid; LMA, Acc3444/PR/01/195.
30. Ibid.
31. J. Oates, *Unsolved London Murders; 1920s and 1930s* (2009), p. 136, TNA, DPP2/2246.
32. TNA, DPP2/2246.

33. *The Middlesex Advertiser and Gazette*, 3 November 1933.
34. Ibid.
35. Ibid.
36. Ibid; LMA, Acc3444/PR/01/198.
37. TNA, HO291/227.
38. Kensington North Electoral Register, 1936, TNA, DPP2/1927; MEPO2/9535; 3/3147; TS58/565; LMA, Acc.3444/PR/01/198.
39. TNA, TS58/565.
40. Kensington Library, plans 4332, 4228; 1871 census, Booth map.
41. Jesse, *Trials*, p. ii-iii.
42. F.E. Camps and R. Barber, *The Investigation of Murder*, p. 57. (1966); LMA, B/BAL/1/225.
43. *New Survey of London Life and Labour*, VI (1934), pp. 12, 427–428.
44. Oates, *Unsolved London Murders*, pp. 115–134.
45. Kensington North Electoral Registers, 1920–1938; TNA, MEPO2/9535.
46. TNA, DPP2/2246; *The Halifax Daily Courier and Guardian*, 26 March 1953.

Chapter 3
1. *The Sunday Pictorial*, 12 July 1953.
2. TNA, TS58/565.
3. *The Times*, 4 December 1965; TNA, MEPO2/9535; 3/3147; TS58/565; Jesse, *Trials*, p. 187.
4. C. Philips, *Murderer's Moon* (1956), p. 137; *The Sunday Pictorial*, 5 July 1953; TNA, HO291/227, CAB143/18.
5. *The Sheffield Star*, 9 July 1953.
6. TNA, MEPO2/9535.
7. Ibid.
8. Ibid.
9. Ibid; Kennedy, *Ten Rillington Place*, p. 42.
10. TNA, MEPO2/9535.
11. Ibid.
12. Ibid; HO396/173.
13. TNA, MEPO2/9535; DDP2/2246; LMA, PS/MS/A1/182; Jesse, *Trials*, pp. 157, 187.
14. *The Sunday Pictorial*, 5 July 1953; Jesse, *Trials*, p. 187.
15. Ibid; MEPO2/9535.
16. TNA, HO291/228, *The Times*, 24 June 1953; *The Sunday Pictorial*, 5 July 1953; Jesse, *Trials*, p. 158.
17. TNA, MEPO2/9535; *The Police Gazette*, 16 October 1943, LMA, COR/LW/1953/147.
18. Jesse, *Trials*, p. 215; TNA, CAB143/21.
19. TNA, MEPO2/9535; DDP2/2246.
20. TNA, MEPO2/9535.
21. Ibid.
22. *The Sunday Pictorial*, 12 July 1953; TNA, HO291/228; Jesse, *Trials*, p. 158.
23. TNA, HO29/228; MEPO2/9535, DDP2/1927; *Sunday Pictorial*, 12 July 1953; Camps, *Medical and Scientific Investigations*, p. 162.

23. TNA, MEPO2/9535.
24. Jesse, *Trials*, p. 189.
25. TNA, CAB143/19.
26. TNA, DPP2/2246, 1927; MEPO2/3147; TS58/565; North Kensington Electoral Registers, 1945–1948; Patricia Pichler's information.

Chapter 4

1. Kennedy, *Ten Rillington Place*, p. 56.
2. Ancestry.co.uk; TNA, MEPO3/3147.
3. TNA, PCOM9/2313.
4. Ibid; HO45/25652; Glamorgan Record Office, Mount Pleasant School Admission Register, North Kensington Electoral Registers, 1936–1946.
5. TNA, PCOM9/2313, CAB143/20.
6. Ibid, TS58/856.
7. Ibid, DPP2/2246.
8. Ibid, MEPO3/3147; CAB143/8.
9. Brabin, *Rillington Place*, pp. 101, 180, 182.
10. TNA, CAB143/12; PCOM9/2313, DDP2/2246, CAB143/8; LMA, PS/WLN/A1/316.
11. LMA, PS/WLN/A1/316; TNA, MEPO3/3147.
12. Kensington North Electoral Registers, 1947–1951.
13. *Kensington News*, 27 March 1953; Birth certificate, TNA, TS58/856; *The Daily Mail*, 3 December 1949, Ancestry.com.
14. TNA, MEPO3/3147.
15. Ibid, MEPO2/9535.
16. Kennedy, *Ten Rillington Place*, p. 60.
17. Jesse, *Trials*, p. 162; Kennedy, *Ten Rillington Place*, p. 56.
18. TNA, MEPO3/3147.
19. Ibid.
20. TNA, MEPO3/3147; 2/9535; PCOM9/2313; Kennedy, *Ten Rillington Place*, p. 58.
21. TNA, MEPO3/3147.
22. Ibid.
23. Ibid.
24. Ibid, CAB143/12; DDP2/1927; HO45/25652, PCOM9/2313.
25. Ibid, HO45/25652.
26. Ibid, MEPO3/3147.
27. Ibid.
28. Ibid, CAB143/8.
29. Ibid, DDP2/1944, TNA, CAB143/12; MEPO3/3147.
30. Ibid, MEPO3/3147.
31. Ibid.
32. Ibid, PCOM9/2313.
33. Ibid, MEPO3/3147.

Chapter 5

1. Brabin, *Rillington Place*, p. 2.
2. TNA, MEPO3/3147.

3. Ibid, MEPO2/3147, CAB143/7.
4. Jesse, *Trials*, pp. 27–8, 40.
5. TNA, MEPO3/3147.
6. Ibid.
7. TNA, MEPO3/3147; Brabin, *Rillington Place*, pp. 41–42.
8. TNA, MEPO3/3147.
9. Ibid.
10. Ibid.
11. Brabin, *Rillington Place*, pp. 37, 38; Kennedy, *Ten Rillington Place*, p. 49; TNA, CAB143/8.
12. TNA, MEPO3/3147)
13. TNA, MEPO3/3147; Brabin, *Rillington Place*, p. 44; Jesse, *Trials*, p. 45.
14. Jesse, *Trials*, p. 20.
15. Ibid, p. 71.
16. Ibid, p. 45.
17. Ibid, pp. 168–169.
18. TNA, MEPO2/9535.
19. Brabin, *Rillington Place*, pp. 2–6; Jesse, *Trials*, p. 46.
20. Brabin, *Rillington Place*, pp. 6–8.
21. TNA, CAB143/20.
22. Brabin, *Rillington Place*, pp. 8–13.
23. TNA, MEPO3/3147, Brabin, *Rillington Place*, pp. 14–15, 18, 19.
24. Jesse, *Trials*, pp. 161–162; TNA, CAB143/8.
25. TNA, MEPO3/3147.
26. Ibid.
27. Brabin, *Rillington Place*, pp. 21–23.
28. TNA, DPP2/1927.
29. Jesse, *Trials*, pp. 158, 162–163.

Chapter 6
1. Brabin, *Rillington Place*, p. 91.
2. K. Simpson, *Forty Years of Murder* (1978), p. 191; Jesse, *Trials*, p. 13; Brabin, *Rillington Place*, pp. 58–59.
3. Brabin, *Rillington Place*, p. 59; TNA, CAB143/12.
4. Ibid, pp. 60–61; Jesse, *Trials*, p. 15; Camps, *Medical and Scientific Investigations*, p. 145.
5. Brabin, *Rillington Place*, pp. 61–62.
6. TNA, MEPO3/3147.
7. Brabin, *Rillington Place*, pp. 65–69.
8. Brabin, *Rillington Place*, pp. 69–71; Jesse, *Trials*, pp. 58–60.
9. Brabin, *Rillington Place*, pp. 69–72, 162.
10. TNA, MEPO3/3147.
11. Brabin, *Rillington Place*, pp. 78–81; CAB143/8.
12. Ibid, pp. 87–90.
13. TNA, CAB143/12; Brabin, *Rillington Place*, p. 102.
14. Brabin, *Rillington Place*, pp. 91–94.
15. Brabin, *Rillington Place*, pp. 234–59; Jesse, *Trials*, pp. 58, 60; TNA, MEPO3/3147.

16. Jesse, *Trials*, p. 115.
17. Jesse, *Trials*, p. xx; TNA, PCOM9/2313; MEPO3/3147.
18. TNA, MEPO3/3147.
19. Brabin, *Rillington Place*, pp. 132–135.
20. TNA, MEPO3/3147.
21. Ibid.
22. Ibid.
23. Ibid.
24. Ibid.
25. F. Cherrill, *Cherrill of the Yard* (1954), p. 233.
26. *West London Observer*, 16 December 1949.
27. Ibid, 30 December 1949; TNA, MEPO3/3147.
28. *The Sunday Pictorial*, 28 June 1953; Procter, *Street*, p. 170; TNA, MEPO3/3147.
29. TNA, DPP2/2246.
30. Brabin, *Rillington Place*, pp. 103–114.
31. TNA, MEPO3/3147.

Chapter 7

1. Jesse, *Trials*, p. 24.
2. Brabin, *Rillington Place*, pp. 142–143; Procter, *Street*, p. 170.
3. TNA, MEPO3/3147.
4. Jesse, *Trials*, pp. 9–13.
5. Ibid, pp. 16–18.
6. Jesse, *Trials*, pp. 18–21, 28; TNA, MEPO3/3147.
7. Ibid, pp. 22–24.
8. Ibid, pp. 25–32.
9. Ibid, pp. 32–33.
10. Ibid, p. 38.
11. Ibid, pp. 38–39.
12. Ibid, p. 40.
13. Ibid, pp. 41–44.
14. Ibid, pp. 45–60.
15. Ibid, pp. 60–61.
16. Ibid, pp. 61–66.
17. Ibid, pp. 66–72.
18. Ibid, pp. 73–74.
19. Ibid, pp. 74–77.
20. Ibid, pp. 77–81.
21. Ibid, pp. 81–82.
22. Ibid, pp. 82–83.
23. Ibid, p. 85.
24. Ibid, pp. 87–88.
25. Ibid, pp. 88–91; TNA, MEPO3/3147.
26. Jesse, *Trials*, p. 92.
27. Ibid, pp. 93–108.
28. Ibid, pp. 109–111.
29. Ibid, pp. 111–114.

30. Ibid, pp. 116–117.
31. Ibid, p. xxviii; *The Kensington Post*, 20 January 1950 and 17 July 1953; TNA, TS58/856; Procter, *Street*, p. 171.
32. TNA, CAB143/22.
33. TNA, DDP2/1944.
34. Jesse, *Trials*, p. 297.
35. Ibid, pp. 297–299.
36. Ibid, pp. 300–301, xxx.
37. Brabin, *Rillington Place*, pp. 174, 182.
38. Ibid, pp. 183–5.
39. TNA, MEPO 3/3147; PCOM9/2313; TS58/565; Kennedy, *Ten Rillington Place*, p. 305.
40. TNA, PCOM9/2313; *The Empire News*, 25 March 1956.

Chapter 8
1. *The Sunday Pictorial*, 26 July 1953.
2. TNA, DPP2/2246; MEPO3/3147; 2/9535, *The Daily Telegraph*, 26 June 1953; R. Maxwell, *The Christie Case* (1953), p. 31, PO Archives, GPO 120/170.
3. *News of the World*, 28 June 1953.
4. TNA, TS58/565.
5. Ibid, MEPO2/9535; *Kensington Post*, 17 July 1953.
6. Kennedy, *Ten Rillington Place*, pp. 209–210; Kensington North Electoral Registers, 1951–1953; TNA, DPP2/2246.
7. Jesse, *Trials*, pp. 194–5.
8. Ibid, p. 209.
9. TNA, CAB143/21
10. Jesse, *Trials*, pp. 209–210.
11. TNA, MEPO2/9535.
12. Ibid, MEPO2/9535; CAB143/21.
13. Ibid, MEPO2/9535.
14. G. Zelland, *Crime in London* (1986), p. 60.
15. Jesse, *Trials*, p. 138.
16. TNA, MEPO2/9535; Jesse, *Trials*, pp. 137, 168.
17. Ibid, p. 166.
18. TNA, MEPO2/9535; Jesse, *Trials*, pp. 148, 195.
19. Jesse, *Trials*, pp. 166–7.
20. *Kensington Post*, 28 March 1953; TNA, MEPO2/9535; HO227/291; *The Belfast Telegraph*, 25, 26 March 1953; Maxwell, *Christie Case*, p. 20.
21. TNA, CAB143/21.
22. Jesse, *Trials*, p. 169.
23. TNA, MEPO2/9535; 3/3147; CAB143/21; *The News of the World*, 28 June 1953.
24. *Kensington Post*, 17 July 1953.
25. Jesse, *Trials*, p. 139; TNA, MEPO2/9535.
26. Ibid, p. 139.
27. TNA, MEPO2/9535.
28. Ibid; HO291/227.
29. Ibid, TS58/856; CAB143/21.

30. Ibid, MEPO2/9535.
31. Ibid.
32. Ibid, MEPO2/9535, CAB143/21.
33. Ibid, MEPO2/9535; CAB143/21.
34. Jesse, *Trials*, pp. 137–138, 195, 205; TNA, DPP2/2246; MEPO2/9535, CAB143/21.
35. Jesse, *Trials*, pp. 139, 143, 167.
36. TNA, MEPO2/9535; Jesse, *Trials*, p. 201, opp.
37. *The Times*, 23 April 1953; Jesse, *Trials*, p. 209.
38. *The Sunday Pictorial*, 26 July 1953.
39. Jesse, *Trials*, pp. 201, 216opp.
40. Jesse, *Trials*, pp. 139, 141–2; TNA, MEPO2/9535.
41. Jesse, *Trials*, p. 139.
42. TNA, MEPO2/9535.
43. TNA, HO291/228; MEPO2/9535; Jesse, *Trials*, pp. 138, 141.
44. Jesse, *Trials*, p. 142; TNA, MEPO2/9535.
45. TNA, MEPO2/9535.
46. Jesse, *Trials*, pp. 143–144.

Chapter 9

1. TNA, MEPO2/9535.
2. *The Sunday Pictorial*, 26 July 1953; Jesse, *Trials*, p. 198.
3. TNA, MEPO2/9535; *The Scotsman*, 27 March 1953.
4. Ibid, *The Southern Daily Echo*, 13 December 1946, 6 July 1949; LMA, PS/BOW/02/030; CLA/003/PR/02/028; *The Reading Standard*, 20 June and 25 July 1952.
5. *The Southern Daily Echo*, 19 September 1950; *The Reading Standard*, 20 June and 25 July 1952.
6. TNA, MEPO2/9535; *The Southern Daily Echo*, 6 July 1949; 19 September 1950; 30 August 1951.
7. TNA, MEPO2/9535; *The Southern Daily Echo*, 26 March 1953.
8. Ibid.
9. Brabin, *Rillington Place*, p. 191.
10. TNA, MEPO2/9535; *The Sunday Pictorial*, 26 July 1953; *Western Morning News*, 23 April 1953; LMA, CLA/003/PR/02/034.
11. *The Sunday Pictorial*, 19, 26 July 1953; TNA, CAB143/21.
12. TNA, MEPO2/9535; *The Belfast Telegraph*, 1 May 1946.
13. TNA, MEPO2/9535.
14. Ibid, *The Belfast Telegraph*, 27, 30 March 1953.
15. TNA, MEPO2/9535.
16. Brabin, *Rillington Place*, p. 189, *Evening Standard*, 26 March 1953; TNA, CAB143/21.
17. TNA, MEPO2/9535.
18. Ibid; *The Scotsman*, 27 March 1953; *Evening Standard*, 26 March 1953; Information from Alice MacLennan.
19. TNA, MEPO2/9535.
20. TNA, MEPO2/9535, 1798; *Daily Mirror*, 8 January 1971; Information from Alice MacLennan.
21. TNA, MEPO2/9535.

22. *Sunday Pictorial*, 26 July 1953; TNA, MEPO2/9535.
23. *The Daily Mirror*, 8 January 1971.
24. *The Times*, 23 April 1953; TNA, MEPO2/9535; Jesse, *Trials*, pp. 175, 200.
25. *The Times*, 23 April 1953.
26. *The Times*, 23 April 1953; TNA, CAB143/21.
27. *The Sunday Pictorial*, 26 July 1953.
28. *The Sunday Pictorial*, 26 July 1953; TNA, MEPO2/9535.
29. TNA, MEPO2/9535.
30. Brabin, *Rillington Place*, pp. 220–221; Camps, *Medical and Scientific Investigations*, p. 175.
31. TNA, MEPO2/9535.
32. Ibid.
33. *News of the World*, 26 April 1953.
34. TNA, HO291/227; MEPO2/9535, CAB143/22.
35. TNA, MEPO2/9535; *The Sunday Pictorial*, 28 June 1953.
36. Ibid.
37. *The Times*, 1 December 1965; TNA, MEPO2/9535.
38. TNA, MEPO2/9535.
39. Ibid; HO227/291.
40. Ibid.
41. Ibid.
42. Ibid.
43. Ibid.
44. *Sunday Pictorial*, 26 July 1953.
45. TNA, MEPO2/9535.
46. Ibid.
47. TNA, HO291/228; MEPO2/1798, 9535; Jesse, *Trials*, pp. 138, 144–5.
48. Jesse, *Trials*, p. 166; *The Belfast Telegraph*, 27 March 1953.
49. Ancestry; TNA, HO291/228; MEPO2/9535.
50. TNA, MEPO2/9535, 1798.
51. Ibid, MEPO2/1798; *News of the World*, 29 March 1953.
52. TNA, MEPO2/9535; Simpson, *Forty Years*, p. 191.
53. *The Times*, 25 March 1953.

Chapter 10
 1. TNA, HO291/227.
 2. Camps, *Medical and Scientific Investigations*, pp. 174–5, Simpson, *Forty Years*, p. 206.
 3. Camps, *Medical and Scientific Investigations*, p. 49.
 4. *The Times*, 28, 30 March 1953; *The Kensington News*, 3 April 1953; TNA, MEO2/9535.
 5. *The Daily Mirror*; 25, 26 March 1953; *The Sunday Pictorial*, 29 March 1953; *The News of the World*, 29 March 1953.
 6. TNA, MEPO2/9535.
 7. Jesse, *Trials*, p. 202.
 8. Ibid, pp. 145–146.
 9. TNA, MEPO2/9535; Jesse, *Trials*, p. 203.
10. Jesse, *Trials*, p. 203; *Manchester Evening News*, 28 30 March 1953; TNA, CAB143/21.

11. TNA, HO291/228; MEPO2/9535.
12. Ibid, MEPO2/9535.
13. Jesse, *Trials*, p. 202; TNA, CAB143/21.
14. Ibid, p. 204; TNA, PCOM9/1668, CAB143/21; Maxwell, *Christie Case*, p. 43.
15. *The Times*, 1, 2 April 1953; *The Kensington News*, 1 May 1953; TNA, MEPO2/9535; Jesse, *Trials*, pp. 147, 204; *Manchester Evening News*, 31 March 1953.
16. Jesse, *Trials*, p. 148; *The Times*, 9, 16, 23 April 1953, J.G. Ballard, *Miracles of Life* (2008), p. 172, Maxwell, Christie Case, p. 47.
17. *The Times*, 2 April 1953.
18. Brabin, *Rillington Place*, pp. 198–200; Procter, *Street*, pp. 170–174.
19. TNA, CAB143/21
20. TNA, MEPO2/9535.
21. Brabin, *Rillington Place*, pp. 200–201.
22. Ibid, pp. 203, 208; *Sunday Pictorial*, 19 July 1953.
23. TNA, MEPO2/9535.
24. Camps, *Medical and Scientific Investigations*, pp. 162, 164.
25. Simpson, *Forty Years*, pp. 192–193.
26. Ibid, pp. 196–198.
27. Jesse, *Trials*, p. 232; TNA, PCOM9/1668; MEPO3/3147.
28. *The Sunday Pictorial*, 19 April 1953.
29. TNA, HO227/291.
30. Ibid, PCOM9/1668.
31. Ibid.
32. Ibid.
33. Jesse, *Trials*, pp. 232–233.
34. Ibid, pp. 234–235.
35. Camps, *Medical and Scientific Investigations*, p. 190.
36. TNA, CAB143/8.

Chapter 11

1. Jesse, *Trials*, p. 242.
2. Ibid, p. 119.
3. Ibid, p. 121.
4. Ibid, pp. 121–123.
5. Ibid, pp. 123–127.
6. Ibid, p. 127.
7. Ibid, pp. 127–130.
8. Ibid, pp. 130–131.
9. Ibid, pp. 133–137.
10. Ibid, pp. 137–146.
11. Ibid, pp. 146–155.
12. Ibid, pp. 156–164.
13. Ibid, pp. 165–169.
14. Ibid, pp. 169–175.
15. Ibid, pp. 175–176.
16. Ibid, p. 176.
17. Ibid, pp. 177–179.

18. Ibid, pp. 179–185.
19. *The Evening Standard*, 26 June 1953; *The Sunday Times*, 28 June 1953; Maxwell, *Christie Case*, pp. 121, 123.
20. Jesse, *Trials*, pp. 185–188.
21. Ibid, pp. 189–192.
22. Ibid, pp. 193–194.
23. Ibid, pp. 194–196.
24. Ibid, pp. 198–199.
25. Ibid, pp. 199–202.
26. Ibid, pp. 202–205.
27. Ibid, pp. 205–209.
28. Ibid, pp. 209–211.
29. Ibid, pp. 211–212.
30. Ibid, p. 213.
31. Ibid, pp. 213–214.
32. Ibid, pp. 215–222.
33. Ibid, pp. 222–224.
34. Ibid, pp. 225–226.
35. Ibid, p. 227.
36. Ibid, pp. 228–231.
37. Ibid, pp. 231–232.
38. Ibid, pp. 233–239; TNA, PCOM9/1668.
39. Ibid, pp. 240–244.
40. Ibid, pp. 245–250.
41. Ibid, p. 251.
42. Ibid, pp. 252–253.
43. Ibid, pp. 254–259.
44. Ibid, pp. 261–265.
45. Ibid, pp. 266–267.
46. Ibid, pp. 267–272.
47. Ibid, pp. 273–289.
48. Ibid, pp. 295–296.
49. Ibid, p. 296.
50. TNA, PCOM9/1668, MEPO3/3147; *The Sheffield Telegraph*, 26 June 1953.
51. TNA, PCOM9/1668.

Chapter 12

1. *The Empire News*, 25 March 1956.
2. TNA, MEPO3/3147.
3. *The Sunday Pictorial*, 5 July 1953; *The Times*, 14 December 1965.
4. *The Sheffield Star*, 9 July 1953; *The Sunday Pictorial*, 26 June 1953.
5. *The Sunday Pictorial*, 5–26 July 1953.
6. Kennedy, *Ten Rillington Place*, p. 249.
7. Ibid, p. 250.
8. Ibid, pp. 267–271.
9. Jesse, *Trials*, pp. 325–326.
10. Ibid, p. 326.

11. Ibid, pp. 328–329.
12. Ibid, pp. 330–331.
13. Ibid, pp. 318–319.
14. Ibid, p. 319.
15. TNA, HO291/227.
16. Ibid, PCOM9/1668.
17. Ibid, HO291/227.
18. Brabin, *Rillington Place*, pp. 231–232; TNA, HO291/227, MEPO3/3147; PCOM9/1668; *The Sheffield Telegraph*, 13 July 1953; *The Kensington News*, 17 July 1953; Procter, *Street*, p. 175.
19. TNA, HO291/227.
20. TNA, PCOM9/1668; Kennedy, *Ten Rillington Place*, pp. 246–247.
21. TNA, PCOM9/1668.
22. *The Empire News*, 25 March 1956.
23. Ibid; TNA, PCOM9/1668; HO27/291; *The Kensington Post*, 17 July 1953; *The Times*, 16 July 1953, C. Richardson, *Nick of Notting Hill* (1965), p. 116.
24. TNA, MEPO2/9535; *The Times*, 28 August 1953.
25. R.T. Paget and S.S. Silverman, *Hanged and Innocent?* (1953), p. 178.
26. Kennedy, *Ten Rillington Place*, p. 16; *The Times*, 7 September 1955.
27. Jesse, *Trials*, pp. xci–xcii.
28. M. Lefebvre, *Murder with a difference* (1958), pp. 240, 250, 167–168.
29. Jesse, *Trials*, p. lxxxiii.
30. H. Scott, *Scotland Yard* (1954), p. 166.
31. Jesse, *Trials*, pp. lxxxi–lxxxii.
32. Kennedy, *Ten Rillington Place*, p. 19.
33. Ibid.
34. *The Times*, 16 December 1965.
35. TNA, CAB143/22; DDP2/1927; MEPO3/3147.
36. Simpson, *40 Years*, pp. 196, 205.
37. TNA, MEPO3/3147; *The Brighton and Hove Gazette*, 27 August 1965.
38. Brabin, *Rillington Place*, pp. 260–261.
39. Ibid, pp. 261–265.
40. Brabin, *Rillington Place*, pp. 267–268; TNA, MEPO3/3147; Simpson, *Forty Years*, p. 204.
41. Brabin, *Rillington Place*, p. 269.

Chapter 13

1. H. Brenton, *Plays*, I (2000?), pp. 4–12.
2. Ibid, pp. 12–24.
3. Ibid, pp. 24–29.
4. *The Times*, 19 September 1970.
5. *The Times*, 29 January 1971; *The Middlesex County Times*, 19 March 1971.
6. *The Times*, 20 October 1994.

Conclusion

1. *The Times*, 17 April 1971.

Bibliography

Primary Sources

National Archives
    CAB143/7, 9, 12, 17–19, 20–22, 24–25
    DPP2/1927, 1944, 2246
    HO291/227–228, 396/173
    MEPO2/9118, 9535, 3/3147
    PCOM2/1668, 2371
    PIN26/16679
    TS58/565, 856

London Metropolitan Archives
    West London Magistrates' Court Registers, 1946, 1949
    Marlborough Street Magistrates' Court Register, 1942
    South West London Magistrates' Court Register, 1929
    Uxbridge Magistrates' Court Register, 1924
    Bow Street Magistrates' Court Register, 1945
    Holloway Prison Register, 1952
    Wandsworth Prison Registers of Prisoners, Acc3444/PR/01/192, 195, 198
    Sales catalogue, B/BAL/1/225
    Coroners' Records, COR/LW/1953/143–168

Ministry of Defence: RAF Disclosures
    Christie's service record

West Yorkshire Archive Service: Wakefield
    Halifax Petty Sessions, P21/8

West Yorkshire Archive Service: Calderdale
    All Souls' Halifax, Parish registers
    Dean and Clough, personnel records, DC/1540

Post Office Archives
    GPO, POST 58/117
    GPO, 120/160, 170

Kensington Local History Library
    Kensington Parish Plans, 4228, 4332
    Kensington Rate Books, 1869–1870, 1937, 1965

Principal Division of the Family
    Will of Ernest John Christie, 1927

Newspapers

The Belfast Telegraph, 1946, 1953
The Brighton and Hove Gazette, 1965
The Daily Express, 1958
The Daily Mail, 1949
The Daily Mirror, 1953, 1971
The Empire News, 1956
The Evening Standard, 1953
The Halifax Courier, 1880, 1911, 1918, 1921, 1927
The Halifax Daily Courier and Guardian, 1915, 1923, 1928, 1953
The Halifax Daily Guardian, 1911, 1912
The Halifax Evening Courier, 1990, 2000, 2002
The Kensington News, 1949, 1953
The Kensington Post, 1950, 1953
Manchester Evening News, 1953
The Middlesex Advertiser, 1924, 1933
The Middlesex County Times, 1965, 1971
News of the World, 1949–1950, 1953
The Police Gazette, 1943
The Reading Standard, 1952
The Scotsman, 1953
The Sheffield Star, 1953
The Sheffield Telegraph, 1953
The Southern Daily Echo, 1946, 1949–1951, 1953
The South Western Star, 1929
The Sunday Pictorial, 1953
The Sunday Times, 1953
The Times, 1953, 1955, 1961, 1965–1966, 1970–1971
The West London Observer, 1949

Other published primary sources

Guide to London (1927)
Halifax Electoral Registers, 1880–1927
Hull Electoral Registers, 1921–1933
Kensington North and South Electoral Registers, 1920–1959
Sheffield Electoral Registers, 1929–1934
J.G. Ballard, *Miracles of Life* (2008)
D. Brabin, *Rillington Place* (1966)
F. Camps, *Medical and Scientific Investigations into the Christie Case* (1953)
L. Kennedy, *On the way to the Club* (1990)
R. Maxwell, *The Christie Case* (1953)
H. Procter, *Streets of Disillusion* (1958).
C. Richardson, *Nick of Notting Hill* (1965)
H. Scott, *Scotland Yard* (1954)
F. Tennyson-Jesse, *The Trials of Evans and Christie* (1957)
K. Simpson, *Forty Years of Murder* (1978)
G. Zelland, *Crime in London* (1986)

Electronic sources

Ancestry.co.uk
www.10rillington-place.co.uk

Secondary Sources

Books (non-fiction)

Lord Altrincham and I. Gilmour, *The Timothy Evans Case: An Appeal to Reason* (1956)
Anon, *Murder Casebook 4: Rillington Place Murders* (1990)
F.E. Camps and R. Barber, *The Investigation of Murder* (1966)
D. Canter, *Mapping Murder* (2007)
M. Eddowes, *The Man on Your Conscience* (1955)
J. Eddowes, *The Two Killers of Rillington Place* (1994)
M. Fido, *10 Rillington Place* (audio-book, 1993)
M. Fido, *A History of British Serial Killing* (2001)
R.K. Furneaux, *The Two Stranglers of Rillington Place* (1961)
F. Gammon, *A House to Remember* (2011)
A. Gekoski, *Murder by Numbers* (1999)
G. Jackson, *Francis Camps* (1975).
L. Kennedy, *10 Rillington Place* (1961)
L. Kennedy, *Thirty Six Murders and Two Immoral Earnings* (2002)
M. Lefebvre, *Murder With a Difference* (1958)
E. Marston, *John Christie* (2007)
F. Mort, *Capital Affairs* (2010)
J. Oates, *Unsolved London Murders: 1920s and 1930s* (2009).
J. Oates, *1940s and 1950s* (2009)
R. Paget and S.S. Silverman, *Hanged and Innocent?* (1953)
C. Phillips, *Murderer's Moon* (1956)
N. Root, *Frenzy: Heath, Haigh and Christie* (2011)
M.J. Trow, *War Crimes* (2008)
T. Vague, *London Psychogeography: Rachman, Riots and Rillington Place* (1998)
R. Van Emden and V. Piuk, *Famous 1914–1918* (2009)
C. Wilson, *Written in Blood* (1990)
C. Wilson, *Serial Killers* (2000)
D. Wilson, *A History of British Serial Killings* (2009)

Fiction

R. Adams, *The Girl in a Swing* (1980)
A. Barron, *The Ballad of John Christie* (1998)
J.N. Chance, *The Crimes at Rillington Place: A Novelist's Reconstruction* (1961)
R. Rendell, *Thirteen Steps Down* (2004)
L. Wilson, *A Capital Crime* (2010)

Index